The Feminine Fifties

By FRED LEWIS PATTEE

SARA JANE CLARKE, "GRACE GREENWOOD"
From an engraving after the portrait by Thomas Buchanan Read, 1848.

The
Feminine Fifties

by

FRED LEWIS PATTEE

Author of "The First Century of American Literature,"
"The New American Literature," etc.

ILLUSTRATED

KENNIKAT PRESS, INC./PORT WASHINGTON, N. Y.

TO
MY DEAR WIFE
GRACE

PREFACE

*I*T SEEMS TO BE THE FASHION NOW TO WRITE HISTORY IN decade units—a new *genre* perhaps. Heartily am I in favor of it. There is need in these journalistic, surface-skimming days for intense study of narrowly restricted areas, for grubbing work to expose the tap-roots of movements and things. Already have I collected a shelfful of these restricted studies, and, for the most part, they have proved to be helpful authorities. Humorous, however, I have found several of them, at least humorous when read simply by title. For instance, yesterday I read a treatment of "The Yellow Nineties," remembering all the time that the decade had once been "mauve," and that its sister, the seventies, had been ruled by a competent judge to be "brown." The last ten years of the century have been the favorite hunting-grounds of this new literary school dubbed by me the "decade-ents." There have been studies of "the gay nineties," "the naughty nineties," and "the romantic nineties." To Irving Bacheller it was "the high-brow decade." Other areas have received similar treatment.

But the most vital and far-reaching of the nineteenth century American decades has been totally neglected. The period of the eighteen-fifties was a true unit, self-contained, highly individual, and tremendously influential. To understand the war that dominated the sixties, one must dig here for its roots. It has been my effort to find the soul of this causal decade. What caused the colossal explosion we call the Civil War? Read the title of my volume. Were I to write a history of the war—and may Heaven keep me from such a crime—this would be Volume I.

F. L. P.

CONTENTS

ILLUSTRATIONS

The
Feminine Fifties

CHAPTER I

BETWEEN TWO WARS

To CHARACTERIZE A DECADE WITH A SINGLE ADJECTIVE is to overload that adjective. Seldom can a word be found so inclusive as to carry even the major elements involved. The 1840's did not always *roar*, nor was roaring their leading characteristic, and the forties were not always *fabulous*, at least not after the ordinary definition. Nor was a certain decade all *brown*, nor another all *mauve*, nor were the nineties *always* gay.

It is the fashion now to describe decades with alliterative cognomens ignoring all sense. How can one word describe the multitudinousness of a decade like the fifties? There are at least ten "f" words that describe phases of the decade: *fervid, fevered, furious, fatuous, fertile, feeling, florid, furbelowed, fighting, funny*—every one of them worth using as a chapter heading. And to find a single adjective that would combine them all—can it be done? Would not such a word be a veritable world in itself? Unquestionably. That I have found this word, however, my title reveals, and that it covers completely

3

ten years of American history it is the duty of my book to show.

First of all, the decade was a fervid one. Feeling ruled it from end to end rather than thinking. It was the hot breathing spell between two wars, the moment of calm between the two halves of a typhoon. In terms of literary history, it was the span between the two halves of *The Biglow Papers*. It opened with Congress a seething cauldron after the Mexican War, and at its close armies were forming for the Civil War. During ten years the United States Senate roared with "squatter sovereignty," "bleeding Kansas," "Fugitive Slave Law," "slave state," "free state," "unconstitutionality"—a cauldron that would have boiled over but for compromises under the leadership of Clay. The 1850 bill postponed the Civil War eleven years.

Great rejoicing there was among the lovers of peace; but even the masses who never think at all felt that the Compromise was but an armistice, that something sinister was coming, an "impending crisis," a sword over them hung by a hair. The result was intensity of feeling, at times even hysteria. To feel how intense it was one needs but to read some of the letters and journals and newspapers of the decade. The placid Emerson, for instance, learning of the Fugitive Slave Bill's passage, threw this into his journal: "The filthy enactment was made in the nineteenth century, by people who could read and write. I will not obey it, by God!"

The decade was fevered. At times of impending crisis long deferred, mob hysteria is always prevalent. Washington, New York City, Boston, were overcharged Leyden jars. Everywhere during the decade were recurrent explo-

sions of emotion. Staid old Boston once became a headlong mob, led by the leading clergyman of the city, even
Theodore Parker,[1] and it would have battered down the
doors of the court house and have released the fugitive
slave about to be taken back to the South, had it not been
prevented by the militia. I quote from Commager's Life
of Parker to show the tensity of feeling in Boston, 1854:

For ten days Boston was in a state of siege, while Loring
ruled on points of law. For ten days the granite Court House
was a Bastile: soldiers guarded the doors, soldiers lined the
stairs, soldiers peered out of the windows. Three cordons of
police were strung around the court, and two more of soldiers.
For ten days the business of the regular courts was suspended.
...What a ferment there was. Rumor flew round the city
like an epidemic: there would be another attack upon the
Court House; the Virginians would be hounded out of town;
Wendell Phillips would be shot; Garrison would be mobbed;
Parker would be arrested. What a ferment there was: law-
abiding men carried pistols and respectable women stood on
the street corners and hissed the guardsmen and the soldiers
as they passed by. Boston was never so crowded; every train
brought a delegation from some country town.

Finally, the owner of the Negro was permitted to remove his property from Boston, and the colored man was
marched out of town at the head of an army: the New
England Guards, the Pulaski Guards, the Independent
Fusiliers, the Washington Light Infantry, the Columbian
Artillery, the American Artillery, the Bay State Artillery,
the Webster Artillery with a cannon. All Boston and part
of near-by New England were on the sidewalks, all flags
at half-mast, Union down, hung with crêpe. And in the

[1] Henry Steele Commager, *Theodore Parker, Yankee Crusader* (Boston,
Little, Brown & Company, 1936).

ABOLITIONISTS IN COUNCIL

"The orator of the day denouncing the Union." *Harper's Weekly,* 1859.

center of the Marshal's Guard, Anthony Burns in a new
suit of clothes, the most astonished "coon" in all America.
"Lot of folks," he remarked, "to see a colored man walk
down the street."

That in Old Boston.

Just as intense the atmosphere of Washington. A veritable mania of anger swept over Congress after Sumner's
"Crime Against Kansas" speech, so intense, indeed, that,
as all know, he was attacked in his seat in the Senate and
beaten until unconscious. And there was the fanatical
John Brown and his battles in Kansas and at Harper's
Ferry. The fifties were furious.

Eighteen-fifty was the closing year of an epoch. Just as
the Revolutionary War dates from 1765, eleven years before the Declaration of Independence, so does the Civil
War date from the Clay compromise. The question of
slavery had been a stormily debated one ever since the
Constitutional Convention, but to the anti-slavery element
in the North it had been largely an abstract matter, a
thing of law and logic rather than an appeal to the emotions. But the Fugitive Slave Law aroused feeling, that
sympathy for the underdog always easily aroused in
America. When the North actually saw individual Negro
slaves who had escaped from servitude, and then saw them
treated as mere chattels, returned to the masters by force
and by law, like cattle, a new element came into the anti-
slavery movement. When an abuse, in an emotional age,
becomes emotional, it is doomed. Dickens had taught the
world that lesson. The result was the double-tracking of
the Underground Railroad; for the Negro, at least in the
feelings of the North, had become a person.

I shall not enter further here into the matter of slavery and anti-slavery, though it was the dominating force of the decade. I wish only to show the fevered emotionalism of the 1850's.

II

THE DECADE was fatuous. The nerves of the nation, stimulated by the intensity of the times, began to crave added emotional stimulants: circuses, melodrama, "shilling-shocker" fiction. Religious emotion, always in America under loose control, expressed itself in a tearful flood of poems and novels and betterment movements. Excess demands always more excess.

To speak in modern terms, it was the "war of nerves" that precedes always the major conflict, and in it women, as always, played a leading part. To the emotionalism of the time they added emotionalism intense and compelling, fanning the flames kindled by the men until, in the midst of the whirlwind that followed, the President, facetiously perhaps, could hail one of them as the little woman who had precipitated the war.

New York City was peculiarly susceptible to mass suggestion, and never did it express appreciation or resentment in measured terms. It took (and it still takes) little to sweep the city off its feet. Just before the opening of the fifties, for instance, there was a fight between two actors, each insanely jealous of the other's popularity—the Englishman Macready and the American Edwin Forrest. The whole city had taken sides, and in May, 1849, when Macready was playing *Macbeth* at the Astor Place Opera House, the theater was mobbed and all but destroyed. When at last order was restored, the heart of the city looked like a battle-field in war time.

Always in New York City extremes: "Do you remember," asked the "Easy Chair" in 1856, "the Dickens ovation—the Ole Bull furore—the Fanny Elssler frenzy—the Jenny Lind enthusiasm—the Kossuth excitement?"

But where can one touch America anywhere during the fifties and not find emotional explosion? The decade had opened with melodrama: the California gold rush; it had shuddered with horror at the newspaper accounts of the murder done by the Harvard professor, Dr. Webster, who had carved up his victim and burned the pieces in the college furnace; it had listened with a thrill of horror to the story of the shipwreck on Fire Island where Margaret Fuller, her husband the Count Ossoli, and their infant son had perished. Sensational, too, had been Webster's "Seventh of March Speech" that swept New England like a storm and was made literary by Whittier's bombshell "Ichabod."

Not all of the excitement of the decade, however, was political excitement, or terror at "acts of God," or shudderings at ghastly crimes. The laying of the Atlantic cable and its breaking again and still again in mid-ocean, then its completion with a national celebration, its use for a week or more, then a final break and no cable for ten years—all this kept interest intense. The Panama railroad was completed across the Isthmus in 1855, and the same year saw the return of the rescue party from the Arctic regions with the lost Dr. Kane and all but three of his entire party, long believed to have perished.

Thus the 1850's, emotionalism in the saddle. Before revolution always it comes. Intuition before experience, and intuition is a feminine endowment.

III

THE DECADE was fertile. Decades of emotion before national explosions always breed reformers, breakers-away, creators of new heavens and new earths. In New England, Transcendentalism, a German ferment added to the religious ferment peculiar to Boston, had at first worked off its expanding energies in lectures and conversations, in sermons and in scholarly articles in the *Dial* and the *Harbinger*. But America, especially in its northern areas, has been pragmatic territory. A theory may for a time be held in debated suspense, but finally it must be put to trial. Sporadic attempts had been made in the forties— the Brook Farm community and Fruitlands and all the various experiments of the New England Reformers described in Emerson's paper. But nothing had borne fruit. By 1850, Transcendentalism no longer had life enough in it to keep alive its club in Boston.

Then suddenly theory had turned to action. With the passage of the Fugitive Slave Law and the opening of the Kansas-Nebraska contest, anti-slavery in the North became a forest fire. The whole decade became the battle time for reformers. Everywhere Abolitionists, temperance lecturers, Woman's Rights agitators.

The Civil War was first fought on forensic platforms, as in the Lincoln-Douglas debates, in lecture courses, on the floors of Congress, at conventions, and in the village stores. And it lasted for ten years.

It is noteworthy that from this intensely emotional,

intensely individualized decade came what is now recognized as our major group of humorists peculiarly American. From excess, whatever its variety, there comes always humorous reaction, often also satire, which is humor embittered. Artemus Ward, John Phœnix, Orpheus C. Kerr, Shillaber, Mrs. Whitcher, Mark Twain, and others began in the 1850's the work for which they are now famous.

IV

A feminine period undoubtedly. Thomas Cholmondeley, of London, to whom Thoreau in 1857 sent a copy of the second edition of *Leaves of Grass*, could sum up the poems and the poet with this startling verdict: "I find reality and beauty, mixed with not a little violence and coarseness—both of which are to me effeminate." Not only did this characterize the early Whitman and his work, but the decade as well which alone had made the man and his writings possible.

CHAPTER II

EL DORADO

*E*IGHTEEN-FIFTY SAW THE CALIFORNIA GOLD FEVER AT ITS height. A veritable army composed of all conceivable human elements had surged across the prairies and over the Rockies, or across the Isthmus to the "Gold Coast." California, a ribbon of wild land between the mountain ranges and the Pacific, had been under the American flag only since July, 1846. Gold had been discovered some two years later, and now in 1850, California had been added to the Union as a state. Thus rapidly do things grow in the vast commonwealth whose motto on its seal is "Eureka."

From the first, tremendously did the state impress the imagination of the East after the gold discovery which was at once magnified to Golconda proportions. Was it not entered from the Pacific through the Golden Gate? Happy augury! Was it not, in all its extent, the land of marvels: the giant forests of redwood trees, the Yosemite Valley, the old Missions behind which lay centuries of Conquistador romance, as yet untold?

Surely the 1850's opened with sensation. The gold rush was a veritable epic, another Argonaut search for the Golden Fleece through perils as deadly and toils as unbelievable as those of Jason, who fought with the Harpies and escaped through the clashing rocks.

By 1850 it had begun to be possible to sift the truth from the mass-mania reports and the wild conjectures that were filling the ears of the eager world. Something like perspective was beginning to appear. With characteristic timeliness, Horace Greeley had dispatched a reporter to the gold fields to send to the *Tribune* the actual truth in a series of articles, and with characteristic good judgment he had chosen for the job the young Bayard Taylor, aged twenty-four, already well known because of his book *Views Afoot,* recording his two years in Europe on money earned on the way, a book that the *Dunciad* of the day had dated as:

> When Bayard Taylor—protégé of Natty,
> Ixion-like walked into the "literati";
> And first to proper use his genius put,
> Like ballet-girls, by showing *Views Afoot.*

Choosing the Isthmus route for his plunge into Golconda, Taylor started in June, 1848, eight months after the famous discovery, and arrived on the Gold Coast in August, fifty-one days later, a journey that fills five chapters of his final volume.

Wild as had been his dreams as to what he was to find, the reality was wilder. Everywhere the mad excitement of a land boom. Money like autumn leaves everywhere. A fellow gold-seeker had loaded up in New York with 15,000 copies of the *Tribune,* and in two hours had sold them all at a dollar a copy. Taylor thereupon had removed the newspaper wrappings from his baggage and sold them for a number of dollars. Everything was in the same key. The boom prices for everything, the speculating in lots, the feverish gambling, impressed him far more than did the gold-mining operations. The greater number of the party he had come with became rich through real-estate speculation in the cities.

Taylor's book, *Eldorado,* published in 1850, is far more than a mere survey of the early placer operations that caused the mass mania of the times. Its sub-title, *Adventures in the Path of Empire,* indicates that its author saw and recorded more than mere newspaper materials. He was impressed more and more by the boundlessness of the land, its promises for rich agriculture, its amazing diversity, its beauty.

Harper's Magazine in a review of *Eldorado* burst for a moment into prophecy: "We shall yet have the poetry, the romance, the dramatic embodiment of the strange life in the country of the yellow sands." In less than two decades the prophecy had been fulfilled. In 1854, Bret Harte was in California.

The frontier lawlessness and the picturesque types of humanity evolved from life in the mines, Taylor makes little of. He was no Bret Harte who saw California through romance-tinted glasses. To him California was a land of hospitality and mutual helpfulness, with a minimum of crime:

There had been, as nearly as I could learn, not more than twelve or fifteen executions in all, about half of which were inflicted for the crime of murder. This awful responsibility had not been assumed lightly, but after a fair trial and a full and clear conviction, to which was added, I believe in every instance, the confession of the criminal.

Taylor saw, however, only the early days of the gold fever. He could report even as he was leaving the state that there is "no cessation to the marvelous reports, and thousands are only waiting a few further repetitions, to join the hordes of emigration."

"Interested parties," wrote H. T. Tuckerman, in 1850, "continually minister to the excited feelings which the El Dorado stories circulated by the press are alone sufficient to keep alive. Enormous quantities of ardent spirits are carried out in every vessel, as well as weapons of all kinds and ammunition."

The numbers that surged across the wild prairie lands, across unbridged rivers, and through fierce bands of mounted Indians have been variously estimated, but it was a veritable army. To realize what they had to endure one needs but to read of Parkman's experiences not four years before the opening of our decade. Read *The Oregon Trail*. Taylor could not consider this modern anabasis without a rush of superlatives:

Considering only the thirty-thousand emigrants who last year crossed the Plains, this California Crusade will more than equal the great military expeditions of the Middle Ages in magnitude, peril, and adventure.... The story of thirty-thousand souls accomplishing a journey of more than two thousand miles through a savage and but partially explored wilderness, crossing on their way two mountain chains equal to the Alps in height and asperity, besides broad tracts of burning desert and plains of nearly equal desolation where a few patches of stunted shrubs and springs of brackish water were their only stay, has in it so much of heroism, of daring and sublime endurance, that we may vainly question the records of any age for its equal.

A mass movement was it, peculiarly American. De Tocqueville, it will be remembered, had observed that "the ties of home and kindred are essentially loose in a mercantile republic," and he was impressed "while observing the extraordinary facility with which men have left accustomed pursuits, local obligations, and family altars to engage in distant and hazardous enterprises." But Americans, it must be remembered, are all of them descendants of adventurous emigrants. The faint-hearted and the unfit remained at home.

Youth—headlong, sentimental, melodramatic—dominated the rush to the new Golconda. Along the thousand miles of the gold route, eager young throngs were singing on the march and around the camp-fires young Stephen Foster's rollicking song, "Oh! Susanna," written in 1848. It became the "theme song" of the gold-rush period. "Maybe it was the care-free, jaunty lilt of the song that endeared it to these pioneers." The words were merest nonsense, but the music of the piece had qualities that carried it around the entire world. Bayard Taylor, writing in 1853, tells how he heard a wandering Hindu minstrel sing "Oh! Susanna" in Delhi.

II

ONE PHASE of the gold-fever period must not be overlooked: its effect upon the America of the fifties. Unquestionably it was an upsetting element in an overtense period. Looked at from an economic standpoint, it was

a stimulant at a time when stimulants of all kinds were
in excess. The first seven years of the decade were flush
times. Hard times were forgotten; money was easy; business was booming; the theaters were full.

Whatever the effect the influx of California gold may
have had upon the banks and upon the national credit,
it had without question a sweeping psychological effect
upon the general public. It was flush times. Was not gold
in a steady stream flowing out of the limitless mines of
California into the whole East? The cry from the mines
was "There is no end to it." A steady stream of returning
gold-seekers was beginning to pour into New York and
Philadelphia and Boston with their pockets loaded with
the yellow metal. One heard it everywhere.

Let me quote from George R. Stewart's stirring novel
East of the Giants, 1938, reviewed by Garrett:

She had watched the miracle and disaster of gold. That
first year, men lived out in the wilderness like the duke in
the Forest of Arden. "Everybody dazzled with the gold, and
nobody stealing because it was easier to find your own gold
than to steal it. Nobody working very hard, for you could
make so much without working hard, and men seemed to
have a feeling that if they worked too hard when gold came
so easily, they might spoil the luck, or wake up and find it
was a dream." Suddenly, it had become a dream. Judith had
waked up, but few others in California had done so. Men had
wrapped greed in a flag and shouted "America" when they
meant dollars.

Publishers were prospering: the best-seller era had begun. Advertising was becoming sensational. But a study
of the book-lists will show a falling-off after the wonder

year 1855. *Uncle Tom's Cabin* and then *Hiawatha* had been launched on a spring tide.

Then had come the financial crash of 1857.

In December of that year the "Easy Chair" in *Harper's Magazine* viewed the depression from the standpoint of its effect upon literature:

This year there will not be so many books published. The glorious days—Saturdays—when whole pages of morning newspapers were not enough to set forth the number, variety, and excellence of books that were issued; when every publisher had that morning ready the most interesting, thrilling, and fascinating book of the season; when the first edition of 20,000 was already exhausted, and purchasers could be served in the order of their coming; when a distinguished literary gentleman had declared, in a private letter to the publishers, that since Professor Ingraham's last there had been nothing of such a startling and commanding character; when the present work was vastly superior to everything else ever written by the world-renowned author; when every book of every publisher was in the twenty-sixth thousand, and the unparalleled demand was increasing at an unprecedented rate; when presses were working night and day; when owing to the extraordinary demand, the issue of the first edition must be postponed from Saturday to Thursday; when not more than fifty thousand copies could be furnished in three days; when the public must have patience, and would finally be supplied; when the cry was "still they come!" When canvassers were wanted by all publishers for the most popular book ever issued; when we were all tantalized with a spicy extract from the chapter "Love, Despair, and Madness"; or when we beheld the "gorgeous Julia Bowen" rushing wildly down a column of nonpareil and pausing from plunging into the fathomless gulf only because "the outside" was only two shillings a line—the days of these glories and triumphs and stupendous successes are past; the enormous editions are all exhausted; there are no more books calculated to create a profound sensation in the social and religious world.

No! the wind suddenly fell. There was a sudden chopping-round, a jibbing, and the encouraging advertisements—cheerful whistlings to keep up the courage of the whistlers—went, down into darkness, and are seen no more. The storm that has touched everything else has not suffered literature to escape. We must have fewer horses and diamonds, and we must also have fewer books. Jewelers and authors must slack work, but bakers must stir up their fires.

...There will be some who will yearn for the resounding Saturdays of yore, and ask, What book can I buy, in which if I can forget my care about the dollar, I shall well invest my dollar?

The California gold undoubtedly was a godsend to the North at the time of the War between the States. According to John Bodwell, "It is a question whether the United States could have stood the shock of the great rebellion, 1861, had the California gold discovery not been made. Bankers and businessmen in New York in 1864 did not hesitate to admit that, but for the gold of California which monthly poured its five or six millions into that financial center the bottom would have dropped out of everything."

CHAPTER III

THE VEDA CROP FAILURE

*I*N AMERICAN LITERARY HISTORY THE 1850's STAND FOR three things: the full ending of the Knickerbocker period; the harvest time of the mid-century group of writers centering in New England; and the seeding time of the literary period that was to end the century. From the standpoint of literature the Brahmins had no sons: only daughters. For a male editor of the *Atlantic* in the next generation—a Westerner—had to be imported, then a man trained by the New York Bohemians, and later a Southerner.

Knickerbockerism for a time was kept alive by blood transfusions furnished by younger writers through the columns of *Putnam's Magazine,* 1853-1857, but it was only a brief delaying of the end. The *Knickerbocker Magazine,* largely because of the popularity of its editor Lewis Gaylord Clark, dragged through the decade, but it was anæmic beyond all hope of resuscitation.

The old Knickerbockers were passing. The death of Poe in 1849 created small comment. Puritanism had re-

jected him, and it was a generation before he was fully
accepted. Cooper died in 1851 and was immediately
hailed as a classic destined for permanence, he who only
a short time before had sued many prominent journals
for libeling him and had won every suit. On February
24, 1852, in New York City, a memorial service presided
over by the enfeebled Webster and made distinctive by
the oration of William Cullen Bryant crowded Metro-
politan Hall to overflowing, and a movement was started
for raising a fund for a monument to the novelist.

The death roll of the decade is a startling one:

> John James Audubon, 1851
> John Howard Payne, 1852
> Robert Montgomery Bird, 1854
> James Gates Percival, 1854
> William Hickling Prescott, 1859
> Washington Irving, 1859
> James K. Paulding, 1860

With them also was passing the old guard political:

> John C. Calhoun, 1850
> Henry Clay, 1852
> Daniel Webster, 1852
> Thomas H. Benton, 1858
> Rufus Choate, 1859

In the order of time, it was the decade when "the flowering of New England" should have been producing its
most distinctive fruitage. As one Brahmin expressed it,
it was harvest time now for early Vedas. The crop had
long been maturing. Transcendentalism had begun on
the intellectual levels, as doctrines to be discussed in lectures and "conversations." The *Dial* had ignored com-

pletely the great American epic that was enacting at its very door, had excluded feeling and humor and life at the human levels of the average homes and had soared in the clouds of theory. It evolved, however, nothing new in the way of philosophy, and it gradually lapsed into "isms" and philanthropy. During the forties it had tried out its Utopian theories at Brook Farm and Fruitlands. These failing, it had thrown its ebbing energies into anti-slavery and temperance reform, and "the rights of women." There were no Vedas. "The decade before the Civil War," wrote Percy H. Boynton, "was a time of unfulfillments."

A glance at the book-lists of the 1850's, however, makes this statement seem at first sight ridiculous. Quantity there certainly was, and enough of quality to give weight to the judgment, sometimes rendered, that during the decade there was produced by the New England group the most notable of the American classics. Three titles are to be found in most lists of the greatest American books:

> Emerson's *Representative Men,* 1850
> Hawthorne's *The Scarlet Letter,* 1850
> Thoreau's *Walden,* 1854

No Vedas here, however; no final classics such as might have been prophesied in the eagerly expectant days of the thirties and the forties. Study the three books. Instead of Vedas tall sproutings from the trunk of Brahminized Kantism—strange growths, experiments, it would seem, rather than rounded finalities.

Emerson, at first the leading Transcendentalist, had seemed in the 1830's like a young David with a sling.

He had had the courage to resign his Boston pastorate with a sermon criticizing church fundamentals. With his "five smooth stones out of the brook" he had appeared at Harvard in 1837 and again at the Divinity School in 1838.

Careless with his sling had been this young Yankee David, and his stones hit their marks:

Thy love abroad is spite at home.

Traveling is a fool's paradise.

A foolish consistency is the hobgoblin of little minds.

As men's prayers are a disease of the will, so are their creeds a disease of the intellect.

We are parlor soldiers. We shun the rugged battle of fate, where strength is born.

Whoso would be a man must be a nonconformist.

In Christendom where is the Christian?

Such sling-stones from a single essay. And Walt Whitman, translating these "sentences incompressible" into his barbaric yawp, was later to hurtle them over the roofs of the world.

But now with the opening fifties the aging Emerson had discarded his sling and his smooth stones and was issuing *Representative Men* in the key of a Carlyle, a book written for English lecture audiences, an American book with no American in it.

Hawthorne, though once a member of the Brook Farm community, was skeptically aloof from Transcendentalism and all its later gropings. The hot intensity of the fifties moved him not at all, and he escaped from it to Europe where he spent most of the decade. His flowering was not a New England flowering and its fruitage was not a New England product. On a cold thin soil of his own creating he produced a stone-crop as apart from the warm currents of actual life as a Utopia dream. His *Scarlet Letter* has in it materials that in the hands of a novelist deeply and emotionally moved by human tragedy might have produced characters like *King Lear,* or the modern *Ethan Frome,* inerasable from the soul of its reader, but his characters are weird and unnatural, and their story is as lacking in warm human naturalness as a treatise on finance.

And as for *Walden,* which came from the same impetus that created Brook Farm, it also was no Veda. To Lowell the book was primarily a Transcendental document. Thoreau would establish a community with a single member, and do it to prove a thesis in social economy. From this standpoint the book, even as Lowell declared, proved to be a "dud." But there were other things in the volume, and these other things, the voicings of something new in the air, caught by him and recorded, have given it its modern rating among American classics.

But other volumes there were of high worth. Every writer in the New England school was creating what he believed to be permanent classics. During the decade came books like these, all of them perhaps as worthy of a leading place among American writings as the three I have first chosen:

Whittier's *Songs of Labor,* 1850
Parkman's *The Conspiracy of Pontiac,* 1851
Hawthorne's *The House of the Seven Gables,* 1851

Stowe's *Uncle Tom's Cabin*, 1852
Longfellow's *Hiawatha*, 1855
Motley's *The Rise of the Dutch Republic*, 1856
Longfellow's *The Courtship of Miles Standish*, 1858
Holmes's *The Autocrat of the Breakfast Table*, 1858

Again to quote Boynton, "Only *Uncle Tom's Cabin* was generated by the times; only *Hiawatha* was also popular. For the rest, neither the works nor the authors were influential on the American people." Thus Transcendentalism, which seemed in its first Boston days like a forest fire destroying old rubbish and creating new tillage land from which a new and original American literature was to spring, lost itself in its own theories and ended in unfulfilment. It talked and lectured and conversed itself to death, but not before it had tried in a last spasmodic way to put its ebbing theories into action, a type of action, indeed, not at all discussed in the early meetings of its club.

The sons of the Brahmins, the second generation of the "flowering" school, were daughters. The men who were to rule the literary ending of the century, born prevailingly in the 1830's, were New Yorkers, Westerners, and Southerners. The literary influence of New York, which had been lost for one generation, was becoming noteworthy. The nationally known newspapers of the metropolis, Bryant's *Evening Post,* Greeley's *Tribune,* and Bennett's *Herald,* were educating a new school of young writers. Willis' *Broadway Journal* and the newly founded *Harper's Magazine* were widely read and widely influential.

Judged by what the young poetic hopefuls were pro-

ducing during our decade, the literary outlook during the
century's second half was not promising. First, and oldest,
was Bayard Taylor, rising newspaper correspondent, trav-
eler, poet. Before 1860 he had issued four volumes of
verse: *Ximena*, 1844; *Rhymes of Travel, Ballads and
Poems*, 1848; *Book of Romances, Lyrics and Songs*, 1851;
Poems of the Orient, 1854. To read them is to ask: What
had happened to American poetry? Why all this borrowed Eastern World finery? Why publish "poems of the
Orient" in the new epic world of America? Sentiment
to mawkishness; nothing new; prettyness instead of
strength.

Read then Thomas Bailey Aldrich's "Ballad of Babie
Bell," 1855, and note that Ferris Greenslet in his biography of Aldrich says that "it struck a chord that found
an instant response in the popular heart," and, "It seems
to have swept through the country like a piece of news."
It sold, in fact, three thousand copies. During the thirteen
years of Aldrich's literary apprenticeship in New York,
1852-1865, he published six volumes. One of them he later
tried to suppress by buying all the copies he could find.
Established in Boston, he later seemed to wish to forget
his New York period. Few poems from these earlier volumes were suffered to enter his later editions.

Richard Henry Stoddard, born the same year as Taylor,
1825, issued five volumes of poetry during the decade,
poetry as remote from America as Arabia. The two young
poets, working hard in New York at non-poetical jobs,
met often of evenings to read together the romantic poets,
pretending to believe that the soul of Keats had been
reincarnated in Stoddard and the soul of Shelley in

Taylor. They were intoxicated with the effeminate early Tennyson, his poems of the "Where Claribel low lieth" period, before he had thrown off the influence of Shelley and Keats.

Edmund Clarence Stedman, almost a decade younger than the two, was old enough to publish at the close of our decade a volume entitled *Poems Lyrical and Idyllic,* poems redolent of Theocritus, whose soul he hoped he had received. His ambition was to make "a complete, metrical, English version of the idyls of Theocritus, Moschus, and Bion." The outbreak of the Civil War with its flooding ghastly realism disturbed his dreamings, but did not awaken him fully to the world in which he was actually living.

No one reads these poets to-day. What had happened to American poetry? We shall see.

CHAPTER IV

MELVILLE AND WHITMAN

*T*WO CLASSICS NOW BY GENERAL CONSENT ADMITTED TO world literature did originate in the 1850's, but their authors were not of the New England group. New Yorkers both of them, born the same year, 1819, in the shadow of the metropolis, and educated in its lower schools without benefit of college. Both were men practically alone, creators, blazers of new trails, stoned by their own generation, and as far as their own day was concerned, exterminated.

The demigods seldom come alone; most often they come in pairs. In the 1850's it was Herman Melville and Walt Whitman.

I

MELVILLE was an unusual blend. His mother was a Knickerbocker of a notable line, a Gansevoort—pure Dutch; his grandfather Melville was a Bostonian from Revolutionary days, the antique embalmed by Holmes in his lyric "The Last Leaf." The Melville father was an

28

importer of French merchandise, often in Paris, a reader
of French novels, a dreamer of a world outside the bounds
of trade. Two natures, therefore, were struggling in the
young lad Melville: the mother Dutch element, restless,
worldly, realistic, impatient of convention and control;
and the father element that could dream of Boston and
of French art. In youth, action comes first. The adolescent
of seventeen escaped to sea, lived in forecastles with ele-
mental men, had dime-novel adventures on Paul and
Virginia islands with beach-combers and the scum of the
tropics; and then served as tramp sailor on whalers and
on a United States man of war.

Home again after years away, he recounted with thrilling effect his tropic adventures, and, wholly untrained as
a writer, endeavored to set them down for publication as
Dana had done in his *Two Years before the Mast,* still a
best-seller. He wrote with no thought of models, simply
to tell his marvelous adventures. Realism, though none
called it that, he wrote all unconsciously: "Nothing but
an earnest desire for truth and good has led him [the
author] to touch upon this subject at all," he declared.
But as he wrote, there awoke within him something he
knew nothing of—his Boston soul. Vivid picturings with
flaming tropic colors, often too extreme after the manner
of the unschooled, began to roll from his pen—philosophy
à la New England—and action presented with a dramatic
intensity that made the reader seem to himself to be an
actual participator; and there was with it all a current
of feeling that the reader at length was sharing to the
full. Whether the story and the picture be true or not,
it is alive and it is compelling. The maiden Fayaway

doubtless never lived as Melville depicted her, but she will never die.

Two natures, indeed, were struggling in the young writer.

His book published, there came the reaction to it of the feminine fifties. Too much Gansevoort: the ladies were shocked. England was the first to raise the cry. The missionaries had been insulted; "He is guilty of deliberate and elaborate misrepresentation." Then the book was branded as grossly immoral. *Omoo,* his second book, was pronounced by the *Living Age* to be scandalously indecent:

"With this tribe he remained about four months, during which he cohabited with a native girl, named Fayaway. We shall not pollute our pages by transferring to them the scenes in which this wretched profligate appears, self-portrayed, as the chief actor." And again:

"When they left jail no captain in the harbor would have anything to do with them on account of their desperate character. They were leagued with a reckless gang of seamen known in the Pacific as 'beach-combers.'"

America was in full accord with the English verdict. Before Harper's would consent to reissue *Typee* they demanded that the text should be thoroughly Bowdlerized. And it was done.

Realism in the feminine fifties was rated with things vulgar and unrefined.

Melville was at the cross-roads now: which road? One area of the 1850's called loudly for moving adventure. "More cannibal stories" they demanded. But the Boston element within him had awakened, and he gave them

HERMAN MELVILLE

From an engraving after the
portrait by J. O. Eaton.

WALT WHITMAN

Frontispiece to the first
edition of *Leaves of Grass*.

instead the volume *Mardi*—New England in an out-rigger canoe, Transcendentalism gone tropic, or, as the critics of the fifties put it, "gone mad."

And yet the volume was in key with the New England times. One phase of the "flowering" period, one that had had little contemporary recognition, was a spirit of revolt from artificiality, from ultra-civilization and convention. Only a few radio-sensitive souls had caught the impulse: Emerson in his earlier period, and then Thoreau. The Walden hut-builder can be rated as a Transcendentalist without doubt, but it is not because of his Transcendentalism that he is alive to-day. He sought for Truth in the primal woods: "My profession is to be always on the alert, to find God in Nature, to know his lurking places." Unconsciously, Melville was with him. The bluebird of peace and happiness had escaped humanity—where look for it? Once he believed he had found it among the naked *Typee* savages with Nature their only law. But it was only for a moment. His volume *Mardi* records his fruitless search. Whitman, escaping from ancient conventions, had thrown poetry into freedom, and in its freedom had found that the elusive bluebird was Democracy, but his idealization of the bird is so extreme that it has become, like Melville's, a fleeting vision.

It is noteworthy that Melville in his pursuit of the bluebird blundered upon Whitman's primitive harp a half-decade before *Leaves of Grass*. Parts of the strange madcap epic *Mardi* are poetry as truly as are Whitman's lawless chants. Seemingly prose they can be thrown into the Whitman line-lengths with Whitman-like effects. This, for example, from Chapter LX, entitled "The Moose":

Hail, mighty brute!—thou feelest not these things;
Never canst *thou* be damned.
Moose! would thy soul were mine;
For if that scorched thing, mine, be immortal, so thine;
And thy life has not the consciousness of death.
I read profound placidity—deep—million—violet fathoms
    down,
In that soft, pathetic woman's eye!
What is man's shrunk form to thine, thou woodland majesty?
Moose, moose! my soul is shot again.

Or this from Chapter CLXXXIV:

Hast ever seen a yellow lion, all day basking in the yellow
    sun:
In reveries rending droves of elephants;
But his vast loins supine, and eyelids winking?
Such Lombardo;
But fierce want, the hunter, came and roused his roar.
In hairy billows his great mane tossed like the sea;
His eyeballs flamed two hells;
His paw stopped a rolling world.

But for all his island ports, the voyager, as recorded in *Mardi,* sailing without chart or compass or known destination, arrives nowhere at all. It is the log-book of a confused genius, and it failed.

New England now took full possession of him. Three years after his return from the Pacific he was married to the only daughter of Chief Justice Shaw of Boston. No more Gansevoort wanderings. Soon with a growing family he moved to the Berkshires and became neighbor to Nathaniel Hawthorne, also an exile. Melville's introspective pessimism, interminably presented, bored the romancer at last, angered him indeed, but when as a wandering Triton he touched upon tropic adventure, there was excitement in the family. Once after a thrilling narrative, intense in its acted realism, the narrator having departed, the children actually searched the room for the spear the cannibal had thrown with deadly effect.

Melville, too, got inspiration from these meetings. It was borne in upon him by Hawthorne that a romance must have in it more than characters and action and background: there must be soul as well as body. Both men had classics within them struggling for delivery. Hawthorne had not yet written *The House of the Seven Gables* and Melville was brooding on a Caliban theme which had taken complete possession of him. Doubtless they discussed together the coming book. It was to be laid, so Melville had determined, on what the Saxons had called "the whale path," and by superficial measurements it was to be the record of a voyage. But it must, so Hawthorne undoubtedly ruled, record more than mere adventure: it must be like a Greek tragedy: the soul of man driven by the gods that are, and though defeated, still "invictus."

The result, wrought in the hell of a New York summer, was the Frankenstein monster *Moby Dick,* a chaos confounded if unity and coherence be objects in fiction. A treatise it is on the whaling industry, even to biology and statistics; a log-book it is of a seemingly actual voyage done with convincing realism; adventure it contains of dime-novel headlongness; sailor psychology and the magic of the sea; and mystic elements even to the ghostly. But soul is in the book. In the old Greek fashion there is in it a new mythology, the addition of a new member to the group of the Eumenides. Few in the fifties saw this, however. The English, nautically minded, saw only sea adventure, and, caustically, they criticized it. It is a hodge-podge, they said, a part of it autobiography and a part in the third person, romance shaken up with ency-clopædia facts.

Considered as fiction or travel or biology or history, the book made no progress. It was not in accord with the fifties that gave it birth. Those who had wept over *The Wide, Wide World,* avoided it as a coarse and brutal thing. There was no love story, no feminine characters, no humor, no religion even remotely orthodox. Parts of it, indeed, reeked, they thought, of the infernal pit.

The French were more lenient. Chasles in the *Revue des Deux Mondes,* 1849, two years before *Moby Dick,* had found Melville to be one of the most notable of the American writers. The best treatment of the man in an American review appeared in 1853 in the first volume of *Putnam's Magazine,* its writer, as we now know, Fitz-James O'Brien, just arrived in New York. With Celtic fervor he dwelt upon the voluptuous picturings of *Typee.* Overlooking entirely the philosophy running through the mazes of *Moby Dick,* he ruled that the most important addition to literary art made by Herman Melville was his insistence upon actuality, upon truth—realism we now term it. Melville had an eye to see and he could tell what he saw:

He is essentially exotical in feeling. Matter is his god. His dreams are material. His philosophy is sensual. Beautiful women, shadowy lakes, nodding plumy trees, and succulent banquets, make Melville's scenery, unless his theme utterly

preclude all such. His language is rich and heavy, with a plat-
ing of imagery. He has a barbarian love of ornament and
does not mind how much it is put on. Swept away by his
sensual longing, he frequently writes at random. One can see
that he uses certain words only because they roll off his pen
lusciously and roundly.

This review, so highly commendatory of Melville's art,
served only to deepen the gulf between him and his religious and prudish contemporaries. And if one knows
these contemporaries one does not wonder. For instance,
note the sensuousness of the Celtic O'Brien's picturings
of the cannibal nymph Fayaway:

Charming, smooth-skinned siren around whose sun-
browned form the waves lap and dimple, like the longing
touches of a lover's fingers, what luxury untold it must have
been to live with thee beneath the shady places of Typee. To
dance with thee in the moonlight in front of the deep-eaved
hut; to hunt with thee for strange flowers in the deep, silent
woods, or sail with thee on the lake when the sunset painted
our tapa sail with finer hues than the work of Gobelius.
How Tom could have left thee surpasseth human understand-
ing. Left thee, graceful, artless child of the forest and the
stream, to dwell among civilized women—dancing machines;
flirting machines, built of whalebone and painted red.

Hardly reading that would commend itself to Lowell
mill-girls, to the Warner sisters, or the Carys, or the
myriad readers of *The Wide, Wide World*.

Melville becomes less and less a problem as time goes
on, but more and more he becomes interesting. Returned
from his adventuring in forecastles and island jails where
he had known intimately the riff-raff of the tropic island
ports, he was as disillusioned as were the trench fighters

of the World War returned after the armistice. Unlike them, however, he came alone, the lost man of his generation, and there was no lost generation to confirm his pessimism or to support him or to listen to him. Before the Civil War had let it loose, the fundamental brute that is in man had been kept concealed. To talk of it was utter vulgarity and obscenity, not to be tolerated.

Melville did not hesitate to present graphically the bestial side of man, but at the same time he had not lost his dream of finding the bluebird love and purity. He was a Gansevoort and at the same time he was a Melville, and his fundamental weakness was that he was neither one thing nor the other—wholly. One can quote him, indeed, to prove him a Transcendentalist, and then one can counter with quotations just as clear that place him at the other extreme. It was for this that the thoughtful ones of his own generation rejected him as a leader. He is great in fragments rather than in wholes. Never completely did he find himself. The last word concerning his work and place was spoken by a writer in the last volume of *Putnam's Magazine,* 1857, ten years after *Typee.* In reality it was his biography, and it needs no change even now in the amazing resurrection era of the man:

Nature said to Herman Melville, "You shall tell the world what you have seen and see, in a warm, quick, nervous style, and bring the realities of life and man before your readers in such a way that they shall know your mind without calling on you to speak it. You shall be as true as Teniers or Defoe, without the coarseness of the Fleming or the bluntness of the Englishman."

Obstinate cultivation rejoined: "No! you shall dissect and divide; you shall cauterize and confound; you shall amaze and electrify; you shall be as grotesquely terrible as Callot, as subtly profound as Balzac, as formidably satirical as Rabelais."

As a result he was both and neither: the two natures within him—Gansevoort-Melville, New York-Boston— warred and clashed and neither reached the powers that might have been his to command.

He disappeared with the feminine decade. Ill luck pursued him. He was threatened at one time with mental break-down. His books sold not well. The great fire that destroyed the Harper's building wiped out his editions, plates and all. He sought in vain a diplomatic position and then went abroad on an aimless tour. The Civil War gave Whitman a second chance; it only rendered more complete the disappearance for two generations of Herman Melville.

II

ON INDEPENDENCE DAY, 1855—the choice of date is noteworthy—was published what was destined to be the most famous book of the decade. A nondescript thing it was, paradoxical from every standpoint. Quarto in size, tall and broad as a family Bible, it contained but ninety-five pages. With its soft green cover over which rambled the title in gold letters made to resemble leaves and roots and tendrils, with its triple-lined border stamped in gold, and its marbled end papers, it had a Fanny Fern look. Its title *Leaves of Grass* suggested the current best-seller *Fern Leaves from Fanny's Portfolio,* a volume with precisely the same binding and cover design. Indeed, according to a late editor of Whitman, he was familiar with the *Fern Leaves* author and her writings and perhaps consulted her concerning his own forthcoming book. We know that Fanny Fern reviewed most appreciatively *Leaves of Grass* for Bonner's New York *Ledger* under the title "Fresh Fern Leaves: Leaves of Grass." Very feminine the volume was in its outer inventory, suggesting at first glance a gift-book of the period, but opening it expecting to find sentimental steel engravings of "Zuleika," or "Sweet Charity," or "The Babes in the Wood," one was confronted by what Lowell termed "a New York rough," or, according to British idiom, a "bloody mucker"—presumably the author, an engraving made from a tintype. No identification under the engraving, no author's name on the title-page, no publishers' imprint. Then ten pages of seeming prose in double columns, smudgily printed, in long paragraphs cut into eccentric fragments by rows of periods used like dashes. Then twelve pieces looking like neither prose nor poetry—long lines strung across the broad pages, each piece headed with "LEAVES OF GRASS" in auction-bill type, or else untitled. Beginning with the first of these, one read:

> I CELEBRATE myself,
> And what I assume you shall assume.

One dollar seems to have been the price of the book in boards, seventy-five cents in paper, if bought in 1855; a thousand dollars or more if bought now.

Sold alongside of *Hiawatha,* then the best-seller on the bookstands, the volume was a "dud." In Whitman's own words, "I don't think one copy was sold—not a copy. The books were put into the stores but nobody bought them. They had to be given away. Yet—I was popular

FIRST EDITION OF *LEAVES OF GRASS*
Brooklyn, New York, 1855. Courtesy of the New York Public Library.

among the dealers then—they liked me. What became of the first edition is a mystery: the books scattered, somehow, somewhere, God knows, to the four corners of the earth."

To study this seeming poetical monstrosity one must begin with the prose introduction, and here, until recently, the student has found himself handicapped. The original text has been butchered and abbreviated in editions like Payne's *American Literary Criticism,* and omitted from later editions of *Leaves of Grass.* It is an important document, the introduction to the Whitman of the fifties. Emerson read the preface straight through and was so moved by it that he wrote its author, who had sent him a copy in paper covers, the most famous letter written during the decade, at least the most famous in the area of American literature. Repeatedly has it been quoted:

Concord, Mass'tts, 21 July, 1855

Dear Sir, I am not blind to the worth of the wonderful gift of "Leaves of Grass." I find·it the most extraordinary piece of wit and wisdom that America has yet contributed. I am very happy in reading it, as great power makes me happy. It meets the demands I am always making of what seemed the sterile and stingy Nature, as if too much handiwork, or too much lymph in the temperament, were making our Western wits fat and mean.

I give you joy of your free and brave thought. I have great joy in it. I find incomparable things said incomparably well, as they must be. I find the courage of treatment that so delights us, and which large perception only can inspire.

I greet you at the beginning of a great career, which yet must have had a long foreground somewhere, for such a start. I rubbed my eyes a little to see if this sunbeam were no illusion; but the solid sense of the book is a sober certainty. It has the best merits, namely of fortifying and encouraging.

I did not know, until I last night saw the book advertised in a newspaper, that I could trust the name as real and available for a post-office.

I wish to see my benefactor, and have felt much like striking my tasks and visiting New York to pay you my respects.

R. W. EMERSON

Later to Carlyle, Emerson wrote that the book was "a nondescript monster, which yet has terrible eyes and buffalo strength, and was indisputably American. Written and printed by a journeyman printer in Brooklyn, New York, named Walter Whitman."

Having been for years in the currents of New York journalism, Whitman knew advertising methods. Three fulsome reviews written by himself soon appeared in friendly newspapers. The second edition, enlarged to thirty-two poems, was issued in 1856 on an Emerson tide, smudgy copies of the letter going with the book. In 1860 appeared the third edition enlarged to 154 poems.

No wonder Emerson approved of the first-edition preface; it was grass from his own meadow: the same Orphic style, the same declamatory ring, the same *ex cathedra* positiveness. The preface was as truly poetry as were the twelve pieces that followed it. Everywhere the Emersonian "free and brave thought" and "courage of treatment." Emerson's extreme statements he had taken with literalness, had even heightened, and then had turned them from the original abstract into concrete application.

To trace the evolution of *Leaves of Grass* beyond the three editions of the 1850's is not my task. Allow me to note, however, that the Civil War caused this section to stand by itself apart, the first movement, as it were, of the Whitman oratorio. The war period so changed him that in a preface written in 1888 he could say "without these three or four years, and the experience they gave, 'Leaves of Grass' would not now be in existence." His physical break-down in the 1870's, and the resulting change from the physical and the mundane to the spiritual and the transcendental, created a third period in his work. With the coming of disciples and the coronation of his poems first by the English and then by the whole world, there came changes in his tones and manner, but these I shall not trace.

The work in the three editions issued before the war, therefore, stands isolate. It reveals the primal Whitman, the Whitman as molded by the feminine fifties. Examining the editions in this light, one is inclined to echo what another critic said of another writer: *had he not appeared as he did, it would be necessary to invent him*. Revolt from the New England florists, from Harvard standards, from imported Victorian refinement was bound to come, and most probably from a critic wholly outside of the New England tradition, wholly devoid of inherited Puritanism. The New York Bohemians talked interminably of revolt, but they were a fugacious lot like all other Gipsy tribes. Lacking stable leadership, they evolved little save hatred of Boston, which to them was what Rome was to the Goths.

Leadership, however, did come from this group, though when the first actual blow was struck in the revolt and *Leaves of Grass* was on the book stands, the group was,

with all the rest of New York, hooting at the unprecedented thing. John Burroughs tells of the "staff of a
leading newspaper of New York waiting to be paid off
one Saturday afternoon in 1855, greeting the passages read
to them from *Leaves of Grass* with peals upon peals of
ironical laughter." Doubtless the reader was giving them
selected passages like this:

Twenty-eight young men bathe by the shore,
Twenty-eight young men, and all so friendly,
Twenty-eight years of womanly life, and all so lonesome.

She owns the fine house by the rise of the bank,
She hides handsome and richly drest aft the blinds of the
    window.

Which of the young men does she like the best?
Ah the homeliest of them is beautiful to her.

Where are you off to, lady? for I see you,
You splash in the water there, yet stay stock still in your room.

Dancing and laughing along the beach came the twenty-ninth
    bather,
The rest did not see her, but she saw them and loved them.

The beards of the young men glistened with wet, it ran from
    their long hair,
Little streams passed all over their bodies.

An unseen hand also passed over their bodies,
It descended tremblingly from their temples and ribs.

The young men float on their backs, their white bellies swell
    in the sun.

  Or, again, this:

Earth! you seem to look for something at my hands,
Say old topknot! what do you want?

Peculiar stuff, this, to found a revolution upon, but the seeds of revolution have seldom a familiar look, and always they refuse to spring up like gourds in a single night.

Whitman, submerged in the newspaper world which he had entered as a printer's devil, self-taught by random reading, had felt revolt from the conventional growing within him for a decade or more. There was revolt in his sensational temperance novel which had fallen flat. Then he had discovered Emerson. As he later expressed it: "I was simmering, simmering, simmering; Emerson brought me to a boil." Undoubtedly he read Emerson, but more likely his inspiration came from hearing the two or three lectures by Emerson which by his own statement he had attended. The influence upon him was great. Traces of the Concord essayist one may find everywhere in the earlier editions of *Leaves of Grass*. Without a question, the sling and the smooth stones of the New England David aroused him from the indolence that had been his besetting sin. He, too, would be a slinger of smooth stones. He pictured himself in the 1850's standing where Emerson had stood in 1837 with his new literary declaration of independence.

Despite Emerson's approval of the primal preface, later dropped, the Concord sage did not long keep pace with his disciple. Emerson was a man of books, Harvard-bred both in letters and theology. He lived his life with Plato and Plotinus, with oriental prophets and seers; but Whitman lived in New York City and Brooklyn and he knew the cities from the water-front slums to the mansions of Fifth Avenue. He went to see plays in the theaters, he enjoyed the opera, he dined in restaurants with the crowd, he rode free on the ferry-boats, he lounged on the docks and the sidewalks, and, sometimes holding the reins, he sat on the driver's seat of omnibuses with "Broadway Jack, Balky Bill, Old Elephant, his brother Young Elephant, Pop Rice, Yellow Joe, Big Frank and the rest. . . . They had immense qualities, largely animal—eating, drinking, women, great personal pride in their way." He read what he enjoyed: George Sand, the New York *Ledger* and other story papers, Dickens. Emerson was bored by Dickens.

Thoreau, touring New York, visited Greeley's farm, heard Henry Ward Beecher preach in his Brooklyn tabernacle, and then visited Walt Whitman in Brooklyn. "He said I had misapprehended him. I am not quite sure that I do. He told me that he loved to ride up and down Broadway all day on an omnibus, sitting beside the driver, listening to the roar of the carts, and sometimes gesticulating and declaiming Homer at the top of his voice."

Leaves of Grass in its first movement—the three earliest editions redolent of the fifties—was not at all transcendental. Its feet were on the ground, or rather on the sidewalks of New York. It dealt with the concrete world. Its creator had before him living people whom he felt he was addressing. I fancy he moved his lips as he wrote his sentences. Emerson was intellectual, an embodiment of the Boston east wind, chilly but impossible to ignore. He was conscious always of the "Oversoul," unseen but none the less felt. Always he worked in the abstract. In his 1837 address he called for American originality and freedom, but wanted it on the intellectual and spiritual levels. He was concerned for "the American scholar." Whitman in his 1855 preface also demanded freedom and originality, but he wanted it for *all* the people—*en masse*. The democratic leaders, he maintained, must come from the ranks of the illiterate, not from the colleges:

There is that indescribable freshness and unconsciousness about an illiterate person that humbles and mocks the power of the noblest expressive genius.

And again:

Take off your hat to nobody known or unknown, or to any man or number of men.... Go freely with powerful uneducated persons, and with the young, and with the mothers of families.... Re-examine all you have been told in school, or church, or in any book, and dismiss whatever insults your own soul.

The Whitman of the 1850's was in key with the pre-war decade that produced the first issue of *Leaves of Grass*. Everywhere violent enthusiasm; Utopian dreamings; humanitarianism become a mania; God's mistakes in creating the world to be rectified. No era was it for thinking; all was feeling. Reason by itself never would have brought the Civil War. As voiced a decade later by Lanier:

"The time needs heart—'tis tired of head,
    We're all for love," the violins said.

And completely was Whitman in tune: all was he of heart and little of head. He voiced the soprano fifties that smothered intellect with emotion. Humanitarianism had captured him early, and now it was capturing even the Transcendentalists who were beginning to leave their studies to become giant-killers. Themes untouched by emotion appealed not at all to Whitman, but when his feelings had been touched nothing could stop him. He let himself go, bring up where he might.

Like all barbarians he hated a refinement that was merely conventional: scholarship hardened into academicism, decorative art, inherited laws reverenced because of their antiquity, Victorianism imported for display. For him, Tennyson was "the bard of ennui and aristocracy"; and the soft cooing of the young Taylor and Stoddard and Stedman and Aldrich angered him. Longfellow, as long as he played only on the emotions, he could endure, but his literary aristocracy, his poems made from books, he could not endure. Thus he assessed the New England poet laureate: "Longfellow, reminiscent, polished, elegant, with the air of finest conventional library, picture gallery, or parlor, with ladies or gentlemen in them, and plush and rosewood, and ground-glass lamps, and mahogany and ebony furniture, and a silver inkstand and scented satin paper to write on."

Conventional prudishness disgusted him, and with adolescent glee he delighted to shock. If Nature put sex life into the open, why try to improve upon Nature? He refused to omit the "Children of Adam" from his collection, though Emerson earnestly pleaded for him to do so. Utterly unacademic, he was like a Vandal breaking in upon a Roman banquet, roaring at artificiality, and smashing the bric-à-brac of an over-refined generation.

In his later periods he expressed his revolt from the New England florists in a series of rules:

Lumber the writing with nothing—let it go as lightly as the bird flies or the fish swims in the sea.

Avoid all poetical similitudes; be faithful to the perfect likelihoods of Nature—healthy, exact, simple, disdaining ornaments.

Do not go into criticisms or arguments at all; make full blooded, rich, flush, natural works.

Insert natural things, indestructibles, idioms, characteristics, rivers, states, persons, &c. Be full of strong sensual germs.

Poet! beware lest your poems are made in the spirit that comes from the study of pictures of things—and not from the spirit that comes from the contact with real things themselves.

Totally, in his first movement, did he combat the refined and the delicate. He lacked courtesy and restraint. To affect him there must be sensation above the ordinary: color, odor—the strong reek of lilacs, resonance, picturesqueness. He loved the "limber, lasting fierce words," aboriginal place names, full-mouthed foreign phrases. The grotesque pseudo-science phrenology, so advertised and exploited during the decade of the fifties, won him completely.

His democracy was what Lanier was to term "love"— the love that knows no distinctions, love without thought of caste or race, love that could hail a felon on the way to execution as "brother," and a common prostitute as "sister":

Not till the sun excludes you, do I exclude you;
Not till the waters refuse to glisten for you and the leaves to
    rustle for you do my words refuse to glisten and rustle
    for you.

Of race prejudice he had none:

The negro holds firm the reins of the four horses ...
I behold the picturesque giant and love him.

For this phase of his democracy—alas, individual with him!—some of his more extreme disciples have gone so far as to compare him with Jesus.

But my study of Whitman is concerned only with the three editions of *Leaves of Grass* created during the 1850's. Despite the fact that Whitman was forty when the 1860 version appeared, youth, even to adolescence, is written on every part of it. It bounds from poem to poem with eager health and animal spirits. For later editions he edited out such lines as,

How dare a sick man, or an obedient man, write poems for these states?

He had matured slowly. As elsewhere I have said, "he was in the very tempest of perfect physical health and he had the youth's eagerness to change things. His early work is as much a gospel of physical perfection as was its contemporary gospel, *Science and Health*. Everywhere in it vigor,

Health chants—joy chants—robust chants of young men.

Of the higher forms of sacrifice, of self-effacement, of character that builds its own aristocracy and draws lines through even the most democratic mass, he knows nothing. He may talk, but as yet it is talk without experience. ... The style of the man, the 'easily-written, loose-fingered chords' of his chants, unrimed, lawless: this was Whitman himself. How he found it or when he found it matters not greatly. He was too indolent to elaborate for himself a deliberate metrical system; he was too lawless of soul to be bound by the old prosody. Whatever he wrote must loaf along with perfect freedom, unpolished, haphazard, incoherent." [1]

The three editions were failures. They did not sell, and despite the fulsome reviews that Whitman himself wrote, they got a poor press—or none. New England ignored the book. Whittier burned his copy; Longfellow ignored it; Lowell, after 1857 literary dictator of Boston and beyond, considered it a gross uncouthness. Even Emerson fell out with the second edition.

Whitman was right when he said that without the war there would be now no *Leaves of Grass*. Not only did the war change Whitman, but it changed the literary atmosphere. And just as truly Whitman might have said that without his physical break-down in the mid-seventies, the Whitman of "The Passage to India" and "The Prayer of Columbus," the Whitman exalting the soul of man rather than the body never could have been.

But naturally I shall not enter the editions that followed the 1860 version.

[1] *A History of American Literature since 1870* (New York, The Century Co., 1915), p. 170.

CHAPTER V

THE SECOND FLOWERING OF NEW ENGLAND

THOREAU IN HIS "SUCCESSION OF FOREST TREES" NOTED the fact that when forest areas are cleared and burned a different variety of trees springs up. The same law seemed to govern the Brahmin literary succession. The new growth from which was to come the second flowering, a growth first discernible during the decade of the fifties, was almost wholly feminine, and it expressed itself to a large degree in a popularized form of fiction, a literary genre not tolerated by early Puritanism.

Women for two decades had been contributing freely to the annuals, to *Godey's Lady's Book* and other magazines, but their offerings had been for the most part poetry. With a few exceptions, the American literary "female," as seen in the 1830's and the 1840's, was a writer of verse. Rufus W. Griswold in 1847, in his *Prose Writers of America* volume which presented selections from the writings of seventy-two authors, admitted to the number only five women: Catharine M. Sedgwick, Eliza Leslie,

Lydia M. Child, Caroline M. Kirkland, and Margaret Fuller.

In 1848, however, one hundred and thirty-one feminine poets were presented to the world, with copious samplings of their work headed by biographical sketches, in three elaborate volumes by three different compilers, each entitled *The Female Poets of America,* one edited by Thomas Buchanan Read of Philadelphia, one by Caroline May of New York, and one by the voluminous compiler Rufus W. Griswold. Of the total number in the three volumes—one hundred and thirty-one—only forty-three were represented in all three collections. The volumes were exceedingly popular, selling many editions. Americans of the 1840's bought feminine poetry; the women wrote it in surprising quantities. Then suddenly in 1850 came a change: feminine fiction began to appear in a flood, and the greater part of it was being produced by New England women or by transplanted New England women, and women and even men were buying it in unheard of quantities.

What had happened?

II

NEW ENGLAND in the 1850's reached in the rural areas its maximum of population. Everywhere, even in the mountain hardscrabbles, little farms strewn with rocks, but always within horse-and-wagon distance of the village with its grocery store, its meeting house, its town hall and its blacksmith shop. Always was there in the town a settled minister, and often more than one, an educated man, often a college graduate. All children without exception went to school in the fall and winter, and most of the population went to church on Sunday.

Rural families were large. My own father and mother had each of them ten brothers and sisters. The boys were forced to leave home early to secure jobs in the city or to seek their fortune in the rising West. All the professions: the ministry, law, medicine, business, politics, were strictly masculine. For girls there were housework or teaching or marriage. Great numbers of girls during the forties and fifties left the farms where they were born and found employment in the mills along the Merrimac as loom-tenders. Many taught country schools and many were held by home ties, often into dreary spinsterhood.

All of them had been trained, more or less, in the red schoolhouses of their day, and all had felt the educating influences of the churches and the pastors who from their childhood had been a part of their lives. All had read in the school readers more or less of good literature, and all had taken out books from the circulating library of the Sunday-school or town.

As a result, literature had fallen more and more into the hands of women. The men of the generation were immersed in business, in professional work, in the driving affairs of a headlong age. And the women remained at home and read—as they could. Willis in his *Home Journal*, 1852, stated conditions with clearness:

While the boys of our country are educated over-practically, the girls are educated over-sentimentally. The universality of cheap and trashy novels impairs both the relish and the right appreciation of the companionship which falls in their way; and no one of them, for some brief period, feels herself properly mated. Hence a stage of girlhood, which is a struggle to build a romance upon commonplace intercourse.

All unknown to the Brahmin classic-makers, a reading class during some two decades had been gathering because of conditions totally overlooked. Large numbers of middle-aged, middle-class women were taking to fiction as a narcotic, as a means for escape. The romantic young girl dreamed over the novels as a picture of her life to be, but the old district school-teacher, the farmer's overworked wife, even the minister's wife, felt at times that life had cheated them, that their dreams had not come true, that they were victims somehow of maladjustment. "In for life" and knowing it, they could, for moments at least and often hours, live on vicarious romance under the spell of a novel that made them forget.

Novels that satisfied them were not easily found, but one day in the late forties came an English book entitled *Jane Eyre*. My mother, then a loom-tender in Lowell, has told me how "Jane Erie," as her companions pronounced it, ran through the mill-girl community like an epidemic. Before she died, aged eighty-eight, she had reread it five times.

The story of its creation fits the setting of the American mid-century as if it were a parable woven for illustration. Three daughters of the manse, marooned on a Yorkshire moor, held in an atmosphere rigidly religious, touching the world only through books that fed their imaginations, and escaping by means of literary creation of a world woven of their dreams and their longings—the novels *Jane Eyre* and *Wuthering Heights*.

So was it in dozens of New England homes, though

no books were created measurable with those written in
the Brontë manse. The new fiction did not come from
ignorance of books. The writers of it had had access to
circulating libraries, and they had read—doubtless too
much. The Lowell mill girls, a fair sample of the middle-
class younger generation, had created for themselves a
literary atmosphere and had published a magazine, *The
Lowell Offering*. *Godey's Lady's Book* was widely read,
as many an attic even to-day will testify. Satisfying novels
were not hard to procure, and girls at home had time for
reading. To read much fiction is to write fiction if one
has resolution enough to substantiate one's desire.

As a result, the new flowering of New England.

III

NEW literary movements begin always in a corner, usually
a corner before unheard of. The movement that was to
start the dominating fiction of the fifties began in a
transplanted New England home on Constitution Island
in the Hudson River near West Point. Here had grown
up two girls in nun-like seclusion, Susan and Anna
Warner, their father, Henry W. Warner, a practising
lawyer, much away from home. So far as they were educated, their education came from him and from their own
eager efforts. No father could have done more for his
daughters—at least so far as good intentions might go.
Every night when he was at home he read to them—the
whole of the Waverley novels, Shakespeare, Dickens,
Paradise Lost, Miss Edgeworth, Boswell's *Johnson*. Faithfully they studied French and Italian, with a tutor, an
old professor who set them rigorous tasks. French novels

they were allowed to read only after their father had marked passages and pages that they were to avoid. Goldsmith they read, and Hume, and *The Swiss Family Robinson,* and Blair's *Rhetoric,* and on Sunday the Bible varied with the singing of sentimental hymns. Religion dominated the home as if it were indeed a nunnery. Out of its atmosphere came two hymns found in most church hymnals:

> We would see Jesus; for the shadows lengthen
> Across the little landscape of our life;

and

> One more day's work for Jesus,
> One less of life for me;

both written by Anna Warner, the younger of the two sisters.

Ill luck in business brought financial stringency in the home and the sisters devised a game which they called "Robinson Crusoe's Farmyard"—cards with pictures of "tame and wild animals judiciously mixed" to be drawn in colors by the two young artists. Then had come Susan's plan to write a novel, and for a year she worked with eagerness. She was melancholy of temperament, subject to tearful overflow, emotionally religious, constantly within doors writing or reading. Her sister, Anna, however was cheerful of soul, loving out-of-doors life, a tonic to her sister as she worked. And the book, christened *The Wide, Wide World,* was finished.

Before approaching the book one must realize that it was created in an atmosphere intensely and emotionally religious. Said Anna Warner of it in later years: "It was written in closest reliance upon God: for thoughts, for power, and for words. Not the mere vague wish to write a book that should do service to her Master; but a vivid, constant looking to him for guidance and help: the worker and the work both laid humbly at the Lord's feet. In that sense the book was written upon her knees; and the Lord's blessing has followed it, down to this day."

The father who had taken it upon himself to market the huge pile of hand-written manuscript found difficulties. "It was refused by almost all of the leading book firms of New York." From Harper's it returned with the word "Fudge!" written upon it. G. P. Putnam received the manuscript while at his summer home on Staten Island. His mother had come for a visit, and to amuse her he handed her the manuscript to read, with the remark, "See if it is fit to publish." She read it and her answer was emphatic: "If you never publish another book, publish this." On her judgment alone the book was accepted and published, and no book published by the Putnams ever had a larger sale.

It was issued December 12, 1850, under the pseudonym Elizabeth Wetherell. In three months it sold 1,500 copies, and by 1852 it was in its fourteenth edition and was selling strongly. In England several editions were published. *Queechy* which soon followed, though more vigorous in style and less doleful in tone, trailed behind the earlier volume even as Mrs. Stowe's *Dred* trailed behind *Uncle Tom's Cabin*.

On the whole the early book reviews were favorable. One who reads the book to-day finds it hard to realize how any critic at any time could speak of "the almost faultless excellence of *The Wide, Wide World"* or could speak of it as an "incomparable work, read with the most heartfelt sympathy and delight." It was the first "best-seller" in the history of American fiction, and like all makers of best-sellers, the author was showered with letters of appreciation, all of them glowing with superlatives.

"Nothing succeeds like success": the era of the best-seller had opened wide.

The novel relies very little on plot for its effectiveness. It has few indeed of those dramatic incidents that usually hold readers of fiction. It is a story of home life, like the day-by-day life in the Warner home on Constitution Island, and it dwells upon the development, moral and religious, of a girl in her teens. In *Queechy,* the leading character is a girl who has been reared in luxury and then has been plunged into comparative poverty, and the reader watches her spiritual and intellectual growth. Instead of action, descriptions of feeling; instead of dramatic sensation, emotion. Like Mackenzie's *Man of Feeling* of the eighteenth century, it should have had an index of tears. By actual count there are 245 tear-flows in the 574 pages of the novel.

But like every other novel, it must be examined against the background of its times. A volume that sold as *The Wide, Wide World* sold cannot be dismissed with an adjective. It is a mirror in which one may see the people who bought it and may study the spirit of its age.

The volume succeeded first of all because of its sensibility. In an emotional age it fed emotion. Then too it was feelingly religious, and it had the atmosphere of home. When mother dies, and little children die, and hardships come to young dreamers, then all will wipe a tear.

One more volume, in a small way a best-seller, came from the Warner home—Anna Warner's *Dollars and Cents,* 1852, issued under the pseudonym Amy Lothrop, a story far more readable to-day than the two her sister wrote, but now completely forgotten.

Mrs. Bayard Taylor, in her autobiography, after recording that the two novels of Susan Warner had been read by her in Germany before she had ever known Bayard Taylor, has recorded this really illuminating anecdote:

Miss Susan was so fully persuaded of the infallibility of her religious views that after making the acquaintance of Thackeray, when he came to New York in 1856, she said of him one evening at a party: "He is an excellent man, but there is a whole world he knows nothing of—a world which I know." Later in the evening, when refreshments were served, Mrs. Stoddard made one of her witty remarks at the expense of the Misses Warner. Alluding to the long necks of these ladies, she whispered to my husband, "Look at the giraffes grazing."

IV

A CONTEMPORARY case, almost parallel with that of the Warner sisters, was that of two other transplanted New Englanders, the Cary sisters, Alice and Phœbe. More completely had they been marooned on their father's little Ohio farm than had the Warner sisters on Constitution Island, or even the Brontës on the Yorkshire moor.

Their father, from a long New England line of Puritan ancestors, had settled early near Cincinnati, and struggling long with mortgages, had had small success as a farmer. He had brought to his family of small children a second

SUSAN WARNER   ANNA WARNER

Courtesy of the Constitution Island Association.

ALICE CARY   PHŒBE CARY

From *Poems of Alice and Phœbe Cary.*

wife, a "hard, uncultured, utilitarian woman" who had small sympathy for anything like idealism in the lives of her stepdaughters. The father, intensely religious, sang hymns to his children and read them the Bible, but he brought them no books and no magazines.

Even had there been books there would have been small time for reading them since work was unending. But like the young Whittier, they dreamed of poetry and they wrote poetry—at night by the light from a burning rag hung in a saucer of lard. And after many attempts, one poem entitled "The Child of Sorrow" was published in a local newspaper. Then had come publication in other newspapers and in the Boston *Ladies' Repository* and *Graham's Magazine*. Their fugitive verses attracted the attention of Horace Greeley, and in the late forties, while in the West, he visited the young poets in their home and assisted them to find a publisher for their poetry. Their first little volume appeared in 1849.

In 1850, when the elder of the two sisters was nearing thirty, they made a tour of the Holy Land of the East— as it had always seemed to them in their dreamings— New York and New England, where they met, as had the Warner sisters on a similar pilgrimage, some of the writers whose works they knew by heart. They had corresponded with Whittier: he had given them advice concerning their poems, and in June 1850, he wrote to Rufus W. Griswold, then located in New York:

I learn from my friend F. W. Kellogg that Alice and Phœbe Cary of Ohio are on their way to the East, and would be glad to see them at my place if they come to Boston. Presuming that thou wilt see them in N. Y. I have taken the liberty to invite them, through thee, to call on me. I have been quite ill this spring, and my sister also is an invalid, and we see little company, but I should feel sorry to have the "sweet singers" of the West so near and not see them.

As a result, they visited the poet's home in Amesbury, a visit that years later Whittier commemorated in his lyric entitled

THE SINGER

Years since (but names to me before),
Two sisters sought at eve my door;
Two song-birds wandering from their nest,
A gray old farm-house in the West.

Timid and still, the elder had
Even then a smile too sweetly sad;
The crown of pain that all must wear
Too early pressed her midnight hair.

Yet, ere the summer eve grew long,
Her modest lips were sweet with song;
A memory haunted all her words
Of clover-fields and singing birds.

Her dark, dilating eyes expressed
The broad horizons of the West;
Her speech dropped prairie flowers; the gold
Of harvest wheat around her rolled.

Foredoomed to song she seemed to me;
I queried not with destiny:
I knew the trial and the need,
Yet all the more, I said, God speed!

What could I other than I did?
Could I a singing-bird forbid?
Deny the wind-stirred leaf? Rebuke
The music of the forest brook?

She went with morning from my door;
But left me richer than before:
Thenceforth I knew her voice of cheer,
The welcome of her partial ear.

Years passed: through all the land her name
A pleasant household word became;
All felt behind the singer stood
A sweet and gracious womanhood.

Her life was earnest work, not play;
Her tired feet climbed a weary way;
And even through her lightest strain
We heard an undertone of pain.

Unseen of her, her fair fame grew,
The good she did she rarely knew
Unguessed of her in life the love
That rained its tears her grave above.

The same year (1850) they removed to New York City, took a small flat on a third-floor back, and wholly without means, save as won from what writings they could sell, started out to make literature their profession:

If my judgment was ever invoked [wrote Horace Greeley in later years] I am sure I must have responded that the hazard seemed to me too great, the inducements inadequate.... We had then scarcely any periodical literature worthy of the name outside of the political and commercial journals. I doubt that so much money was paid, in the aggregate, for contributions to *all* the magazines and weeklies issued from this city, as were paid in 1870 by the *Ledger* alone.

The story of Alice Cary's literary evolution illustrates the evolution in progress during the early fifties. In the 1840's women wrote poetry and published poetry when they could find a publisher. By 1850 they were writing prose sketches like those in Grace Greenwood's *Green-wood Leaves* and Fanny Fern's *Fern Leaves*. Alice Cary, seeking eagerly for a market, found it in 1852 with her *Clovernook*, but after the sensational sales of *The Wide, Wide World* and *Uncle Tom's Cabin* all the women made haste to trim their sails for the new breeze. Alice Cary had a novel, *Hagar*, ready in 1852, and another, *Married not Mated*, in 1856; but Alice was no novelist.

Her greatest success was with her volume of sketches and short narratives, *Clovernook, or Recollections of Our Neighborhood in the West*, 1852, a volume that may be ranked as a minor best-seller in its period. Especially did it find favor in England where it appeared in five different editions. That she got little for these popular editions pirated abroad filled the gentle editor of *Putnam's Magazine* with a mild rage:

Some of the foreign pirates [he stormed] have had the decency to offer her a small sum for the republication, but the others, like our own book-purveyors, have not said even "thank ye." If there is a future place of retribution, as the theologians assure us, and men are punished according to the wrongs they have afflicted on other men, what a sad fate awaits those who have fared sumptuously every day on the brains of poor authors.

But fame for an American author in England, even if not paid for in pounds and shillings, often has meant fortune at home, and so it was with *Clovernook*. A second series was issued in New York in 1853 which was more successful even than the first.

The English undoubtedly had been attracted to the book because of its local color. To them the "West" meant utter wildness, buffaloes, Indians. And *Clovernook* was something utterly new. Caroline M. Kirkland, a decade before, with her *A New Home; Who'll Follow?* and her *Western Clearings,* had romanticized the new Western settlements. Her work seemed like propaganda for a land boom, but these sketches and narratives by a woman who had been born on the prairie and who had lived on a small farm there for thirty years were manifestly the whole truth. Often over the sketches hung a softened atmosphere of remembered youth, an atmosphere created by homesick memories. Mostly are the sketches "grim and realistic accounts of bare and unlovely lives" with little omitted of the harshness and privations of farm life on a newly-broken frontier. It was the first piece of Hamlin Garland-like reaiism to come out of the Middle Border lands, and it came some ten years before Hamlin Garland was born. Tremendously serious books they were, written, as all of Alice Cary's other ten volumes were written, without humor and without reservations. Life to her had meant sorrow and heart-ache. When, in 1853, she issued *Lyra and Other Poems,* even the decade of tears criticized it harshly for its uniform somberness.

By 1856 her two *Clovernook* series and her books for children had been so successful that she was enabled to buy a modest little house on Twentieth Street, New York City, and make of it a home that in time became a national and even an international literary center. The sisters had found influential friends, and now more and more for the next fifteen years their Sunday Nights became famous, so famous indeed that no treatise on the literary 1850's and 1860's can neglect it. Horace Greeley never missed a Sunday evening visit, and with him he brought always distinguished foreigners visiting the city, like Robert Chambers of Edinburgh, or Justin McCarthy. Always was there a merry gathering of writers like Richard and Elizabeth Stoddard, George Ripley, who had been the founder of the Brook Farm Community. E. P. Whipple, Robert Bonner, R. W. Raymond, Dr. Chapin, T. B. Aldrich—indeed, everybody went sooner or later to see the Cary sisters. As hostesses they seem to have been charming, more charming, indeed, than any of their surviving volumes. They were totally unaffected, they were genuine, and everything about them had the atmosphere of home.

Alice wrote and published the books that paid expenses and bought the tea and cakes always served on Sunday nights. She was the Mary of the establishment, and Phœbe was the Martha upon whom fell all the work of the housekeeping. Alice in later years has been the one mentioned in literary histories and anthologies. Phœbe always is dismissed as a single-poem poet. She wrote a hymn which is still sung. But Phœbe was, in truth, the more gifted of the two. She was as sunny as her sister was somber. She was the soul of the Sunday evening gatherings, pronounced by all who knew her as "the wittiest woman of her generation." Her puns were quoted everywhere, and her parodies, not many of which she allowed to be printed, were really humorous. She could even make light of her old friend Whittier's "Maud Muller" which in her parody "Kate Ketchem" she reversed, making the miserly rich man's daughter look with favor on the young farm worker, and finally, to his consternation, marry him. The conclusion, perhaps, is better even than Whittier's:

> And alas for any who find to their shame,
> That two can play at their little game,

> For of all hard things to bear and grin
> The hardest is knowing you're taken in.

> Ah well, as a general thing we fret
> About the one we didn't get,

> But I think we needn't make a fuss
> If the one we don't want didn't get us.

Though, like the younger of the Warner sisters, she could write a hymn still to be found in the church hymnals:

> One sweetly solemn thought
> Comes to me o'er and o'er;
> I am nearer home to-day
> Than I ever have been before;

and though religion runs through her poems, as it does through her sister's like a major chord, she was not sentimental. Alice had had a disastrous love affair that had filled her poems with tears, but not Phœbe. "Believe *me,* I never loved any man well enough to lie awake half an hour, to be miserable about him."

A very human soul. If either of the two sisters had genius, it was Phœbe, but hers was a genius that never had time to express itself in books. Would that she and not Alice had written the two novels.

Having read the work of the two sisters, I am convinced that the definitive word concerning it was spoken by the *Christian Union* after the death of Alice in 1871:

They began to write verses which treated of sorrowful experiences, of unrequited love, of painful illnesses, of hopes and
fears plaintively mingled, and of untimely deaths. It was linkéd
sadness long drawn out. Tender regret and weak sentiment
seem to us—we say it unwillingly—the staple of what they
wrote. Their sobbing lyrics do not melt;—they ruffle and vex
us.

The elder sister wrote more, was better known and her
talent thought to be greater than the younger's. With this
opinion we cannot agree... Phœbe seems to have been freer
from false sentiment, less given to gentle preaching, and less
affected in style than Alice... Phœbe has a more natural, a
plainer tone; is far less morbid, and shows us now and then
something very like humor, of which we find no trace in her
sister.

v

THE FLOOD of novels that came after the early best-sellers
had covered all the newsstands came almost wholly from
the pens of New England women. It was the work of the
rising second generation—the children of the literary
Brahmins—and it was mostly feminine. The roll of the
young New England women who began their work in
the fifties is a long one. I name them in the order of their
appearance: "Grace Greenwood"; Caroline Lee Hentz,
whose novels in three years sold a hundred thousand
copies; "Fanny Fern"; Ann S. Stephens; "Fanny Forester"; Sarah Josepha Hale, who, sensible of the rising
tide, launched again her novel *Northwood;* Maria S.
Cummins; Lucretia P. Hale; Mary Jane Holmes, who in
the fifties launched the first five of her interminable series
of novels that ultimately sold over two millions of copies;
Rose Terry (Cooke); Harriet Prescott (Spofford); Louise

Chandler (Moulton); Louisa M. Alcott; and three non-
New Englanders—E. D. E. N. Southworth; "The Widow
Bedott" (Mrs. Whitcher); and Augusta Jane Evans
Wilson.

All of them began their work in the fifties, and with
them, also, the poets Lucy Larcom and Julia Ward
(Howe). The second flowering of New England was
indeed feminine.

CHAPTER VI

THE SHADOW OF DICKENS

UNTIL WELL PAST THE CIVIL WAR, AMERICAN LITERATURE inch-wormed along, always at least one decade behind the English. Wordsworth kindled Bryant two decades after the *Lyrical Ballads;* Scott got to Cooper a decade after *Waverley;* and Dickens, who had toured America in 1842, did not reach full circle in America until the 1850's. *Harper's Magazine* was founded in 1850 with Dickens its major reason for being. *Bleak House* and *Little Dorrit* ran their interminable length as serials through the magazine, and in nearly every number during the whole decade there were excerpts from *Household Words.*

Scott, who ruled American fiction for three decades, had been aristocratic in his materials and his atmospheres; Dickens, who was the leading influence after the mid-thirties, was plebeian in his picturings of life. Scott emphasized the trappings of royalty and caste, using the peasant class to create amusement; Dickens could make a street waif and pickpocket his title character. Scott made his reader *see* cloth of gold and tournaments; Dickens made his reader *feel* the sufferings of the poor. The American South took to Scott. In the patrician mansions of the slave states he was a necessary classic; but the North read Dickens and *felt* "life among the lowly." When an abuse reaches the emotions of the people it is doomed.

Chauncey Depew, who was graduated from Yale in 1856, has declared that during his later boyhood the excitement when the novels of Dickens would appear "equalled almost the enthusiasm of a political campaign. ... The characters of Dickens became household companions. Everyone was looking for the counterpart of Micawber or Sam Weller, Pecksniff or David Copperfield, and had little trouble in finding them either in the family circle or among the neighbors. ... Speaking of Dickens one picture remains indelibly pressed upon my memory. It was the banquet given him at which Horace Greeley presided. Everyone was as familiar with Mr. Pickwick and his portrait by Cruikshank in Dickens' works as with one's father. When Mr. Greeley arose to make the opening speech and introduce the guest of the evening, his likeness to this portrait of Pickwick was so remarkable that the whole audience, including Mr. Dickens, shouted their delight in greeting an old and well-beloved friend."

Despite the storm in the newspapers after *American Notes* and *Martin Chuzzlewit,* the two volumes harmed not at all their author's popularity with the reading masses of America. Late in the fifties, great pressure was brought to bear on him to make a second trip to conduct a reading tour of the States, or, as he expressed it in a letter to a friend, "Evans, of New York, proposed that I should sign a conditional agreement to go to America for eighty readings within a month after the receipt of ten thousand pounds." He was greatly tempted, but it was 1867 before he was free to make the trip.

According to Bret Harte in his *Condensed Novels,* certain devices and mannerisms of Dickens haunted nearly all the writers of fiction of his period:

I see a child . . . a most unnatural child, a model infant. It is prematurely old and philosophic. It dies in poverty to slow music. It dies surrounded by luxury to slow music. It dies with an accompaniment of golden water and rattling carts to slow music. Previous to its decease it makes a will; it repeats the Lord's Prayer, it kisses the "boofer lady.". . .

I see a good woman, undersized. I see several charming women, but they are all undersized. They are more or less imbecile and idiotic, but always fascinating and undersized. They wear coquettish caps and aprons. I observe that feminine viritue is invariably below the medium height, and that it is always simple and infantile. . . .

I see a haughty, proud and wicked lady. She is tall and queenly. I remark that all proud and wicked women are tall and queenly. . . .

I see several things continually impending. I observe that whenever an accident, a murder, or death is about to happen, there is something in the furniture, in the locality, in the atmosphere, that foreshadows and suggests it years in advance. I cannot say that in real life I have noticed it. . . .

I see the influence of this in the magazines and daily papers; I see weak imitators rise up and enfeeble the world with senseless formula. I am getting tired of it. It won't do, Charles! it won't do!

Weak imitations there were indeed, shoals of them. All through the decade and beyond one finds them everywhere, even in the writings of Harte himself. Dickens did not start sentimentalism in America. It would be foolish to charge him with that crime, but he fed abundantly the increasing appetite for it, and unquestionably he was to blame for a Herod-like slaughter of innocents. To cite a single instance, consider Fanny Fern's *Fern Leaves from Fanny's Portfolio,* 1853. In her first series alone there are recorded with heart-throbs the deaths in detail in twelve stories of twelve different children, even as Paul Dombey and Little Nell. Best are these sobful tales read, like legislative bills, by title and passed. Here are six of the titles: "A Night Watch with a Dead Infant," "Little Charley the Child Angel," "The Transplanted Lily," "The Angel Child," "The Wail of a Broken Heart," "Two in Heaven." The funerals I did not count; the anguished widows were four, and two of them died in a lunatic asylum. And there are two stepmothers, one invalid wife, and one "stray lamb."

More greatly did Dickens influence America by his type of purpose novel. He attacked abuses in his fiction, but he did not argue or condemn or preach. He simply presented individuals and made the reader see and feel them. He did not strike at the crime of the London slums: he presented Fagin; he did not argue against the poorhouse schools: he pictured Nicholas Nickleby.

Unquestionably, Dickens prepared the ground for the feminine best-sellers of the fifties. In England and America he created a new reading public. Early in the decade, the "Editor's Table" of *Harper's Magazine* was inclined to deplore the fact that the contagion of fiction-reading had reached the masses:

Literature has gone in pursuit of the million, penetrated highways and hedges, pressed its way into cottages, factories, omnibuses, and railroad cars, and become the most cosmopolitan thing of the century. The working man considers cheap literature as a domestic necessity, and he enters it, like bread and raiment, on the account current with his pocket.

The people followed him for one thing because of the strangeness of his material. He had humor, too, he had sympathy with the poor, he had feeling, and he saw always what heretofore had never been noted. He was attracted most strongly by incongruities and picturesque individualities. During his tour of America the romance of the New World history, the drama of the American past, the new Republic, the vast epic enacting on wild frontiers, and the mighty promise of empires yet to be, moved him not at all. He saw nothing of it. He saw only a woodsman on an Ohio river-boat spitting tobacco juice with accuracy into a knot-hole. A cockney Londoner, he damned the frontier because it was not England. All that makes America great he saw not at all; he saw only spittoons.

Unquestionably his influence, coming at the time it did, was bad. During a long period no other writer in America had so devoted a following, and undoubtedly more than any other individual he was responsible for the spirit of an era. In an over-emotional age he added emotion. He taught nothing; to a people near the verge of hysteria he brought only feeling. To the uncritical he was a realist. He seemed to be presenting scenes and characters drawn from actuality, but no eye has ever seen just such a background and just such characters. We may have seen a

Sam Weller back or a Pickwick hat, but not the entire character. Dickens created his own world out of London fragments, just as the medical student Frankenstein created his monster man out of scraps from the dissecting room; and after he had created his new world he compelled his reader to live in it. As a result American readers learned to divorce the world of books from the world of actuality they knew, and as a result soon they were able to enter without protest the impossible worlds created by the feminine creators of best-sellers and afterwards by the makers of the wild-cat fiction later called "dime novels."

One weapon that Dickens forged for his propaganda fiction attacking current abuses proved highly effective. Who can stand against humor, especially if it be barbed with satire? Charles Kingsley used only emotion for his *Alton Locke,* 1849, and his reader emerges from the novel too upset to think of doing anything about remedying the abuses portrayed. They are too awful to be human. So with Mrs. Gaskell's *Mary Barton,* 1848. Harriet Beecher Stowe made the combination, and as movingly as Dickens himself could have done it, and for the first time the foundations of slavery, that had stood against the logic of a generation of orators, really trembled.

As Dickens had been the first prominent novelist to use fiction as a weapon against social abuses, so he was the first to use for his materials "life among the lowly." It was because of his success, undoubtedly, that Mrs. Stowe, when invited by the *New Era* to use her pen in the anti-slavery battle, made her appeal in the form of a novel. Like Dickens, she would not argue or present logical proof, but would attack the evil by stirring up emotion against it, by presenting individual cases of martyred slaves or devil-like slave-traders so vividly that they seemed to the reader to be actually present as a part of his own experience. After *Uncle Tom's Cabin* no longer was slavery a far-off evil to be debated by senators: it had come into the reader's own home.

Then, too, Mrs. Stowe, like Dickens, wrote with intense emotion. The biographer of Dickens records that once a lady calling on Mrs. Dickens heard hilarious laughter long continued in the room above them, and at length remarked that Mr. Dickens must have with him a very jovial visitor. "Oh no," was her response, "he is all alone. He is writing on his story." It is safe to say that his readers also laughed when they came to what he was writing.

In the introduction to the 1879 edition of *Uncle Tom* it is recorded that:

The first part of the book ever committed to writing was the death of Uncle Tom. This scene presented itself almost as a tangible vision to her mind while sitting at the communion-table in the little church at Brunswick. She was perfectly overcome by it, and could scarcely restrain the convulsion of tears and sobbings that shook her frame. She hastened home and wrote it and her husband being away, she read it to her two sons of ten and twelve years of age. The little fellows broke out into convulsions of weeping, one of them saying through his sobs, "Oh! mamma, slavery is the most cursed thing in the world."

Instead of two boys, soon the whole world was weeping over the story. We know that recording the death of

Little Eva Mrs. Stowe cried herself sick and was unable to work for two weeks.

Emotion begets emotion. First Dickens and then Mrs. Stowe awoke to a realization that they were using the most deadly of all human weapons, aroused emotions, a force that no entrenched evil can long withstand.

II

THE SECOND evil during the decade to be attacked with fiction in the Dickens manner was intemperance in the use of liquors. It was indeed a crying evil. Willis in his *Home Journal,* 1852, told of a walk he had taken up Broadway on New Year's day:

The amount of *well-dressed* drunkenness, in the streets, on New Year's day, surprised every one. Between Grace and Trinity, at 4 P.M., we saw a crowd, almost without exception presentable as to broadcloth and linen, yet every third man, at least quite intoxicated. Either clothes have gone *down* in the scale of society, or drunkenness has gone *up*. Either rowdies are more respectably dressed, or respectability is more "addicted." A statistic may drive a nail into this. There are 5,000 licensed bar-rooms in New York—one to every eighty inhabitants.

In 1842, Walt Whitman had published his *Franklin Evans, or The Inebriate. A Tale of the Times. By a Popular American Author*. The notice that appeared in the *New World,* November 5 of that year, written undoubtedly by Whitman himself, is noteworthy:

THIS NOVEL, which is dedicated to the Temperance Societies and the friends of the Temperance Cause throughout the Union, will create a sensation, both for the ability with which it is written, as well as the interest of the subject, and will be universally read and admired. It was written especially for *The New World* by one of the best Novelists of this country, with a view to aid the great work of Reform, and rescue Young Men from the Demon of Intemperance. The incidents of the plot are wrought out with great effect, and the excellence of its moral, and the beneficial influence it will have, should interest the friends of Temperance Reformation in giving this tale the widest possible circulation.

In 1846, when Whitman assumed the editorship of the Brooklyn *Eagle* he reissued the novel in its columns. It is a harrowing tale of a country boy who goes to the city, falls into temptation, becomes a drunkard, and has a grim series of maudlin adventures. But after losing children, wife, honor, and after prison and crime, he reforms and the book ends with joy in heaven over another sinner who has been converted.

But just as the decade was to produce the greatest abolitionist novel of all time, so was it also to produce the most widely distributed temperance novel that ever was written. Its author, Timothy Shay Arthur, had learned from Dickens his art of fighting abuses, the presentation of sentimentalized individual cases instead of logical arguments. Always he played upon the emotions. His stories are full of weeping Little Evas, pathetic victims of drunken fathers, innocent lamb-like babies of the variety made lyric in the early poem declaimed by a whole generation of school girls:

> Father, dear father, come home with me now,
>   The clock in the steeple strikes one;
> You said you were coming right home from the shop
>   As soon as your day's work was done,

and so to the tearful end.

TIMOTHY SHAY
ARTHUR

From an engraving in pos-
session of the New York
Historical Society.

FIRST EDITION OF
*TEN NIGHTS IN A
BAR-ROOM*

Philadelphia, 1854. Courtesy
of the New York Public
Library.

After a miscellaneous career as a magazinist, he had established in 1850, *Arthur's Home Magazine,* and its editor he remained until his death in 1885. With this receptacle open for him he produced a mass of writings that it is impossible to count with exactitude. Great numbers of his writings were moralized fictions, sugared advice on all human problems, sentimental and sensational stories of victims of the drink habit. The classic among his writings, however, the one that despite his enormous output makes him like Mrs. Stowe, a one-book novelist, is his *Ten Nights in a Bar-Room and What I Saw There,* 1854. Its sales in the 1850's have been estimated as second only to those of *Uncle Tom's Cabin.* Undoubtedly it has been one of the leading American best-sellers even to the present. It is a lurid, sensational tale of the doings of rum as sold by the public house called the Sickle and Sheaf, and through it runs a tide of sentimentalism unlimited. Gamblers, murderers, hopeless wrecks of once noble men totter out of the rum-hole to crime and shame. The proprietor's own son becomes the most tragic victim.

Arthur's output of volumes in 1875 was estimated at seventy-five; ten years later at the time of his death it must have been at least one hundred.

CHAPTER VII

ENGLISH GENIUS DISCOVERS THE
YANKEE DOLLAR

*D*URING THE WHOLE OF THE NINETEENTH CENTURY AN American could not talk with a literary Englishman for ten minutes without being charged with piracy. The Yankee nation, it was charged, dollar mad, was fighting international copyright because of the profits to be made from stealing English books. Literary piracy in America had become a national industry, so the charge ran. To the countercharge that the English were stealing American books, the reply would be that there were few American books worth stealing and that English books worth stealing were all but infinite. Dickens, whose volumes in multitudinous editions were sown thickly over America with not a cent paid to him, in hot rage once declared that whenever he had told the Americans that they had "no literature of their own ... the universal answer (out of Boston) is 'we don't want one. Why should we pay for one when we can get it for nothing? Our people don't think of poetry, Sir. Dollars, banks, and cotton are our books, Sir.' "

THE BRITISH LION IN AMERICA
Caricature in *The Daily Joker*, 1867.

Dickens had come to America in 1842 hoping that he might further the cause of international copyright. Several times during his tour he had presented the matter with directness and force, but, according to his own report, he had been warned not to press the matter. The general opinion of America, as he gathered it, was in favor of continuing to steal, and to oppose public opinion was dangerous business.

This may have been true, but Dickens as he was touring from city to city was making a discovery—a tremendous discovery, as it proved. He, a mere writer of books, was being everywhere fêted as if he were the crown-prince of a realm. As Mr. Ticknor had expressed it before Dickens had arrived in America, "A triumph has been prepared for him in which the whole country will join. He will have a progress through the States unequalled since Lafayette's."

And so indeed it proved. America was eager, so it seemed, to honor men of genius, to greet them in shouting masses, and to fill great halls at highest prices to hear them lecture or read—a tremendous discovery. Despite the lack of international copyright, English authors could get veritable fortunes out of America. His second tour of America netted Dickens more than $100,000. The money side always was uppermost. He noted in a letter that "we had 450 in the house last night and the New York hall holds five hundred people more." Time and again during his reading tour, Dolby, his business manager, would stagger from the box-office loaded with dollar bills tied up in tall bundles. Leigh Hunt had thought of America as "one great shop counter extending

all down the coast from Massachusetts to Mexico," and
now, under the guidance of Dickens, the English had
found how to leap over this counter and get to the till.
Let the Americas steal the English copyrights, and strew
the books over the land till the author's name had become
a household word, and then let him go over and reap his
reward.

Dickens had made his second harvesting after the
ground had been made fallow through the publication
of his *Bleak House* and *Little Dorrit,* each of which during the fifties had dragged its length through nineteen
issues of *Harper's Magazine* with side dishes from Dickens' *Household Words* in every issue as appetizers. And
American publishers were everywhere issuing his writings, and extending his fame.

II

THE FIRST prominent author to follow up Dickens' discovery in the 1850's and come to America to reap from
his non-copyrighted popularity was Martin Farquhar
Tupper, laureate of the wistful for culture and tone.
Thousands there were in America who rated his *Proverbial Philosophy* with Solomon's. Of the English poets
of the decade he, perhaps, was the best-seller in America,
but his readers—let Dr. Holmes draw for us a typical
specimen. Meet "my landlady's daughter." ... "Age 19.
Tender-eyed blonde. Long ringlets. Cameo pin. Gold
pencil case on chain. Locket. Bracelet. Album. Autograph
book. Accordion. Reads Byron, Tupper, and Sylvanus
Cobb, Jr., while her mother makes the puddings. Says
'Yes?' when you tell her anything."

Byron in Boston in the 1850's was naughty reading, so considered by prudent mothers; a book to be read as boys read yellow backs in fearful secrecy. To read Sylvanus Cobb, Jr., would require copies of the New York *Ledger*, for Cobb was in print nowhere else. Doubtless they were subscribers, for what were single copies of a paper with exciting serials always at breath-taking moments suddenly to be stopped with a "To be continued"? Even mothers read the *Ledger*. But Martin Farquhar Tupper!

Tupper to newly-rich débutantes ignorant of books, to aspiring landladies' daughters who had boarders like the Autocrat, to sighing old maids with longings for culture, was refinement. Tupper was to be found on parlor tables with the family Bible, with *The Female Poets of America,* and *Lives of Eminent Christians* in scarlet and gold. To read Tupper was it not to breathe the Air of culture? Here was a genius who knew his own worth. Had he not published his "Hymn to the Nations" in a volume containing translations of the poem into thirty languages so that no refined person on earth could complain that he was unable to read the classic since it was in a foreign tongue? And he was coming to America.

In June, 1851, he sailed into New York harbor and so impressed was he at his dawning upon the New World that he overflowed in a sonnet that, by his own arrangement, greeted him in the New York papers when he landed:

> Not with cold scorn or ill-dissembled sneer,
>   Ungraciously your kindly looks to greet,
> By God's good favor safely landed here.
> Oh friends and brothers, face to face we meet.

Now for a little space my willing feet,
  After long hope and promise many a year,
Shall tread your happy shores; my heart and voice
  Your kindred love shall quicken and shall cheer,
While in your greatness shall my soul rejoice—
  For you are England's nearest and most dear!
Suffer my simple fervors to do good,
  As one poor pilgrim happy may and can
Who knit to heaven and earth by gratitude
  Speaks from his heart to touch his fellow men.

As reported by Bayard Taylor, he had followed this in a speech after his landing with, "America, be not afraid. *I* will protect you."

It is small wonder that he visited America. In the 1881 illustrated quarto edition of *Proverbial Philosophy* it is stated that a million copies of the volume had been sold in America and a quarter of a million in England. "Vast numbers of fairly-educated middle-class people perused these singular rhythmical effusions with genuine enthusiasm and thought that Tupper had eclipsed Solomon."

How he impressed literary New York we may learn from the "Easy Chair":

Tupper oozed sonnets at every pore while he made his triumphal progress through the country. Tupper, wreathed and encircled by his multitudinous editions, sang from the ship, and the car, and the steamer. An admiring nation hung upon his steps. I hope America cherished no hostile feeling toward Britain, because Tupper is indigenous to English soil. I hope that this young and flourishing country, which has everything, even Tuppers, to hope for in the future, does not begrudge Martin Farquhar to his native land.

Thereupon the "Easy Chair" professed to quote from "a young poet of whom America has the highest hopes, whose genius has already proved itself by its records of meetings with similar genius in other lands, but whose modesty forbids the mention of his name. ... I venture to quote the first lines of 'An Ode to the Proverbial Philosopher' by R ---- t D --- e:

> Oh Mr. Tupper, when your glances bland
> Did first irradiate my native land,
> 'Twas then I somehow felt a sudden blow,
> O, Martin Farquhar—Martin Farquhar, O!"

To account for his phenomenal popularity among "high-brow" women allow me to quote a review from *The Ladies' Wreath* of 1848. Reviewing the latest issue of *Proverbial Philosophy* it said:

This remarkable book constitutes the 32d and 33d Nos. of Wiley & Putnam's "Library of Choice Reading," and never was the expressive motto of the Series, "Books which are Books," more justly imprinted on the title page of a book, than on this. We have not yet had time to glance at half its beauties —as to reading it, that is quite another affair. It is not a book to be devoured at one sitting, like most of the literary ephemera of the day. Every page contains enough valuable ideas to furnish out some half dozen volumes of ordinary reading, with the raw material so scantily used in their manufacture. The quaintness of the style—the originality of the thoughts, which yet commend themselves to the common sense of the reader—the exquisite beauty of the abundant imagery, and the pure morality everywhere inculcated, all combine to give this volume a power of fascination we have seldom experienced. Each chapter resembles a string of diamonds of the purest water, bright, sparkling, and valuable no less for their intrinsic worth, than for their rarity.

Hawthorne in 1856 visited Tupper at his home in Albany, England, and Julian Hawthorne in his life of his father filled nine pages with a letter Hawthorne wrote describing his reception. On the whole he liked the man. At the sight of his American visitor the poet had rushed out effusively to meet him:

"Oh, great Scarlet Letter!" he cried. I did not know what the Devil to say, unless it were, "Oh, wondrous Man of Proverbs!" or "Oh, wiser than Solomon!" and as I was afraid to say either of these, I rather think I held my tongue. I felt in an instant that Mr. Tupper was a good soul, but a fussy little man, of a kind that always takes one entirely aback. He is a small man, with wonderfully short legs, fat (at least very round), and walks with a kind of waddle, not so much from corpulence of body as from brevity of leg. His hair is curly, and of an iron-gray hue; his features are good, even handsome, and his complexion very red. A person for whom I immediately felt a kindness, and instinctively knew to be a bore.

After dinner he "opened one of the book-cases, and showed it packed quite full of American editions of his works, all splendidly bound and gilt—talking with evidently intense satisfaction of his American fame."

During his first visit to America he seems to have made little impression on the Boston Brahmins. Longfellow noted that he was in town and Mrs. Stowe dismissed him with the remark that he was "a little man with fresh, rosy complexion and cheery, joyous manners." Despite his million copies sold and his idolization by what Willis called "japonica-dom society," among the judicious he has always been a synonym for literary gilding made to look like gold. Holmes, however, in the first *Autocrat* volume, could speak of "the ocean of Tupperian wisdom" and confess that he himself at times may have dipped from it.

III

IF THE FORTIES talked Dickens, the fifties certainly talked Thackeray. He had come to America in October, 1852, with James Russell Lowell and Arthur Hugh Clough as shipmates. On January 5, Lowell gave him a supper with Felton, Clough, Dana, Dr. Parsons, Fields, Edmund Quincy, Estes Howe, and Longfellow as guests. From Longfellow's journal comes a tiny bit of the Jovian wit of that Boston night:

We sat down at ten and did not leave the table till one. Very gay with stories and jokes:—
"Will you take some Port?" said Lowell to Thackeray.
"I dare drink anything that becomes a man."
"It will be a long while before that becomes a man."
"Oh, no," cried Felton, "it is *fast turning into one.*"
As we were going away Thackeray said, "We have stayed too long." "I should say," replied the host, "one long and two short—a dactylic supper."

Thackeray, touring the cities, lectured on "The English Humorists of the Eighteenth Century." Willis, voicing many, had believed that Thackeray was making a mistake in coming to America:

Thackeray is about taking the bold step of coming over bodily to displace his ideal—an experiment which Dickens and Kossuth found so disastrous, and upon which few authors or heroes that ever lived could safely venture. The soul and the body seldom look alike. Once demigod-ed a man had best stay in his cloud. What sort of descriptions do you suppose the "correspondents of the country papers" would give of Milton, if he were to re-appear and walk Broadway for a month? America is, to English authors, an optional posterity—the

MARTIN FARQUHAR TUPPER
From a portrait by F. Rochard, 1846.

WILLIAM MAKEPEACE THACKERAY
Harper's Weekly, 1857.

broad Atlantic being a well-adjusted magnifying glass which produces the same effect as the trans-envy and competition of the Styx. I used to know Thackeray in London...He is more likely to be personally popular, I think, than any other English author would be, on this side of the water.

Willis' judgment was at fault. Thackeray's lecture-halls were full night after night despite the fact that he lectured only to the well-educated and the well-read who would understand his unexplained allusions, and as a result he took home with him in the spring of 1853, $12,500, over and above his expenses for six months. So successful was he that according to the "Easy Chair" the winter of 1853 could be dubbed the season of "the Henry Esmond–Thackeray fever." In November, *Harper's Magazine* began the serialization of *The Newcomes,* a Gargantuan feast that endured until August, 1855.

The mistake, if any, was his second tour of America so closely following his first. He arrived in October, 1855, and began a series of lectures, this time on "The Four Georges." The subject aroused no enthusiasm. It was criticized in England. It was wrong, they said, to display the weakness of British royalty to Americans. He extended his tour into the South as far even as New Orleans, but his lectures were felt to lack the verve and wit of his earlier course. His novels, however, were holding up. From December, 1857, *Harper's Magazine* serialized *The Virginians*—a most unconscionable time it was before it died. The "Easy Chair" tried to make easy its last hours by explaining "Unless you read them (Thackeray's novels) in monthly parts, you will not read them at all. You are likely to be so appalled by the magnitude of the compiled work as not to read it at all. . . . One must yield to the literary customs of the times." It was complained, too, that there was no story to be read with excitement as in *Jane Eyre,* and that it was hard to remember after months and months what the earlier parts had been.

Moreover, the magazine began to be showered with complaints concerning the treatment of Washington. Thackeray was stripping him of his glory, reducing him to the ranks, making him even as you and I. "The Americans," said one letter, "hold Washington too sacred a character to be handled in this trifling manner. With almost an equal propriety might Thackeray have manufactured a novel from the Bible, and made the Saviour and Saint Paul its leading characters. . . . Washington should be represented as history proves he was, the heaven-chosen, miraculous founder of our nation."

In vain the magazine argued that "When you make him a demigod you lift him out of human sympathy"— the American people did not take to *The Virginians.* But despite the criticism, two more novels by Thackeray the Harpers were to serialize, as well as the completed *The Four Georges.*

IV

THACKERAY and the English writers who followed him to America were helped greatly by the habit, firmly fixed in the American people, of patronizing lecture courses. The 1850's were the flood-tide years of the Lecture Lyceum, which had arisen spontaneously to supply a need. Small towns and cities, especially in the new and growing West, had awakened to a realization that they had left behind them much of the riches of an older civilization; and they did what they alone could do: they clubbed together and brought in prominent lecturers to keep them in touch with culture and progress. A piece in the *Utica Herald* of 1887 pictured vividly this important phase of the mid-century:

The lecturers who were most sought at that time (the 1850's) were almost without exception men of very strong convictions upon the great question which, however evaded and dextrously hidden, was the vital thought of the country; and every successive week from November to April, in the largest cities and the smallest cities, along the belt of country from the Kennebec through New England and New York westward through Ohio and the Northwest to the Mississippi, before thousands of the most intelligent American citizens, this band of lecturers advanced, like a well-ordered platoon of sharp-shooters, and delivered their destructive volley at what they felt to be the common enemy...

The singular success of the lyceum lecture of that time was due, undoubtedly, to two causes—the simultaneous appearance of a remarkable group of orators, and their profound sympathy with the question which absorbed the public mind. The weekly lecture was not merely a display of oratory, not only an amusing recreation, but it brought wit and accomplishment and eloquence to strengthen the public feeling and arouse the public conscience, and to confirm the earnest spirit which was universal, and which forecast the great events and the noble elevation of the public mind that followed. Emerson, Wendell Phillips, Gough, Beecher, Chapin, Starr King, Theodore Parker, could of themselves carry any course of lectures, and each in his own way was thoroughly in accord with the truest American life of that time. The situation and the condition of the public mind would not have availed, indeed, without the happy chance of such orators to create the lyceum, but with that chance the lyceum of that day was as remarkable a continuous display of various and effective eloquence as has been ever known.

Hardly one of the prominent men of the decade who at one time or another did not find his mail full of requests from lyceum-lecture groups. Bayard Taylor, "the great traveller," was in constant demand. Just to see such celebrities as Dickens, Thackeray, Emerson, Horace Greeley, Edward Everett, would bring together anywhere in America enough of an audience to pay the lecturer's fee. The most sought of them all was Emerson, who might have told a census enumerator that his profession was lyceum lecturer. Many who could not follow at all the threads of his lecture went home nevertheless delighted with him, even Mrs. Partington:

"I 'tended the lectur' last night—one of the eternity course." "Fraternity," we suggested; "Who spoke?"—"O, Mr. what's his name—he that made the refrigerator, you know, for warming houses in summer and cooling 'em in winter—Emerson—T. P. Emerson."—"You mean R. W. Emerson," we hinted; "Did he lecture on refrigerators?"—"O, dear no! 't was on chance; and sich a lectur'! I thought I'd heerd lecturs before, but that succeeded 'em all."—"Indeed!" we said, somewhat interested, though there were eleven letters unopened on the table, "Tell us about it."—"Well," she continued, "it was about chance, and he is sich a queer man that you have to watch every word or you can't understand him. If you lose one word, it's jest like a stitch broke in a seam made by some of the sowing-machines—the work is good for nothing. Well, he said there was no sich thing as chance, and that everything was planned out beforehand. And, to prove it, he spoke of a ship on the sea, knocked about by the winds and waves, and showed, just as loosed as anything I ever saw, that she was not there by chance, or that she was, and I declare I don't know which."

Undoubtedly many could give similar reports, but there never was a time when Emerson could not fill a town hall with eager people.

To quote from Old South Leaflets, No. 139, "The American Lyceum":

Emerson once said, "My pulpit is the Lyceum platform." When he retired from the pulpit in 1832, he simply transferred his ministry from the church to the platform. It was on the lecture platform above all other places that he was at home. He was *par excellence* Emerson the Lecturer. Someone has said that he created a new profession, that of the lecturer; and another has said that he gave to the Lyceum in this country its form and character, and made it the efficient instrument of instruction and reform which it was for the third of a century and more during which he occupied the platform. Almost everything that he wrote after *Nature* was written originally for the platform.

CHAPTER VIII

FEMALES MILITANT

*D*URING THE 1850'S, AMERICAN WOMEN HAD REACHED A point where they were handed everything a woman could dream of possessing with one single exception—their "Rights," and for these the sex arose in a rebellion that made the decade a battlefield—of words. According to N. P. Willis, as expressed in his *Home Journal*, read by all aspiring females, there was perfect *"pluribus-unum-imity"* that "the present is the first century, and this the first country, of the world in which the female sex is (collectively and all qualities taken into account) *superior to the male."*

And yet the women were refused their "Rights." The men cheerfully would grant everything else. The ballot and an open door to the masculine professions and the colleges they would not grant. As one chivalrous bachelor phrased it, "Since boyhood I have been taught that women are angels and I have believed it, and the voting place with its sawdust floor and tobacco juice is no place for an angel." Withholding the single grant of masculine rights from the women, the men were willing to admit to the full all that had been claimed for women, even to the limits set forth in a paper on the "Rights of the Sex" read at the Ohio Female Convention early in the decade. As reported in the *Home Journal,* it was contended that woman is man's superior in four different fields:

First, she is on the whole superior physically. Men have degenerated in America under the "slavery of business" and women have increased in stature and strength. Second, women are on the whole more intellectual. "It is the women who read. It is the women who are the tribunal of any question aside from politics or business. It is the women who give or withhold a literary reputation. It is the women who control clergymen and churches, patronize and influence the Arts, and exercise ultimate control over the Press." Third, "morally the women of America are superior to the men, to a degree (the mere fact scarce need be asserted) which was never known before in the history of nations." And, finally, "in religion, in taste, in general elevation of sentiment and in consistency of standard of opinion, the women of America are superior to the men, as probably no one will deny."

What would one expect to hear at a "Female Convention" in the 1850's? It was the "Woman's Rights" decade, and "females" all through the decade fought for their rights by word of mouth in lecture tours and conventions. John Phœnix reports such a convention even in gold-rush California, himself attending—prone under a church pew. The Widow Bedott pictured a Woman's Rights lecturer of the period—"a wonderful tall, slab-sided, coarse lookin' critter. Her hair looked singular, 'twas all raked

THE WOMAN'S RIGHTS CONVENTION

"The orator of the day denouncing the lords of creation." *Harper's Weekly*, 1859.

back off her forrard, and made her phizmahogany look amazing broad and brazen." And Artemus Ward, who saw everything worth seeing in America during his apprenticeship decade, the fifties, and preached always a sermon to those who needed reproof, found women militant even on the western frontier:

I pitcht my tent in a small town in Injianny one day last season, & while I was standin at the dore takin money, a deppytashun of ladies came up & sed they wos members of the Bunkumville Female Moral Reformin & Wimin's Rite's Associashun, and thay axed me if thay cood go in without payin.

"Not exactly," sez I, "but you can pay without goin in."

"Dew you know who we air?" sed one of the wimin—a tall and feroshus lookin critter, with a blew kotton umbreller under her arm—"dew you know who we air, Sir?"

"My impreshun is," sed I, "from a kersery view, that you air females."

"We air, Suh," said the feroshus woman—"we belong to a Society whitch beleeves wimin has rites—whitch beleeves in razin her to her proper speer—whitch beleeves she is indowed with as much intelleck as man is—whitch beleeves she is trampled on and aboozed—& who will resist hense4th & forever the incroachments of proud & domineering men."

Durin her discourse, the exsentric female grabed me by the coat-koller and was swinging her umbreller wildly over my hed.

"I hope, marm," sez I, starting back, "that your intensions is honorable. I'm a lone man hear in a strange place. Besides, Ive a wife to hum."

"Yes," cried the female, "& she's a slave. Doth she never dream of freedom—doth she never think of throwin of the yoke of tyranny & thinkin & votin for herself?—Doth she never think of these here things?"

"Not bein a natral born fool," sed I, by this time a little riled, "I kin safely say that she dothunt."

"O whot—whot!" screamed the female, swingin her um- breller in the air— "O, what is the price that woman pays for her expeeriunce!"

"I don't know," sez I; "the price to my show is 15 cents pur individooal."

"& can't our Sosiety go in free?" asked the female.

"Not if I know it," sed I.

"Crooil, crooil man!" she cried, & bust into tears.

"Wont you let my darter in?" sed anuther of the exsentric wimin, taken me afeckshunitely by the hand. "O, please let my darter in—she's a sweet gushin child of natur."

"Let her gush!" roared I, as mad as I cood stick at their tarnal nonsense; "let her gush!" Whereupon they all sprung back with the simultanious observashun that I was a Beest.

"My female friends," sed I, "be4 you leeve, Ive a few re- marks to remark; wa them well. The female woman is one of the greatest institooshums of which this land can boste. It's onpossible to get along without her. Had there bin no female wimin in the world, I should scarcely be here with my un- paralleld show on this very occashun. She is good in sickness —good in wellness—good all the time. O, woman, woman!" I cried, my feelins worked up to a hi poetick pitch, "you air an angle when you behave yourself; but when you take off your proper appairel & (mettyforically speaken)—get into panty- loons—when you desert your firesides, & with your heds full of wimin's rites noshuns go round like roarin lyons, seekin whom you may devour someboddy—in short, when you under- take to play the man, you play the devil and air an emfatic noosance. My female freinds," I continnered, as they were indignantly departin, "wa well what A. Ward has sed!"

II

SAMPLES, these, of the public mind during the 1850's. In 1848 the first Woman's Rights Convention, called to meet at Seneca Falls, N. Y., by Lucretia Mott, Martha Wright, Elizabeth Cady Stanton, and May Ann McClintock, had been roughly handled. The women were stoned, and even jailed, and the newspapers had treated it under such head-lines as "The Reign of Petticoats." As late as March, 1857, the "Easy Chair" could record after a later convention:

The newspapers have had their annual joke over the Woman's Rights' Convention two or three months since. It is hard to say which was the poorer fun—the convention itself, or the mock reports and criticisms upon it...Consider for a moment the humorous resources open to it. Here are women who have especially studied womanly diseases, and who now wish to have a hospital in which women shall treat sick fe-males. The joke is patent. In the first place, is it not the duty of women to bear children and nurse them? Has not the Reverend Dinglydiddlely shown at length that the true sphere of women is the family?

Transcendentalism, as we have seen, had endeavored to express itself in pragmatism, in Yankee schemes for sup-plying blessings which had been overlooked by the Crea-tor in His days of creation; but reforms cannot be rushed. Anti-slavery projects got bullets, temperance reform was opposed with bad eggs and dead cats, and Woman's Rights got a barrage of newspaper jokes, like those in later years hurled at the Ford car, or at the WPA. The militant women furnished the newspapers with fun for a decade, and seemingly that was as far as the women got with their campaign. But single battles they won even in the jeering fifties.

Margaret Fuller had been the first feminine writer of prominence to turn the Transcendentalist ferment into feminine holders. Her series of papers, "The Great Law-suit, or Man *vs.* Men, Woman *vs.* Women," had been published in the *Dial* in 1842, and so had perished unread. Ten years later, however, it had been dug up, dusted off, and, with a foreword by Horace Greeley, had been re-published as *Woman in the Nineteenth Century,* thus giving it a second chance. But again few read it.

The admission of women to the literary peerage, de-spite their sudden prominence in fiction, and despite the advertising given them by Griswold's volumes, did not fully come until the century was in its penultimate dec-ade. The aristocracy of letters as recognized by such edi-torial boards as those of the *North American Review,* or *Knickerbocker's* or *Graham's* or the *Atlantic Monthly,* the baby of the magazines in the late fifties, were, in heart at least, with Dr. Samuel Johnson, whose opinion of "blue-stockings" is well known. In 1854, *The Knicker-bocker Gallery,* a volume issued as a testimonial and benefit to its editor, Lewis Gaylord Clark, with contri-butions from the leading writers whose work had ap-peared in the magazine since its start in 1833—fifty-four writers in all, contained the work of no woman. Only five women were represented in Griswold's *Prose Writers of America*—five out of seventy-two sampled. When, in 1866, the *Independent* issued its large engraving of the "Authors of the United States," forty-four in all, the women numbered nine.

To the Reverend Rufus Griswold, literary pack-rat, enamored of rubbish, the literary "female" was a poet. His *Gems from the American Female Poets* and his *Female Poets of America,* an amazing scrap-heap, he prefaced with superlatives: "The proportion of female writers at this moment in America far exceeds that which the present or any other age in England exhibits." Then to superlatives he added prophecy: "A school of art, original and special . . . the infusion of our domestic spirit and temper into literature" was quickly to come to America "through the poetry of our female authors." And the same year had been laid out two other poetic graveyards, entitled *American Female Poets,* one by Caroline May and the other by Thomas Buchanan Read.

But before one dubs the Reverend pack-rat the "Gullible Griswold," one should look at his sales-sheets. A novel issued at $1.50 on a 10 per cent royalty basis yields only $150 for each edition of 1,000 copies. Griswold's *Poets and Poetry* volume sold ten editions before the fifties opened and many more afterwards. The ladies bought the books and Griswold, knowing their weaknesses, threw his feminine volumes into elaborate purple and gold bindings like gift-books, selling them at $5 and more a volume. The Yankee editor was looking not for literature but for the main chance.

That women could write poetry and fiction that could command the market the men were forced to admit, but they stood inflexible when it was a question of admitting women to the masculine professions. Even to this day they have been denied entrance to the priesthood. Even the tolerant and liberal Oliver Wendell Holmes voted against the admission of women to the Harvard Medical School, considering them "too impressionable and imaginative" to be successful as physicians, and he could end a letter with the question, "Am I a woman, that I should fill eight pagelets with less than nothing?" A whole generation later Howells was to issue his novel *Dr. Breen's Practice,* the story of the woman physician who married her first patient and quit the profession, and Miss Phelps was to answer it with a novel entitled *Dr. Zay.*

III

THE FIRST WOMAN of note to take the Woman's Rights question to the platform as a lecturer was Elizabeth Oakes Smith, wife of Seba Smith who wrote the Jack Downing papers. She had begun as a poet. Her poem "The Sinless Child" was rated high. Griswold classed her "among the first poets of her sex." But her greatest triumphs were in prose. When her husband issued his volume of stories, *'Way Down East; or Portraitures of Yankee Life,* in 1854, which sold six editions, she issued her novel of New York City life, *The Newsboy,* which sold twelve editions the first year.

Her entry into the Woman's Rights battle was in 1851 when she published in Greeley's *Tribune* a series of papers entitled "Woman and Her Needs," later issued as a pamphlet and spread broadcast. At once she was rated as a radical, extreme in her demands for her sex. Even Sarah Josepha Hale, who for years had spoken for women in *Godey's,* could not go with her. Mrs. Sigourney turned thumbs down on the whole movement: "Woman should keep in her own sphere," she said, "and not attempt to fill men's places." Seba Smith, husband of the militant Elizabeth Oakes, had no sympathy with his wife's doctrines, and even while she was supporting the family with the proceeds of her lecturing tours, wrote for the *United*

States Magazine, "Billie Huggin's Wife," a story cheaply ridiculing the advocated new deal for women.

After 1857 for seven years she was constantly before the American public as a lecturer. It was her claim that she was the first woman to be admitted to the lyceum group of lecturers. She addressed with effectiveness the second Woman's Rights Convention at Worcester, Massachusetts, in October, 1851, and followed it with lectures in most of the American cities, complaining always that more men came to hear her than women. When she appeared at Concord, Thoreau escorted her to the hall, but he who once had confided to his journal that he could not understand why a man should be attracted by a woman just because she had regular features, was not highly impressed by the exquisite champion of her sex who had come under his care:

She was a woman in the too common sense after all. You had to substitute courtesy for sense and argument. It requires nothing less than a chivalric feeling to sustain a conversation with a lady. I carried her lecture for her in my pocket wrapped up in her handkerchief; my pocket exhales cologne at this moment.

Curtis in *Harper's,* 1853, pictured her with a sentence: "Mrs. Oakes Smith with pleasant voice, and with eloquent language, is beguiling very many into her notions about womanhood." But Richard Grant White has reproduced her best of all:

A fair sweet presence rises before me, that of Elizabeth Oakes Smith. America has known no truer poetess than this lady in all her years of nurture. No womanly face was ever more perfectly chiseled than hers, due regard having been had meanwhile, to the fact that a woman and not a statue, was being formed. That calm, pleasant face, those soft and kindly luminous brown eyes, and that wealth of waved dark hair, drawn low over her fair white forehead, in the fashion of the time, won many a heart, the homage of which was kept by the always kind and tender words flowing from the faultless lips, seldom opened but to emit a sparkle. Her mouth was exquisitely small, with a chin to correspond. Her bearing was majestically grand, her manners refined and dignified, yet cordial, and taking her all in all, she looked, acted, and moved the born patrician.

Curtis was perhaps the fairest and most judicial of the contemporary critics of the movement. In 1855, this he confided to the "Easy Chair":

We have observed and read to very little purpose, if we have not long ago felt that there is something in the conditions of modern society which bears very severely upon women. The civilized world is purely Hindoo in its social organization. And the Woman's Rights movement is a blind effort to grasp what women feel is denied them—though it would be hard to say how, who, or by whom. Every woman in modern society who has strong character, great intelligence, a fine and fastidious taste, a nature which demands unusual scope, and a heart capable of all that makes the love of women the theme of poetry and the substance of history, feels the want of a career. They try to find it in a hundred ways.

But the women, though they were not to win a complete victory for years to come, fought on as women will. They filled the book-stands with volumes. Sarah Josepha Hale edited a gigantic tome of 900 pages, with enormous toil and expense, its title *Woman's Record, or Sketches of All Distinguished Women from the Creation to 1851.* A year later was issued *Noble Deeds of Woman; or examples of Female Courage and Virtue,* by Elizabeth Starling. And so the work went on.

But the outbreak of the Civil War stopped the movement for years. In wartime there can be in the nation but a single war.

IV

ONE SKIRMISH in the long fight, the women won with finality. In 1855, Mrs. Hale (in the trenches of *Godey's Lady's Book*) had begun a barrage upon the word "female." Such expressions, she declared, as "He went over to the females" were ambiguous and insulting. "The 'females,'" she argued, "could be mares or she-asses."

Early fiction, both English and American, had swarmed with "females." To cite but a single example, Cooper's novels were almost wholly without ladies and even women, but here and there one found "females." Open *The Pioneers:*

"Curiosity induced the females to approach this spot."

"He approached the young females."

"There is no fear of anything unpleasant occurring to a female in this new country."

"The noise of the female servant awoke the females."

It was a period when "female seminaries" were multiplied for the finishing of aristocratic daughters, and "female boarding schools" for others. In his *Home Journal,* 1850, Willis could say:

America is the Canaan of women. In what other country is there a "Female Medical College" like that opened this month in Philadelphia? Where else is there a "Female Academy of Design" to give instruction in Drawing, free of expense, to such women as have not the health for other means of livelihood, or such as have more talent for the pencil than for the needle?

All this is as it should be, argued Mrs. Hale, save for that insulting adjective. "Omit the 'female!' from every seminary and from every institution where it stands to degrade women" became the war-cry of *Godey's* for a decade. And the embattled woman always wins.

She had begun her anti-"female" campaign by making fun of the opposition. In all her editorials in *Godey's* she substituted "male" for man. Once she recorded that the arrest had been made of certain "males who had robbed the mails." Her insistent demand that women be accorded the same educational privileges as men bore fruit early in the next decade when, in January, 1861, the New York Legislature chartered a college endowed by Matthew Vassar "designed to accomplish for young women what our colleges are accomplishing for young men."

Victory for Sarah Josepha, but the charter had as the name of this first American college designed for the education of women only and offering the same courses of study offered previously to men alone, VASSAR FEMALE COLLEGE:

"Female!" thundered the lady editor of *Godey's* in a letter to Mr. Vassar. "What female do you mean? Not a female donkey? Must not your reply be, 'I mean a female woman?' Then ... why degrade the feminine sex to the level of animals? ... I write this earnestly because I wish to have Vassar College take the lead in this great improvement in our language."

But the main building that soon arose had on its front in letters of stone VASSAR FEMALE COLLEGE, and all the stationery of the institution bore the same name. But a woman always wins her fight. In 1867 the New York Legislature, at the demand of Mr. Vassar, deleted the "Female" from the college name and a mason chiseled the word from the main building. Thus can be explained the most peculiar inscription on an American college building: "To this day the uninitiated visitor on the campus is immediately struck by so strange a grouping—'Vassar   College.' But the pride of Vassar's heart is that long, blank space on the stone—symbol of 'the honor of womanhood.' "

V

WHILE the feminine militants were demanding more room in the masculine world of affairs, suddenly, by a noiseless revolution, in 1856, they were granted *per force* double the room they had ever occupied before. The hoop-skirt had arrived with a diameter that exceeded belief and a circumference that kept all men at a distance. As a cartoon in the "Editor's Drawer" department of *Harper's Magazine* makes clear, the style was extreme. The fashions, as Willis once expressed it, always "peacockified women," but never, it would seem, had they given them such a peacock-spread of feathers. Note the bellows in the cartoon. The fashion plates of the late fifties in *Godey's* resemble caricatures rather than actual fashions. According to a recent volume entitled *The Rise of New York Port*, 1939, by Robert G. Albion, the hoop-skirt, unlike Greek Helen, *un*-launched a thousand ships

DRESSING FOR THE BALL

"Editor's Drawer," *Harper's Magazine*, 1857.

and all but destroyed the topless towers of Manhattan. He estimates that before the advent of the hoop-skirt, the ample petticoats worn by the women required sixty-three yards of cotton materials. Under the spread of the hoop-skirt these became an impediment, and they were reduced until at length only three and one-half yards of cloth went into a woman's underwear. Less underwear less cotton, and less ships to transport cotton to England and to reship the finished goods to America. *Ergo,* the hoop-skirt greatly damaged New York's shipping industry.

VI

Femininity, indeed, during the decade crept even into politics, the supposed stronghold of masculinity. In the campaign of 1856, the newly organized Republican party ran as its candidate John C. Frémont, who could, as the times seemed to demand, be played up like a dime-novel hero. Had he not fought Indians in the Rockies and had he not been an important part of the blood-stirring California epic? The Tippecanoe campaign of a decade before had also been run as a western thriller, but it had had no heroine for its hero. Not so the Frémont campaign. Its heroine all but stole the play. The "Pathfinder" hero, under the merciless campaign search-lights, was suspected of being something of a "stuffed shirt" even as an explorer. Wholly without political and governmental experience, would he not be a failure as a president? Possibly, but there was a compensating element: he had a wife who would more than supply any deficiencies he might have as an executive. Was she not the daughter of Senator Benton who for a generation had been a dominating force in Congress? And had she not inherited all of her father's political astuteness, executive force, and personal charm? The campaign slogan became at once: "Give 'em Jessie!!"

Judging from the campaign songs, one might conclude that the candidate was in reality Jesse Benton Frémont, with the Pathfinder as advertising material and window dressing. Over and over during the campaign were repeated notes like this:

> Frémont has got a better half,
> And what must be the whole?

One of the most popular songs of the campaign was labeled to be sung to the old Scotch tune "Jessie, the Flower of Dumblane":

> The sunburst has dawned over all the glad mountains,
>   While Freedom and Glory rise up hand in hand,
> To meet our young chieftain from Liberty's fountains,
>   With Jessie, sweet Jessie, the flower o' the land!
>
> How blithe is the summons o'er all the wide Nation!
>   How swells the bold music that marshals our band!
> He comes like a hero to fill the proud station,
>   With Jessie, sweet Jessie, the flower o' the land.
>
> She's wise and she's prudent; she's good and she's bonnie;
>   For Virtue and Freedom she takes a brave stand;
> For the Chieftain's White Mansion she's better than onie;
>   So give her God speed! there, the flower o' the land.
>
> Let honest hearts greet her, and victory meet her;
>   You'll never repent it,—so join hand in hand,
> Till firm with our leader in rapture we seat her,—
>   Our noble young Jessie, the flower o' the land!

Another song, to be sung to the tune "Wait for the Wagon," had this as its chorus:

> We'll give 'em Jessie,
> We'll give 'em Jessie,
> We'll give 'em Jessie,
>   When we rally at the polls!

It is perhaps noteworthy that a prominent song during the campaign, as in a more modern losing campaign, was set to the music of Foster's song "Oh! Susannah." This was its chorus:

> Rise, bold freemen,
>   Rise from hill and dale;
> Your watchword, "Jessie and the Right,"
> There's no such thing as fail!

Much was made of the fact in song after song that Buchanan, the opposing candidate, was "A fine old fossil bachelor—the doughface candidate"—

> A rusty old codger, who ne'er—as 'tis said,
> Had children to speak of, and never was wed

But,

> With pride we can point at our own candidate,
> Who doubled his value by taking a mate,
> And who found in his Jessie a treasure more bright
> Than all Mariposa will e'er bring to light.

Buchanan, as all know, was elected, but there was no landslide. "No candidate had a majority of the popular vote."

CHAPTER IX

"A D----D MOB OF SCRIBBLING
WOMEN"

I

BY 1856, FEMININE FICTION WAS RUNNING AT HIGH TIDE. From Liverpool in January, 1855, Hawthorne wrote his publisher, Ticknor, that he was inclined to abandon fiction writing because of literary conditions in America. Only one other novel, in fact, did he ever complete—*The Marble Faun,* four years later.

> America [he wrote] is now wholly given over to a d---d mob of scribbling women, and I should have no chance of success while the public taste is occupied with their trash— and should be ashamed of myself if I did succeed. What is the mystery of these innumerable editions of *The Lamplighter,* and other books neither better nor worse? Worse they could not be, and better they need not be, when they sell by the hundred thousand.

And yet, strangely enough, a month later, in a letter to his publisher, we find him throwing bouquets at the most tearful and convulsingly "female" moralizer of the whole modern blue-stocking school, "Fanny Fern":

In my last, I recollect, I bestowed some vituperation on female authors. I have since been reading *Ruth Hall;* and I must say I enjoyed it a good deal. The woman writes as if the Devil was in her; and that is the only condition under which a woman ever writes anything worth reading. Generally women write like emasculated men, and are only to be distinguished from male authors by greater feebleness and folly; but when they throw off the restraints of decency and come before the public stark naked, as it were—then their books are sure to possess character and value. Can you tell me anything about this Fanny Fern? If you meet her, I wish you would let her know how much I admire her.

That Hawthorne found *The Lamplighter* intolerable is easily understood, but this sudden infatuation for Fanny Fern requires explanation. *The Lamplighter,* published in 1854, was written by a native of Salem, Massachusetts, Maria S. Cummins, 24 years old. *Jane Eyre* undoubtedly she had read and reread, and *Wuthering Heights,* and Dickens, and over them she had dreamed school-girl dreams. Like the rest of her feminine clan of New England romancers, she had been careful to mix her sentimentalism and melodrama with a saving dash of morals and religion. Her resulting blend proved to be perfect, and the American reading public, mostly women, found it delightful. Forty thousand copies of the novel were sold in its first eight weeks, and by the time Hawthorne got his copy the circulation was nearing a hundred thousand.

Plot now was entering the feminine novel, and romantic love described in *Jane-Eyre*-like moving superlatives. Realism, so far as Miss Cummins was concerned, was a device wholly out of place in romance that was to be read by the women who had reread *Jane Eyre* and

cried over *The Wide, Wide World*. To illustrate what
The Lamplighter really was, allow me to quote from an
anonymous parody of the volume, an early condensed
novel, published in *Harper's Magazine* in May, 1855.
Relying wholly upon intuition gathered from its style
and mannerism, I have guessed that it was written by
N. P. Willis, or by one of his New York circle.[1]

In Chapter I of the parody, the hero, a cadaverous poet,
has induced an old lamplighter to allow him to climb his
ladder and light a lamp opposite a window where he has
caught the glimpse of a face. He is now on the ladder:

With suspended breath the young poet stood at that dizzy
height, and looking into the room with one eye, and at his
ostensible task with the other, he succeeded in lighting the
lamp, at the cost of smashing one side of glass. A mob was
speedily gathered around the lamp-post, but the youth heeded
neither their laughter nor their execrations. He saw—oh, pity!
what saw he not?

The furniture of the room was excessively mean, but on
one side stood a cottage piano of gorgeous workmanship, before which sat a maiden of perfect beauty—the beauty of rich
golden hair, pearl-white skin of softest vermeil shade, eyes of
dewy violet, and form of gazelle-like lightness. Oh, but she
was lovely!

At the sound of the smashed glass she naturally turned
around and looked up.

A youth with long hair, turn-down collar, and poetic eye,
at the top of a lamplighter's ladder is not an ordinary object.
Isabel gazed wonderingly. An elderly female, of majestic port,
entered the room.

"Look there, *chère maman!*" said Isabel.

---

[1] Dickens' facetious sketch "The Lamplighter," published in his *Pic Nic
Papers* in 1841, is entirely different from the *Harper's Magazine* sketch described above.

"What, *ma chère?*"

But before another word was spoken, the youthful bard rapidly retraced his steps down the ladder, and clasped the arm of the friendly lamplighter in a half swoon of delicious emotion. There was an interval of silence.

"Friend!" said the lamplighter, "if thy look betray me not, thou art noble—thou art gifted."

"I write for the *Hearthrug Excruciator,*" murmured the youth with ill-concealed pride.

"I knew it! I knew it! Enough! Would you know the maiden—sit at her side—speak to her—press her hand—"

"Oh heaven!" interrupted the young poet.

"Speak!"

"I would!"

"No more! We meet again—give me your card—good—farewell!"

The lamplighter disappeared hastily round the corner. Uncertain whether he was awake or dreaming, Edward (for his name was Edward) stood "Like one that hath been stunned and is of sense forlorn," till the taunts of the hustling mob around him suggested his moving on.

Still the lamps shone, and the stars twinkled while the rattle of an engine and the cry of fire in the main street diverted the crowd.

When they were gone, Edward returned and lingered by the charmed spot. The voice was silent, but it was now late and there was a light in the front room up stairs.

"Ah!" said he, "she sleeps!"

He was mistaken. It was the room of a lodger who played in the orchestra of the "Royal Pavilion Theatre." Isabel slept in the back parlor with her mother.

Still the stars and lamps shone on.

CHAPTER II

Joy comes and goes.

The next morning as Edward was bewailing his empty

purse—for his pocket had been ruthlessly picked on the previous evening—a letter arrived for him. It was in a disguised hand, and contained these words:

"Be *there* at eight to-night, and ask for Isabel. Be bold and fear not! Your destiny is in your own hands.

THE LAMPLIGHTER.

How the youthful poet passed through that day; how he performed its dreary, monotonous duties; how he endured his agony of suspense; how he found his way to the Commercial Road in the evening—are all among the things that may not be written; save that, with respect to the last point, it is definitely known that he went in a fourpenny omnibus, having borrowed a small sum from his landlady.

.　　.　　.　　.　　.　　.　　.

A mist swam before his eyes. He said faintly,
"Isabel? I was told to ask for Isabel—"
"Edward?" said the beautiful maiden, advancing with a smile and a blush.
"All right?" inquired Edward.
"Quite," said Isabel meaningly.
There was a sweet, soft moan of tender unrest and she flung herself on his bosom....
At this moment Edward heard a slight clicking noise outside, and turning his head, caught a glimpse of the lamplighter at his nightly occupation...Was there not something Satanic in his half-suppressed smile?...Gracious powers! Could it be that he was....No! No! the thought was too wild. But in spite of himself, a tremor seized his limbs, a cold sweat bedewed his brow, his hair stood almost on end....

The plot, now in full swing, finishes Chapter II, runs headlong through Chapters III and IV and culminates with a crash in Chapter V in which is revealed the joyful news that the Lamplighter is the Earl of Bradcliffe, that he is Isabel's papa, and that in his will is the provision that Edward, now the husband of Isabel, is to succeed him as Earl of Bradcliffe.

This undoubtedly is extreme criticism of Miss Cummins. E. P. Whipple, the critic of the New England group, commended *The Lamplighter,* "owing to the simplicity, tenderness, pathos, and naturalness of the first one hundred pages." But taking the book as a whole and realizing its kinship with the great mass of feminine fiction that poured from the presses of the early fifties, it is not overdone. *The Lamplighter* was perfectly in key with its day: it sold 70,000 copies in its first year.

II

THE FEMININE novel was now under full steam, and what Mrs. E. D. E. N. Southworth, Ann S. Stephens, Caroline Lee Hentz, Mary J. Holmes, Augusta Evans Wilson and similar "females" were to do to it we shall see. But first, why was Nathaniel Hawthorne so infatuated with *Ruth Hall?* And that brings us to Fanny Fern.

First of all, she was the sister of Nathaniel Parker Willis. Born in Portland, Maine, she had been reared in Boston where her father was editor of *The Youth's Companion,* she had attended the public schools, and had been "finished" at Catharine Beecher's Female Seminary at Hartford; married early to a Boston bank clerk, and then after his death, which left her in poverty, married again most disastrously. Divorce had followed, and at the age of forty, wholly without literary experience, she had settled down with her children to support herself with her pen. Naturally she had turned for help to her brother, then editor of the *Home Journal,* but Willis, as can be easily gathered from his voluminous writings, had small sympathy for "blue-stockings," even when they were in his own family. According to Henry A. Beers, in his life of Willis, "she offered some contributions to the *Home Journal;* but Willis, whose literary taste, though certainly not severe, was fastidious in its way, could not see merit enough in his sister's writings, and disliked what he regarded as its noisy, rattling style."

But something deeper than this lay under the episode. From her childhood she had been "the *enfant terrible* of the family." Beers admits that there had always been an "opposition in character and taste between the two." Willis' attitude toward her early marriages has never been revealed. Certainly she never had been one to take opposition with meekness.

The sub-editor of the *Journal,* James Parton, later to be famous as a biographer, read the submitted manuscripts "which had a heart-throb in them," as one contemporary commentator has declared, and disagreed with his chief and accused him of cruelty to his sister who was struggling to support her small children. "There was a scene, in consequence, in the office of the *Home Journal,*" records Beers, "and Mr. Parton retired from the paper, his place being supplied by T. B. Aldrich." "And then," records Greenslet in his life of Aldrich, "so far did he carry his championship, that despite the lady's somewhat disconcerting matrimonial record and her eleven years seniority, he contracted an engagement of marriage with her."

The marriage, however, did not take place until 1855,

Title-page engraved for the edition of 1853.

when Fanny Fern had become widely known as the author of *Fern Leaves from Fanny's Portfolio,* a volume composed of her gathered-up contributions to many magazines. Completely was the book in key with the times, a tear-drenched section of goody-goody inanity, carved alive from the feminine fifties. And, believe it or not, the book speedily sold 70,000 copies, another series was demanded, and the book-reviewer of *Putnam's Magazine* welcomed it as a classic:

They are acute, crisp, sprightly, knowing, and, though sometimes rude, evince much genuine and original talent, a keen power of observation, lively fancy, and humorous as well as pathetic sensibilities.

Amazing! But *Fern Leaves* was only the beginning of the incredible vacuum in the history of American letters that we call "Fanny Fern." "Hell has no fury like a woman scorned," and one may add, no fight is so relentless as a family row. She threw her grievances into the novel *Ruth Hall,* a book characterized by Beers as a "caricature." In it, he says, she "washed a deal of family linen in public":

Willis figures therein as Hyacinth, a "heartless puppy," who worships social position, has married an heiress, inhabits a villa on the Hudson, and is the prosperous editor of the *Irving Magazine.* When Ruth asks him to help her by printing her pieces in this periodical, he coldly assures her that she has no talent, and advises her to seek "some unobtrusive employment." But when she becomes famous and begins to get letters from college presidents, begging her for her autograph, and from grateful readers, saying "I am a better son, a better brother, a better husband, and a better father than I was before I commenced reading your articles. God bless you!" then, under these triumphant circumstances, Hyacinth, who had given $100 for a vase when Ruth was starving, is proud to point out to a friend, as they sit together on the porch of his country seat, a beautiful schooner tacking up stream with "Floy," his sister's *nom de plume,* painted on the bows.

To understand a book, the reviewer must, so far as possible, forget modern standards, and surround himself with the atmosphere of the times that produced it. To be perfectly fair to *Ruth Hall,* I shall reproduce the review in *Harper's Magazine* one month after the volume was published, a review that to-day seems definitive:

Here lies *Ruth Hall.* Has it a single great literary merit? Is there any story at all? Is there any individualization or development of character? Is there any sentiment which is not sentimentality, of the worst kind? Is there any thought which is not a thin echo of some noble word of one of the great minds that warm the age with their humane wisdom, and so distorted in the echo that it becomes untrue? Is there any pathos that is not puerile and factitious? Is there anything more in the book than an easy smartness?

Its pictures are like life as the portraits of an itinerant painter are like the sinewy farmer and red-cheeked wife whom he paints. They are executed and then hung on the parlor wall...

The characters have a dull and distorted resemblance to the characters of life, as a face inked on blotting paper may vaguely resemble a face. But as they figure on the pages of the story they have no point, no moral, no interest. The whole book is embittered. It is not easy to see why, nor to what good result. If the book was written to sell, it has succeeded. It has sold universally and that profoundly interesting question whether Ruth Hall is Fanny Fern has been debated from the Penobscot to the Mississippi. Let us suppose that it is. How glad we are that Fanny Fern has raised herself from penury to plenty. Let us suppose that it is not. How glad we are there is one less victim of poverty.

Doubtless Hawthorne, totally unaware of the family feud and the rage of the scorned author, attributed the intense atmosphere of the novel and its over-done picturings of the effects of extreme poverty upon a struggling feminine soul for genius, and had commended it just as he might have commended the vastly superior *Wuthering Heights.*

III

THE EVOLUTION from *The Wide, Wide World* to Augusta Evans Wilson's gorgeous and Byronic melodrama *St. Elmo* was the work of only a decade, but what a gulf to jump in a tiny ten years. When plot and sensation and *la grande passion* began to be tolerated in the novel, and the New York *Ledger* began weekly to increase in circulation, the movement became a flood. In the evolution one notes first the work of Caroline Lee Hentz.

She was of Puritan stock, born in Lancaster, Massachusetts, the daughter of General John Whiting. At the age of twenty-four she married N. M. Hentz, teacher of French in Bancroft's Round Hill School. Teaching positions they held later in Chapel Hill, North Carolina; in Covington, Kentucky; in Cincinnati; and in Florence, Alabama, where for nine years they conducted a prosperous "female" academy, and finally superintended schools in Georgia.

She was forty-six when she began writing fiction— short sketches gathered up, after the fashion of the time, into a collection—*Aunt Patty's Scrap Bag,* and she was fifty when appeared her first novel, *Linda, or the Pilot of the Belle Creole*. It is noteworthy that she turned to fiction after a successful run as a dramatist. While in Kentucky, she had won a prize of $500 for a tragedy, *De Lara, or the Moorish Bride,* and it had had a successful run. She had followed it with *Lamorah, or the Western Wild, a Tragedy,* and by *Constance Werdenberg, a Tragedy*. A book of poems also she published.

As a result of this training, her novels, when she began to write them, had plot and movement and dramatic atmosphere. For the most part she used Southern backgrounds and Southern life, and had she been content to modify her sensationalism and her overdoneness in romantic picturings, and to present actuality as she must have known it after her many years in the South, she could have made herself a literary pioneer, and her books to-day might still be in circulation.

True to her New England blood and training, she salted her novels heavily with morality, a device that undoubtedly increased the numbers of her feminine readers. She was the most cultured, perhaps, of all the woman writers of her period. To her undoubted talent she added a literary finish and a style undoubtedly influenced by her husband's French scholarship and French library, and by her early studies of French dramatic art.

In all, her novels number fifteen, and they were issued in a series of twelve volumes in 1870. Very uniform are they in quality, but if six were to be selected they would be, perhaps: *Linda,* 1850; *Marcus Warland, or the Long Moss Spring,* 1852; *Helen and Arthur, or Miss Thusa's Spinning Wheel,* 1853; *The Planter's Northern Bride,*

1854; *Robert Graham, a Sequel to Linda,* 1855; and *Ernest Linwood,* 1856.

The one that made the most sensation in the North was doubtless *The Planter's Northern Bride*—an "Anti-Uncle-Tom novel"—the slavery question as viewed by a Northern-born woman who had lived the most of her mature life in the South. Again let me quote a contemporary review, an anonymous estimate in *Putnam's Magazine,* May, 1854:

It is the story of an accomplished and wealthy Southerner who marries the daughter of a New England abolitionist and who by means of his own excellence and the agreeable light in which his relations to his slaves are placed, by actual experience, converts the entire family into good pro-slavery people. The intention is to do away with Northern prejudices, which are supposed to exist and to exhibit society in the South in its true aspects. But we object to the book apart from our general objections to all novels having a set moral purpose, that it proves too much, and consequently proves nothing. It paints the South so entirely *couleur de rose* that the reader, knowing there are some and great evils in all societies, suspects it to be untrue.

IV

EMMA DOROTHY Eliza Nevitte Southworth wrote in the fifty years of her literary life sixty novels, all of them bulky volumes. Her early life, in some of its years, was full of Southworth-novel stuff. She was twice married. Deserted by her second husband, she had returned from Wisconsin where he had left her, and had settled in Washington, her native city, as a school-teacher. As she could, she wrote, sketches at first, after the fashion of the

ANN S. STEPHENS
Graham's Magazine, 1844.

SARAH JOSEPHA HALE
Godey's Lady's Book, 1850.

AUGUSTA JANE EVANS WILSON
From a daguerreotype in possession of
Florence A. Slade, Columbus, Georgia.

SARA PAYSON WILLIS
"Fanny Fern." Courtesy of the
New York Historical Society.

times, then a propagandic novel, *Retribution,* serialized in the Washington *National Era,* the paper that soon was to serialize *Uncle Tom's Cabin.* In 1849, the novel had appeared in book form, and Whittier, his eye sharp for anti-slavery documents, found it and commended it highly, advising its author to quit school-teaching and devote herself to fiction. This she did at once, and the fictional flood began. During the fifties her best work, perhaps, was *The Curse of Clifton,* 1852, and *The Missing Bride,* 1855. Then had come her masterpiece, *The Hidden Hand,* 1859, run first as a serial in Bonner's New York *Ledger,* a plot novel, written in the exuberant splendor of style for which she became noted. Made into a melo-drama, it long held the stage, John Wilkes Booth at one time starring in the rôle of Black Donald.

"Contemporary criticism praised her sentimental and melodramatic plots immoderately, and her large reading public, mostly women, encouraged her to an abundant production." Undoubtedly she was a victim of her times. It was the *Ledger* that made her what she became. Pathetically, she explained in later years that her one thought at first had been to please the readers of the *Ledger* and that she would have written differently if she had been freed from financial pressure.

Year by year her gorgeous fictions greeted the reading public, always introduced with such elaborate "blurbs" as this:

Gloria: a Novel by Mrs. E. D. E. N. Southworth, author of *The Hidden Hand, The Unloved Wife, Lilith, Unknown, A Leap in the Dark, Nearest and Dearest, For Woman's Love, The Lost Lady of Lone, David Lindsay,* etc. etc.

We are not claiming too much when we say that Mrs. Southworth is one of the most engaging writers of fiction that this country has produced. Her novels have a larger circulation among the people than those of any other American writer. She has the gift of making her stories interesting, and filling them with pleasing incidents and characters, so that when the reader has finished one he wants to take up another.

What would a history of American fiction be were the writer to draw his materials wholly from the "blurbs" and advertising matter of publishers?

V

EVEN the names of the feminine novels that flooded the late fifties and all of the sixties would fill a chapter. It is useless to dwell on such ephemeræ as Ann S. Stephens' melodramatic *The Heiress of Greenhurst*, 1857, though it could be described by a contemporary as "gleaming with the splendor of a warm Spanish atmosphere." And when one comes to the all but infinite chaos known as Mary Jane Holmes, whose net circulation has been estimated at over two million copies, one realizes one's meager supply of superlatives.

She was born in 1825 in a parsonage in Brookfield, Massachusetts; she taught school; she married a lawyer and lived with him for a time in Kentucky where she got much stuff to use in her fictions. Beginning her life as a novelist in 1854 with *Tempest and Sunshine, or Life in Kentucky,* she wrote at least one novel a year until her death in 1907. During the fifties she published five other novels. Her greatest vogue, however, came after the Civil War when she ran neck and neck in popularity with

E. P. Roe. Many of her later novels were issued in paper covers at low popular prices.

Feminine fiction with her reached a low ebb, a lowness exceeded, perhaps, only by the later Laura Jean Libbey. Her characters always were snow-white or coal-black. All her heroines, usually the fairest lilies of an exclusive society, had "beautiful bosoms which were perpetually heaving." Her style was rococo to the extreme, over-florid, fantastic, feebly pretentious.

Along with her, in 1856, had come Augusta Jane Evans Wilson with *Inez,* following it in 1859 with *Beula,* and in 1866 with *St. Elmo,* in gorgeous ultra-romantic atmospheres out-*Jane-Eyreing* even *Jane Eyre.* Her Byronic, Mr. Rochester-like hero bowled over a whole generation of romantic school-girls. "A perfect revel was it of saccharine delight."

But the climax of the feminine period did not come in its fullness until there arrived, in the next literary period, the glamorous Laura Jean Libbey. But my prosy pen fails me. Allow me to page Heywood Broun, who wrote in his column in the New York *World* after her death:

So Laura Jean Libbey is dead. What recollections her name calls up! School days, strawride days, days when the bees bumbled outside and the smell of flowers floated in; days when boys, as though by psychic agreement, stoutly refused to work and hid Nick Carter and Dick Merriwell behind their geometries. And those terrifying, mysterious, alluring creatures across the aisle, those perverse creatures with ribbons on their hair, and ringlets to their waists—what were they hiding behind their geometries? Laura Jean Libbey. Laura the incomparable, the delightful; Laura who could evoke pink-and-lavender glamour right from page 1; Laura who never failed to deliver the loving couple into each other's arms, while bells banged the nuptials and friends wept into their kerchiefs. She is said to be the author of eighty-two novels and forty plays. She once said she never had any trouble writing; no halting or doubt, no tramping the floor at midnight to capture an elusive concept, no temperamental fits, starts, or sulks, no waiting for inspiration. She always knew where she was going; right always conquered might, wrong, or what-not, and right was always perfectly easy to perceive. Well, all honor to her. Her works may not be great literature, but they were in key with youth. If she was not profound, girls found her readable; and who shall say that her influence was not as good as the movie, which has usurped her place?

What more is there to say?

VI

MOST of the rising school of humorists found in the growing feminine movement materials in abundance for their fun-making. Nearly all of them began with parodies of the feminine fiction that was so loading the news-stands and the book-stores. Robert C. Newell beginning as a columnist, as he would now be called, on the staff of the New York *Mercury* in the late fifties, using the pseudonym "Orpheus C. Kerr," began his career as a humorist with a diagnosis of the feminine disease of the decade, one of the symptoms of which was the desire to create romantic fiction. This was his philosophy:

Long and patient study of womanly works teaches me that woman's genius, as displayed in gushing fiction, is a power of creating an unnatural and unmitigated ruffian for a hero, at whose shrine all crinoline and immense delegations of inferior broadcloth are impelled to bow. Such a one is that old humbug, Rochester, the beloved of Jane Eyre. The character has been overdone scores of times since poor Charlotte Brontë gave her famous novel to the world, and is still much used in respectable families.

The great difficulty with the intellectual women of America is, that they will persist in attempting to delineate a phase of manly character which attracts them above all others, but which they do not comprehend. Woman entertains a natural fondness for that which she cannot understand, and hence it is that we very seldom find her without a wildly vague admiration for Emerson.

There is in this world, my boy, a noble type of manhood which unites dignified reserve with the most loyal integrity, relentless pride of manner with the most kindly humility of heart, rigid indifference to the applause of the world with the finest regard for its honest respect, and carelessness of woman's mere frivolous liking with the most profound and chivalrous reverence for her virtue and her love.

This is the type which, without comprehending it, the intellectual women of America are continually striving to depict in their novels; and a pretty mess they make of it, my boy,— a pretty mess they make of it.

Their Rochester hero is harder to understand than Hamlet, when he falls into the hands of our schoolgirl authoresses.

Thereupon, to illustrate the feminine fiction of the fifties, Newell presents what he declares to be a novel sent him by "one of the young and intellectual women of America." In the *Jane Eyre* manner, grotesquely exaggerated, as Harte was to do it some years later in the "Miss Mix" of his *Condensed Novels,* he was unsparing in his attack upon the *St. Elmo* types of fiction. One may find this "Woman's Novel" as he called it, in his *Orpheus C. Kerr Papers,* 1862, Letter 9.

VII

IN LATER years Newell was to throw his youthful philosophy to the winds and marry perhaps the most glamorous "female blue-stocking" of the pre-war period or of the decade beyond—a Jewess, born in New Orleans, Adah Isaacs, but later to be known by her *nom de guerre,* Adah Menken—Menken, a merchant of her native city, having been her husband number one.

Her earliest ambition, after the fashion of the times, had been a literary career, and she even published a volume of verses, now happily extinct; but the stage offered greater glory, and she was soon thrilling Southern audiences with *East Lynne* and other stock melodramas of the era. She then escaped to New York where she prospered as a Bowery soubrette. With Ada Clare, she discovered the Bohemians at Pfaff's, Walt Whitman among them, and for a moment she was one with the group. Divorcing her first husband, as she supposed, she next married Heenan, the much-exploited prize-ring hero of the period, and a son was born to them. A divorce, however, speedily followed, and then came husband number three, the young humorist Newell.

With him as manager, she next took her mad-cap dramatics to San Francisco, where she at once became a sensation. The new California school of writers, brilliant but fugacious—Bret Harte, Artemus Ward, Mark Twain, Joaquin Miller, and the others—held court for her in the offices of the *Golden Era,* hailing her as a genius of their own order, as if a princess had arrived in Roaring Camp.

To the little adolescent city this impetuous whiff of

personality and melodrama was a thrilling thing. In a dramatization of *Mazeppa,* with her playing the title part, she was stripped seemingly naked and lashed to a maddened horse which at a climactic moment crashed through the stage wings and to all intents out into the wild steppes. A moment it was to remember. There was a seeming oriental atmosphere about the woman, a mystery, a memory, which she seems to have emphasized with color and costume. She was emotional, with a voice peculiarly winning, with sex appeal and vivacity, and to the little group of young poets which for a moment dreamed of a new Pacific school of literature and art, she seemed a veritable new Helen of Troy.

For the moment she was always irresistible, but swift change was her very life. Like a night-moth she was gone. Divorcing Newell, she was off to Europe where her later amorous and Thespianic triumphs read like a Bertha Clay romance. But this brings me into the sixties.

CHAPTER X

THE NOVEL THAT PRECIPITATED
A WAR

THERE IS LITTLE THAT ONE CAN SAY NOW ABOUT *Uncle Tom's Cabin* that has not been said many times before. It has become an American myth, a historical document for students of American history, the best-known and most widely presented drama the country has ever had. Who does not know of Eliza's escape across the ice, of Little Eva's death, of Uncle Tom whipped to death by Simon Legree? I shall consider the book only as it throws light upon the characteristics of the 1850's. And no book ever written enlightens the period more.

First of all, the book did nothing that it was expected to do and it has defied classification in a way that is now humorous. Gentle Mrs. Stowe, who cried so easily and who was so motherly and tender of heart, had no intention of throwing a bombshell into the South and helping to bring on a ghastly Civil War. She thought the South would approve of her book and be led by it to see slavery

130

as she saw it. Her worst men, like Legree for instance, were Northerners who had gone South, and her best men, like Tom's first two masters, were ideal gentlemen who made their slaves a part of their family life. Joel Chandler Harris once declared that the first third of *Uncle Tom's Cabin* made slavery really attractive. The earliest words from the South were indeed as commendatory as Mrs. Stowe ever could have wished. Mrs. Child in one of her letters cites this instance:

Mr. Pierce, Senator from Maryland, read *Uncle Tom's Cabin* lately and when he came to the sale of Uncle Tom he exclaimed with great emotion, "Here's a writer who knows how to sympathise with the South. I could fall down at the feet of that woman! She knows how to feel for a man when he is obliged to sell a good, honest slave."

The North it was which first brought criticism. Garrison, arch Abolitionist, objected to the book since it did not carry out his program outlined in the *Liberator,* and Mrs. Stowe, in turn, later attacked his abolitionism with severity for he had left God and the Bible out of his argument. The New York *Observer,* however, condemned *Uncle Tom's Cabin* for running counter to God's word. The Bible, it said, countenanced slavery. The South did not awake in anger until the book had sold 100,000 copies and had been reviewed by the London *Times* and other English journals. Nor did the North awake to a full appreciation of the book's significance until England had made of it a sensational best-seller. According to James Truslow Adams, "In 1852, Mrs. Stowe's *Uncle Tom's Cabin* sold in one year one million copies in London with only one hundred and fifty thousand in the United States."

Everywhere one touches the book one finds paradox. The leading publisher in Boston misjudged it, refused to publish it, giving as his reason that it would injure the firm's Southern trade. Those beginners to-day who receive rejection slips may find balm perhaps in contemplating this master rejection slip of all time, the rejection of the best seller America has ever produced. Had the firm never sold another book in the South until the present day it still would have made money for them to publish *Uncle Tom*. It is paradoxical that the book at length was brought out by a totally unknown young publisher who thought he might be taking a risk by publishing a first edition of 5,000 copies, the number that would have been assigned to a potential best-seller like *The Lamplighter*. The *National Era,* where it had run as a serial for ten months, misjudged it: they paid the author $300.

Academic critics of three generations have condemned its structure and its artistry. It was carelessly written, they have contended, loosely constructed, faulty in its English. It is not one book but three, with three different casts of characters, Uncle Tom only remaining permanent. Moreover, it is in parts, they contend, utter melodrama, as pronounced even as can be found in the *Gunmaker of Moscow* school of fiction; it is sentimental to an extreme unbearable to-day; and it uses types for characters rather than actual individuals studied from life. From the South soon came the cry that it falsified Southern life. The author located, for instance, St. Clair's

UNCLE TOM'S CABIN;

OR,

LIFE AMONG THE LOWLY.

BY

HARRIET BEECHER STOWE.

VOL. I.

BOSTON:
JOHN P. JEWETT & COMPANY.
CLEVELAND, OHIO:
JEWETT, PROCTOR & WORTHINGTON.
1852.

Title-page of the first edition.

summer home on the shore of Lake Pontchartrain, an utter impossibility as all knew who had seen the black-mud borders of this lake. Little Eva was buried in a garden on the lake shore, or in other words plunged into black, quaking mud. All who have visited New Orleans know of the burial vaults of the city and will be told that only paupers were buried in the ground. Uncle Tom is compared with "the Christian Bishops of Africa... men of color in their days," a statement that would make of Christians like Cyril, Athanasius, and St. Augustine, African Negroes. It is needless to continue this academic criticism. Even as the critics have written and carped and muck-raked for errors, the book has become a world classic, more widely translated, more multitudinously sold, and more vital in its influences than any other novel ever written. And to this may be added another paradox: for every critic who has attacked the book there has been always another equally eminent who has defended it. The chorus of condemnation has been all but overwhelming, but, *per contra,* the chorus of eminent praise has been equally overwhelming. At this point let it rest.

That the novel caused the Civil War, as Lincoln is said once to have intimated, is of course a matter for argument, and neither side can speak with positiveness. Let me appoint, therefore, a loyal Southerner to say for us the last word, Thomas Nelson Page. This is his verdict: "By arousing the general sentiment of the world against slavery, it (the novel) contributed more than any other one thing to its abolition in that generation," and "did more than any one thing that ever occurred to precipitate the war."

II

In 1853, "Harry Franko" (Charles F. Briggs) published in *Putnam's Magazine* an article entitled "Uncle Tomitudes." To sample the atmosphere of America and the world during the first four months of *Uncle Tom's Cabin,* allow me to quote:

It is but nine months since this Iliad of the blacks, as an English reviewer calls Uncle Tom, made its appearance among books, and already its sale has exceeded a million of copies; author and publisher have made fortunes out of it, and Mrs. Stowe, who was before unknown, is as familiar a name in all parts of the civilized world as that of Homer or Shakespeare. Nearly two hundred thousand copies of the first edition of the work have been sold in the United States, and the publishers say they are unable to meet the growing demand. The book was published on the 20th of last March, and on the first of December there had been sold one hundred and twenty thousand sets of the edition in two volumes, fifty thousand copies of the cheaper edition in one, and three thousand copies of the costly illustrated edition. The publishers have kept four steam presses running, night and day, Sundays only excepted, and at double the ordinary speed, being equal to sixteen presses, worked ten hours a day at the usual speed. They keep two hundred hands constantly employed in binding Uncle Tom, and he has consumed five thousand reams of white paper, weighing seventy-five tons. They have paid to the author twenty thousand three hundred dollars, her share of the profits on the actual cash sales of the first nine months. But it is in England that Uncle Tom has made his deepest mark. Such has been the sensation produced by the book there, and so numerous have been the editions published, that it is extremely difficult to collect the statistics of its circulation with a tolerable degree of exactness. But we know of twenty rival editions in England and Scotland, and that millions of copies have been produced...We have seen it stated that there were thirty different editions published in London within six months of the publication of the work here, and one firm keeps four hundred men employed in printing and binding it. There have been popular editions published also in Edinborough and in Glasgow; and it has been dramatized and produced on the boards of nearly every theatre in the Kingdom. Uncle Tom was played in six different theatres in London at the same time.

Rev. Calvin E. Stowe, college professor, had been content to sign a contract with the publisher Jewett for 10 per cent of all sales of the novel. The English editions brought in practically nothing, since the foreign copyright act was in the far future—1891 in fact. He has been criticized that he did not secure the dramatic rights for the novel so as to secure a percentage on all presentations of dramatized versions, but the first law to grant such a right was not passed until 1856. That he had small hopes of receiving financial benefit from the novel we can feel sure. As a preacher he was prejudiced against fiction. Some weeks after the first printing of the book he visited the publisher. "How much do you suppose I owe you now?" asked Mr. Jewett. "Oh, I suppose enough to buy my wife a silk dress," answered the minister, whereupon he was handed the first check with the astonishing figure upon it of $10,000.

To "Harry Franko," writing nine months after the book first appeared, the amazing popularity of the novel came not because of its subject and the timeliness of its message, but because it was a living thing:

"When I am reading a book," says Dean Swift in his *Thoughts on Various Subjects,* "whether wise or silly, it seems to me to be alive and talking to me." This is the secret of *Uncle Tom's Cabin;* it is a live book, and it talks to its readers as if it were alive. It first awakens their attention, arrests their thoughts, touches their sympathies, rouses their curiosity, and creates such an interest in the story it is telling, that they cannot let it drop until the whole story is told. And this is done, not because it is a tale of slavery, but in spite of it. If it were the story of a Russian Serf, an evicted Milesian, a Manchester weaver, or an Italian State prisoner, the result would be the same. It is the consummate art of the story teller that has given popularity to *Uncle Tom's Cabin,* and nothing else. The anti-slavery sentiment obtruded by the author in her own person, upon the notice of the reader, must be felt by everyone to be the great blemish of the book; and it is one of the proofs of its great merits as a romance, that it has succeeded in spite of this defect... We can name no novel, after *Tom Jones,* that is superior to *Uncle Tom* in constructive ability. The interest of the narrative begins in the first page and is continued with consummate skill to the last. . Mrs. Stowe, like Fielding, seizes upon the attention at the outset, and never lets go for a moment. It matters not by what means this is done, it is the chief object aimed at by the romancer, and the greatest artist is he who does it in the most effectual manner; if the writer of fiction fails in this point, he fails altogether.

Her attack upon slavery was not obvious. She did not preach and she did not argue and she made no frontal attack. Like Dickens, she aroused emotion; she created characters that her reader could feel as if they were present in the room. The victims were under-dogs, and in America they were therefore to be pitied. The oppressors were all utter villains. The novel came in the one moment in history when it would have been received as a world classic. For America was tense with emotion, and that emotion was almost as intense in Europe, especially in England. As a period novel it had every element that would make for popularity: it was melodramatic, with a hero and heroines and villains; it was sentimental even to the Dickens extremes; it had humor of the Jim Crow type; it had negro spirituals sung by slaves; and it had a strong religious motif such as could come only from one reared, as she had been, in such an atmosphere as she was later to present in her *Oldtown Folks*.

Dickens with his *Pickwick* and his *Oliver Twist* and the novels that followed undoubtedly created a new reading public. Hostlers and weavers and servant girls who never before had thought of books as things to be read laughed over Sam Weller and the fat boy and cried when Paul Dombey died and Little Nell. In the same way *Uncle Tom's Cabin* enlarged greatly the American reading public. For one thing it broke down a long stretch of the stockade that had guarded Puritan families from the "contagion" of novels, long believed in Christian homes to be works inspired by the devil. Everybody read *Uncle Tom*. Was it not history? Was it not a weapon against slavery? Was not Mrs. Stowe saying that the hand of God held her hand as she wrote it? And they followed it into the theater and saw Little Eva go up to Heaven on a wire which they did not see, with "not a dry eye in the house." They saw Eliza cross the ice with her baby in her arms and the awful bloodhounds leaping at her throat, and they went home shuddering at the death of Uncle Tom ready to canonize him as a veritable saint. Surely uncounted thousands went to see a Tom drama who never before had seen the inside of a theater.

HARRIET BEECHER STOWE

LITTLE EVA READING THE BIBLE TO UNCLE TOM

An illustration in the first edition of *Uncle Tom's Cabin*, 1852.

And the novel stirred eager pens North and South to write and publish Uncle Tomized and anti-Uncle Tomized books—a whole alcove of them. Sarah Josepha Hale reissued her *Northwood, or Life North and South,* first published in 1827, a remarkable book. William Gilmore Simms awoke with a roar and attacked *Uncle Tom* as if it had been a personal insult, and F. A. Adams "late of Charleston" answered him with *Uncle Tom at Home, a Review of the Reviewers and Repudiators of Uncle Tom's Cabin,* 1853. To Mrs. Stowe's *A Key to Uncle Tom's Cabin,* a "Lady of New York" retorted with *The Patent Key to Uncle Tom's Cabin.* The list is a long one and it belongs to the alcove of curiosities of American Literature, but all of it long ago has disappeared, "gone with the wind," while *Uncle Tom's Cabin* endures and will endure. Complete surveys of American Literature with voluminous extracts for the use of college classes, like J. B. Hubbell's *American Life in Literature,* or Jones and Leisy's *Major American Writers,* may be found with no mention made of Mrs. Stowe, but geography sometimes warps the judgment of critics.

III

THE FIRST thought of Mrs. Stowe, with sudden riches in her hands, was a trip to Europe from which was pouring by every mail a shower of invitations and letters of praise from all the eminent men and women of the period. On her first trip in 1853 she was received everywhere like a visiting empress. England and Europe generally showered her with honors, and when she returned home to write her account of the tour, *Sunny Memories of Foreign*

Lands, 1853, she was undoubtedly one of the best-known women in the world, as famous almost as Victoria who had so graciously received her.

In 1855 she republished her early volume, *The May-flower,* a series of New England sketches which she had first read before the Semicolon Club of Cincinnati in 1843. In it one finds her beautiful hymn, now in all church hymnals:

When I'm Awake I Am Still with Thee

Still, still with thee, when purple morning breaketh,
    When the bird waketh and the shadows flee;
Fairer than morning, lovelier than the daylight,
    Dawns the sweet consciousness, I am with thee!

Alone with thee, amid the mystic shadows,
    The solemn hush of nature newly born;
Alone with thee in breathless adoration,
    In the calm dew and freshness of the morn.

As in the dawning o'er the waveless ocean
    The image of the morning star doth rest,
So in this stillness thou beholdest only
    Thine image in the waters of my breast.

Still, still with thee! as to each new-born morning
    A fresh and solemn splendor still is given,
So doth this blessed consciousness, awaking,
    Breathe, each day, nearness unto thee and heaven.

When sinks the soul, subdued by toil, to slumber,
    Its closing eye looks up to thee in prayer,
Sweet the repose beneath thy wings o'ershading,
    But sweeter still to wake and find thee there.

So shall it be at last, in that bright morning
   When the soul waketh and life's shadows flee;
O, in that hour, fairer than daylight dawning,
   Shall rise the glorious thought, *I am with thee!*

Then had come *Dred,* 1856, a second novel woven about slavery problems, a novel more successful than the general run of fiction, but a flat failure when compared with *Uncle Tom's Cabin* and its miraculous run into all the civilized languages. In 1856 she went abroad again, and still again in 1859. For a year she ran in the *Atlantic* her *The Minister's Wooing,* a novel of the New England of her childhood, a true study of the actuality of a period, one of the best pieces of work she had ever done, but like *Dred* it was lost in the fierce glow of *Uncle Tom's Cabin.* Despite her long row of published volumes she seems destined to go down to posterity as a one-book novelist.

IV

UNCLE TOM as a drama has become a subject almost apart from the history of Uncle Tom as a novel. It was dramatized by several actors, but the first version to succeed was made by George L. Aiken for his uncle George C. Howard, who produced it for the first time in September, 1852, at the Museum in Troy, New York, with the manager's wife as Topsy and her little daughter Cordelia as Eva. By careful doubling of parts the family troupe of seven presented eleven characters. Its success was instantaneous and overwhelming. It ran in Troy for one hundred nights, and transferred to New York, ran for more than two hundred nights, sometimes two and three presentations a day, the actors forced to eat their meals in full costume and make-up. That was the beginning. The play so tremendously pleased the people that troops of barn-stormers soon were covering the whole nation. Indeed, for one whole generation the Uncle Tom show could almost be rated as a national industry. Hardly an actor of any prominence who did not at one time or another essay the part of Uncle Tom or Marks or Simon Legree.

The original version was changed almost from night to night. New "gags" were added constantly and new features. Bloodhounds, not in Mrs. Stowe's story, chased Eliza over the ice; Little Eva was taken to heaven by a band of angels; versions appeared with Marks riding in on a mule; or with two Topsys. The comic little pickaninny was given a song to sing, "I'se So Wicked," and audiences from Maine to Nevada rolled off their seats with laughter:

> Oh, white folks, I wuz nebber born;
> Aunt Sue she raise me on de corn,
> Send me errands night an' morn,
>   Ching-a-ring-a-ring-ricked!

> She used to knock me on de floor,
> Den bang me haid again de door,
> An' tear ma wool out by de core.
>   Oh, golly! I's so wicked!

Wesley Winans Stout, in a fascinating article in the *Saturday Evening Post,* "Eva Is Seventy-Five," said this of the interpolations:

They had a way of being cumulative. For example, Mrs. Stowe was innocent of Legree's order, at the conclusion of the whipping scene, to Sambo and Quimbo to take Tom out "and throw him to the hogs." This in turn suggested another liberty with the script. In the book Legree died very satisfactorily of delirium tremens. Aiken built up the action by having him die at the hand of Cassy, settling a private score of her own and incidentally avenging Tom. At some early but unfixed date an equally unknown artist devised yet another end for Legree, so superior in hokum that it was adopted generally.

In the book St. Clair was the accidental victim of a barroom brawl between two strangers, and Marks was a minor character who appeared only in that part of the story concerned with George Harris and Eliza. The new twist made Legree the assassin of St. Clair. No motive was advanced, but it permitted Marks to appear at the Red River plantation with a warrant for Legree charging him with murder, and when the villain resisted, the comic lawyer shot him down. And now Marks whirled his umbrella, and ordered Sambo and Quimbo to take Legree out "and throw him to the hogs"—a Nemesisian boomerang that stirred the gallery to a frenzy of whistling and foot stamping.

The whole history of the dramatic versions of *Uncle Tom* and their presentations during thirty years and more should be made at volume length, and when such a book is made it will throw much light upon the people of America during one peculiar stage of their development.

Let the inimitable Otis Skinner, who played Uncle Tom in the earliest years of the drama and who was the last to represent him in the famous revival of 1933, say for us the last word:

Early Victorian drama partook of something of the character of the antimacassar, the worsted flowers, the horsehair sofa, the steel-engraving lady, the morocco-bound, gilt-edged volume of poems on the marble-topped table, and the sea-shells in the corner "what-not." Virtue and vice ran in clearly-defined stripes: the good were good, the heroes were paragons of virtue and valor, the wicked were fiends incarnate, the comic gentlemen fairly oozed whimsicality, lovers were deco-rous beings who described their amorous symptoms in long perorations, heroines were modest violets and chambermaids pert, intriguing minxes.

Into this conventional mold of the theatre George Aiken poured the life and substance of Harriet Beecher Stowe's in-spired story of *Uncle Tom's Cabin*. It was an easy task. The book is largely in dialogue form and speeches were transferred entire to the play manuscript. You may find the yellow-covered play book, with its Victorian verbiage trickling through its pages, at your bookseller's, but you will look in vain for the name of Harriet Beecher Stowe. Its cover bears the caption: "A Domestic Drama in Six Acts, Dramatized by George L. Aiken."

V

FROM the veritable library of articles and reviews and books which have discussed phases of the *Uncle Tom's Cabin* mania affecting two peoples, I select one written by Samuel Warren, the English author who wrote *Ten Thousand a Year*. Reviewing *Uncle Tom's Cabin* for *Blackwood's Magazine,* October, 1853, he joined the prophets and projected himself a century into the future. As the century has nearly elapsed it may be well for us to know what has happened and what is to come:

The present United States of America, after having been perhaps more than once split asunder and soldered together again—or the whole or a large portion voluntarily reannexed to the mother country and by and by detached—after these and other possibly more or less sudden, violent and bloody

vicissitudes—may have become a great empire, under the
stern but salutary one-willed sway of the Emperor of America, his Majesty a jet black who has shown consummate and
unexpected high qualities for acquiring and retaining the fear
and submission of millions of the stormiest tempers of man-
kind, but his lovely empress a white.

Then after some elephantine capers, he imagines his
own successor as a writer for *Blackwood's* coming across
a copy of *Uncle Tom's Cabin:*

From a preliminary dissertation prefixed to the book our
critic of 1953 learns that it excited, almost immediately on its
appearance, a prodigious sensation among all classes, both in
Europe and America; that both sexes high and low, young
and old, literate and illiterate, vulgar and refined, phlegmatic
and excitable, shed tears over it and wrote, talked and even
ranted about it everywhere; that within a few months' time
impressions of it were multiplied by millions and in most
languages of the civilized world... Inflamed with curiosity,
our shadowy successor sits down to peruse a work then possibly little, if ever mentioned—anxious to see what could have
produced such a marvellous effect in the middle of the intelligent nineteenth century on all classes of readers, and whether
it produced permanent results or passed away as a nine days'
wonder. Having at length closed the pages of *Uncle Tom's
Cabin* and judged it according to the critical standards of
1953, will he deem it adequate to have produced such effect?
What estimate will he form of our intellectual caliber?

"We cannot tell and shall not attempt to conjecture,"
he concludes, but since the emphasis of the book is on a
moral basis, he had no fears.

CHAPTER XI

DEMENTIA GOTHAMIANA

*E*RAS OF INTENSE EMOTION BLOW OFF AT TIMES LIKE superheated engines. New York City seemed to be the blow-hole of the fifties. To characterize the New York City of any decade requires strong adjectives. To attempt to cover it with a single descriptive term is doubtless to essay the impossible. The city is temperamental, it is sensational even to the utmost of the melodramatic, it is explosive, subject to recurrent intoxications non-alcoholic, it is all this and it is more.

To Martin Chuzzlewit, as reported by Dickens in 1844, New York was a peep-hole into a sewer. Note how the newsboys greeted him as he landed from England:

"Here's this morning's New York Sewer!" cried one. "Here's this morning's New York Stabber! Here's the New York Family Spy! Here's the New York Private Listener! Here's the New York Peeper! Here's the New York Plunderer! Here's the New York Keyhole Reporter! Here's the New York Rowdy Journal! Here's all the New York papers. Here's full particulars of the patriotic loco-foco movement yesterday, in which the Whigs was so chewed up; and the great Alabama gouging case; and the interesting Arkansas dooel with Bowie-knives; and all the Political, Commercial, and Fashionable News! Here they are! Here they are! Here's the papers, here's the papers!"

"Here's the Sewer!" cried another. "Here's the New York Sewer! Here's some of the twelfth thousand of to-day's Sewer, with the best accounts of the markets, and all the shipping news, and four whole columns of county correspondence, and a full account of the ball at Mrs. White's last night, where all the beauty and fashion of New York was assembled; with the Sewer's particulars of the private lives of the ladies that was there! Here's the Sewer! Here's some of the twelfth thousand of the New York Sewer! Here's the Sewer's exposure of the Wall Street gang and the Sewer's exclusive account of a flagrant act of dishonesty committed by the Secretary of State when he was eight years old; now communicated, at great expense, by his own nurse. Here's the Sewer, in its twelfth thousand, with a whole column of New Yorkers to be shown up, and all their names printed. Here's the Sewer's article upon the Judge that tried him, day before yesterday, for libel, and the Sewer's tribute to the independent jury that didn't convict him, and the Sewer's account of what they might have expected if they had! Here's the Sewer, here's the Sewer! Here's the wide-awake Sewer; always on the lookout; the leading journal of the United States. Now in its twelfth thousand, and still a printing off. Here's the New York Sewer!"

Always had New York been temperamental, subject to explosions, dominated for moments by mass dementia. Shortly before 1850 there had been the Macready-Forrest riots caused by the jealousy of two actors, riots that had destroyed theaters, erected street barricades, and had been subdued after a veritable battle in which 26 had been killed and 36 wounded.

In its celebrations, too, its welcoming of lion-hearts and artists, its tremendous receptions and banquets and farewell dinners, and its mob-like gatherings to celebrate unexpected achievements, always has it been extreme. Willis in his *Home Journal* in 1851 said this of his city:

We love to be subjected to a new "complete *furore*." We love to have a new singer astonish, overwhelm, and make a fortune out of us. And of the indispensable preliminary process —the puff, the humbug, the appeal to popular enthusiasms and nationalities, the anecdotes, portraits, and biographies— we are anxious watchers, encouragers, and willing enchant*ees*. .. New York is *now* the artist's Golden Gate.

But, he could add, defending the city that was so dear to his heart:

Second-, third-, and fourth-rate celebrities, for whom in Europe there is attention justly measured, pass wholly unnoticed through our city. It must be a full-blooded nobleman, or the *first* singer or danseuse of the world, or the *most* popular author, or the *very first* actor, or the miraculous musician, if there is to be enthusiasm. This lack of a scale of tribute to merit is one reason why we so ridiculously overdo our welcomes to great comets, as in the case of Dickens.

Surely a city that had as citizens P. T. Barnum, James Gordon Bennett, Horace Greeley, Robert Bonner, Commodore Vanderbilt, Edwin Forrest, A. T. Stewart, Henry Ward Beecher, and a dozen others like them, could not drone along like a country village.

II

THE DECADE was opened with characteristic sensation by P. T. Barnum, in 1850 already world-famous as the exhibitor of Tom Thumb. The news that he had secured for exhibition Jenny Lind, "the Swedish Nightingale," at the height of her European fame came to America like a "believe-it-or-not" tall story. It was a Barnum sensation. But soon it was found that a contract actually had been drawn. The great prima donna had agreed to come to America for 150 concerts at a cost that staggered the imagination of even New York. One thousand dollars was to be paid for each concert, and, in addition, one half of all receipts each night above this amount. In addition to this, Barnum was to pay all expenses of the voyage from Europe and all expenses in America of a party consisting of the singer; a feminine friend; a secretary; two servants; a composer and pianist, M. Benedict, at a salary of $25,000; and a baritone, Giovanni Belletti, at a salary of $12,500—something like a half million of dollars.

All Europe chuckled. Barnum had embarked upon a gambling venture which would be his ruin. But not for a moment did the figures disturb Barnum. For the first time, now, he had a veritable "greatest show on earth," and he handled it with characteristic methods. He knew his New York and he knew the American people. Jenny Lind he was sure had a combination of characteristics that would sweep America off its feet. First of all, she could indeed sing. No superlatives could exceed her real powers. Then, too, she was unspoiled, peculiarly naïve and winsome; she was genuinely religious; she was kindly and amazingly generous, a veritable saint with the winnings from her God-given powers; and in addition to all this, and perhaps the most moving attraction of all, she was an emotional artist. To N. P. Willis, as he re-

ported it for his *Home Journal,* her emotional quality
was supreme: "her capacity of expressing feeling—pure
feeling—to its utmost depth and elevation, is beyond
cavil."

No detail of his preparation for the advent of the great
singer was suffered by Barnum to go unnoticed. In the
city of sensational advertising he was the leading advertiser always. First, he offered a prize of $200 for the
words of a song to be sung by the prima donna on her
first night in New York. Seven hundred and fifty poems
were submitted, and the song written by Bayard Taylor,
then twenty-five, won the prize:

GREETING TO AMERICA

Words by Bayard Taylor—Music by Jules Benedict

I greet, with a full heart, the Land of the West,
    Whose Banner of Stars o'er a world is unrolled;
Whose empire o'ershadows Atlantic's wide breast
    And opes to the sunset its gateway of gold!
The land of the mountain, the land of the lake,
    And rivers that roll in magnificent tide—
Where the souls of the mighty from slumber awake
    And hallow the soil for whose freedom they died!

Thou Cradle of Empire! though wide be the foam
    That severs the land of my fathers and thee,
I hear, from thy bosom, the welcome of home,
    For song has a home in the hearts of the Free!
And long as thy waters shall gleam in the sun,
    And long as thy heroes remember their scars,
Be the hands of thy children united as one,
    And Peace shed her light on the Banner of Stars!

The famous singer and her entourage arrived at Quarantine, New York, September 1, 1850. Barnum met her there with a reporter to see him climb up the ladder "with a choice bouquet stuck in the bosom of his white vest." The newspapers issued extras to record the great event, and when the party landed the next morning, they were, received, as recorded by the press, with a "demonstration of popular enthusiasm which has seldom been equalled in this country. More than 20,000 people gathered upon the wharf where she landed and crowded the streets through which she passed." An amazing demonstration for "a young woman who has not yet seen thirty years."

England, who not long before had herself gone to extremes in her approval of the young singer, was manifestly jealous. The London *Athenæum* in its report headed "Jenny Lind in America" declared that:

The whole people of New York are now reeling to and fro under the Lind intoxication. The event of the Swedish singer's touching their shores marks an era in the history of that great and go-ahead people. The arrival of Columbus in the West was a less significant event... The Liverpool penny-a-lining on the subject of the Nightingale made men turn away sick and ashamed, but even in Liverpool, though they did their best, they have no notion of a folly on the American dimensions. The genius of hyperbole seems here to have exhausted itself on a negation. The gentle little lady has come amongst them to sing a few of her pastoral airs "for a consideration,"—and they greet her with a perfect Niagara of welcome... Meantime, we know not what the next American arrivals can well bring us in the way of climax to all these things—if it be not the announcement that Jenny Lind has sung "Yankee

Doodle," and that the Americans have elected her as a separate and independent State into the Union.

Punch also reported the arrival. Under the heading, "Coronation of Jenny the First—Queen of the Americans," it described at length the voyage and the reception:

...As the ship neared the pier, every mast seemed to be made of eyes, noses and mouths; every window was a mass of heads; and the roofs of the houses looked as if they were slated with human beings, and had men and women for chimney-pots...The progress to Irving House was one tremendous crush of beings, so densely packed together, that an exceedingly ripe cheese, in spontaneous motion, is the only thing to which it would bear comparison...We should not be surprised if the next "Latest from America," should announce the dissolution of the republic, and the proclamation of Jenny Lind as Queen of the United States, with Barnum as Chief Secretary for Foreign Affairs—a post for which his long acquaintance with such foreign affairs as Tom Thumb, the sea serpent, and other contents of his museum, renders him fully qualified.

Barnum, who in his autobiography has told in detail of the welcome to Jenny Lind and the incidents connected with his tour as her manager, has given his opinion that

never before had there been such enthusiasm in the city of New York, or indeed in America...At twelve o'clock that night, she was serenaded by the New York Musical Fund Society, numbering on that occasion, two hundred musicians. They were escorted to the Irving House by about three hundred firemen, in their red shirts, bearing torches. There was a far greater throng in the streets than there was even during the day. The calls for Jenny Lind were so vehement that I led her through a window to the balcony.

During the eleven days before the first concert New York was in a veritable fever. "Presents of all sorts were showered upon her." "The carriages of the wealthiest citizens could be seen in front of her hotel at all hours of the day":

Songs, quadrilles, and polkas were dedicated to her, and poets sung in her praise. We had Jenny Lind gloves, Jenny Lind bonnets, Jenny Lind riding hats, Jenny Lind shawls, mantillas, robes, chairs, sofas, pianos—in fact everything was Jenny Lind. Her movements were closely watched, and the moment her carriage appeared at the door, it was surrounded by multitudes, eager to catch a glimpse of the Swedish Nightingale... Jenny Lind's first concert was fixed to come off at Castle Garden, on Wednesday evening, September 11th, and most of the tickets were sold at auction on the Saturday and Monday previous to the concert. John N. Genin, the hatter, laid the foundation of his fortune by purchasing the first ticket at $225.

Needless to say, the Castle Garden auditorium, which Jenny Lind once declared looked like a vast wash-tub, was packed to its uttermost capacity. Barnum estimated the number to be over seven thousand:

The reception of Jenny Lind on her first appearance, in point of enthusiasm, was probably never before equalled. As Mr. Benedict led her toward the foot-lights, the entire audience rose to their feet and welcomed her with three cheers, accompanied by the waving of thousands of hats and handkerchiefs. This was by far the largest audience to which Jenny Lind had ever sung. She was evidently much agitated, but the orchestra commenced, and before she had sung a dozen notes of "Casta Diva" she began to recover her self-possession, and long before the *scena* was concluded, she was as calm as if she was in her own drawing-room. Toward the last portion of the *cavatina* the audience were so completely carried away by their feelings, that the remainder of the air was drowned in a perfect tempest of acclamation. Enthusiasm had been wrought to the highest pitch.

The receipts the first night were $17,864.05. No one ever was more generous with earnings. Before leaving New York, she gave $10,000 to worthy charities of the city and it was noted by one writer that "already she has bestowed upon benevolent objects half a million of dollars not inherited or won at throw."

The quality of the art of a singer or an orator or an actor must be judged by later generations wholly through descriptions written by contemporaries. As to the color and the feeling and the technic of Jenny Lind's renditions we are forced to depend upon the reports of adequate critics who heard her sing. The *Tribune* employed the best musical critic in America, John Sullivan Dwight of Boston, to report the first concert in New York:

Hers [wrote Mr. Dwight] is a genuine soprano, reaching the extra high notes with that ease and certainty which makes the highest one a triumph of expression purely, and not a physical marvel. The gradual growth and sostenuto of her tones; the light and shade, the rhythmic undulation and balance of her passages; the bird-like ecstasy of her trill; the faultless precision and fluency of her chromatic scales; above all, the sure reservation of such volume of voice as to crown each protracted climax with glory, not needing a new effort to raise force for the final blow; and indeed all the points one looks for in a mistress of the vocal art, were eminently here in "Casta Diva." But the charm lay not in any point, but rather in the inspired vitality, the hearty, genuine outpouring of the whole—the real and yet truly ideal humanity of all her sing-

ing. That is what has won the world to Jenny Lind; it is that
her whole soul and being goes out in her song, and that her
voice becomes the impersonation of that song's soul, if it have
any, that is, if it *be* a song. There is plainly no vanity in her,
no mere aim to effect; it is all frank and real and harmoni-
ously earnest.

In every audience there are two audiences, the culti-
vated and the uncultivated. To the musical specialists the
high points of the concerts were her renditions of classic
masterpieces from Handel or Mozart and colorful inter-
pretations of the overture to *Der Freischütz* and *A Midsummer Night's Dream.* But the multitude preferred her
simple melodies like "The Flute Song" and "The Echo
Song," "The Pasture Song," and other folk-songs of her
native Sweden. The most effective of her simple songs
was "The Bird's Song," the text of which I am reproduc-
ing, since I feel that it brings us nearer to Jenny Lind
than any other surviving fragment of her art:

> Birdling, why sing in the forest wide?
>   Say why! say why!
> Call'st thou the Bridegroom or the Bride?
>   And why? and why?
> "I call no Bridegroom—call no Bride,
> Although I sing in forest wide,
>   Nor know I why I'm singing."
>
> Birdling! why is thy heart so blest?
>   O say! O say!
> Music overflowing from this breast!
>   O say! O say!
> "My heart is full, and yet is light,
> My heart is glad in day or night,
>   Nor know I why I'm singing."

Birdling! Why sing you all the day?
    O tell! O tell!
Do any listen to thy lay?
    O tell! O tell!
"I care not what my song may be,
Now this, now that I warble free,
    Nor know, yet must be singing."

Before New York could allow her to return to Europe she gave there thirty-five concerts. In addition, she gave eight in Philadelphia, twelve in New Orleans, seven in Boston, five in St. Louis, five in Cincinnati, and others in Providence, Baltimore, Washington, Richmond, Charleston, Havana, Cuba, Natchez, Memphis, Louisville, Madison, Wheeling, Pittsburgh—ninety-five in all. The total receipts were $712,161.34, an average of $7,496.43 for each concert. Barnum's business ability is not to be discounted.

At the end of her tour came a surprising climax. In Boston, in June, 1851, the Sweetheart of all America was married to her pianist, Otto Goldschmidt, a native of Hamburg. Like all the rest of America the "Easy Chair" was jealous:

Poor Jenny! that she should have gone the way of all the world is not a little saddening! That her angel habit of song and charity should not have lifted her forever into a sphere, above the weaknesses of human attachments, may point the moral of a ditty.

III

HARDLY had America recovered from what the English had termed its "Lind lunacy," when news came that the famous "Hungarian Patriot" Louis Kossuth was to make

THE HUNGARIANS

Cartoon by F. O. C. Darley, *The Lorgnette*, 1850.

a tour of America, making his first stop at New York. Again the city went wild. According to a contemporary account, "The roar of cannon and the huzzas of immense multitudes honored his disembarkation at Castle Garden, and the subsequent military and civic parade through the great thoroughfare of the city, which had been decorated with surpassing magnificence, exceeded any demonstration of a similar nature in honor of heroic virtues or public worth."

When the pompous deposed dictator, resplendent with decorations and gold lace, was escorted to his hotel, he satisfied to the full the romantic expectations of the crowds. He looked like an emperor. On December 13, 1851, a colossal banquet was given him with America's best as speakers and entertainers, and the "great patriot" as an orator exceeded all expectations. And he used with amazing facility the English language. Soon, as one contemporary expressed it, "he was flashing over the country like a meteor." But the hero, it was soon discovered, had come to America for money, and he had no Barnum to act as his financial agent. Unlike Jenny Lind, he was not wholly sincere. The "Easy Chair," while free to admit that "the manifestations of popular regard and admiration of which he has been the object have been most remarkable and are entirely without example," was inclined, even while the hero was still touring the country, to believe that New York had gone too far. "We are an impulsive people, and take off our hats, one moment, with a hearty good will and devotion, and thrust them over our ears, the next, with the most dogged contempt."

Longfellow in his Journal, December 19, 1851, wrote:

Every day brings a new speech of Kossuth—stirring and eloquent. All New York is in a blaze with his words—quite mad, wonderful power of oratory and the pleading of a sincere heart in the cause of human rights! But why need people go *clean daft?*

Kossuth undoubtedly, as later years have seen him, was a "stuffed shirt," glorifying himself first and Hungary second. He was dissolute, and he had little to offer America save gold lace and decorations and bouquet oratory.

IV

THE MASS-MINDED enthusiasms of New York centered always about a personality—a hero, a supreme artist, an accomplisher of the seemingly impossible. In 1855 came the actress Rachel, a torrent of emotion, in *Camille* "a wild whirl of tragic force." "Rachel," in the words of Curtis, "has come and seen and conquered. Here in New York all have been talking of her.... Jenny Lind's first night was an event; Rachel's a great event. She was truly triumphant." To the over-emotional New York City of the 1850's she brought emotion intense and compelling.

In the summer of 1858, New York, in a wild mass-celebration, elevated one of its own citizens to the realm of the demigods—Cyrus W. Field. Seemingly he had accomplished the unaccomplishable.

Beginning in 1854, he had concentrated his whole powers upon the realization of what the world at large rated as a wild dream—a cable-line across the Atlantic. He secured a charter for the enterprise, pledged his entire property to the furthering of the work, raised funds amounting first and last to millions of dollars, crossed the ocean fifty times, and personally superintended the construction of the telegraph line across Newfoundland. The cable wire completed, in 1857 two naval transports, one from England and one from the United States, started to lay it across the Atlantic. When 335 miles had been laid the cable broke. A second attempt was then made with a new cable, and that, too, broke in mid-ocean. With the whole world prophesying failure, a third attempt was made, and on August 9, 1858, blazed out the news: "The cable is laid: and now the most honored name in the world is that of Cyrus W. Field."

"Churches rang their bells, factories blew their whistles, and in the evening the river front blazed with fireworks flashed across the sky. Buildings were illuminated; one thousand lights were said to have shown from the windows of the Everett House." Before a formal celebration could be arranged, a procession of 11,000 laborers and 800 carts from Central Park paraded the city with a procession three miles long.

The first message to pass over the wire was Queen Victoria's, and with the news of its receipt the city burst into an uproar. Then had come the "Cable Carnival." The New York *Herald's* headlines were all in the superlative:

ACHIEVED THE GLORIOUS WORK
THE METROPOLIS OVERWHELMED WITH VISITORS
OVER HALF A MILLION OF JUBILANT PEOPLE
BROADWAY A GARDEN OF FEMALE BEAUTY
A BOUQUET IN EVERY WINDOW
GLORIOUS RECOGNITION OF THE MOST GLORIOUS WORK OF THE
  AGE

"The crowd on Broadway was so great that the military had much difficulty getting through it, and so the procession was somewhat retarded." Illuminations covered all the buildings. On one could be read in letters of fire:

> With wild huzzas now let the welkin ring,
> Columbia's got Britannia on the string.

Another ran:

> Lightning caught and tamed by Franklin,
> Taught to read and write and go errands by Morse,
> Started in foreign trade by Field, Cooper & Co.

And another:

> Married, August 1858, by Cyrus W. Field,
> Old Ireland and Miss Young America.
> May their honeymoon last forever.

On September 2, a dinner given by the Common Council of New York City to 600 guests was pronounced "the most sumptuous banquet ever laid on any great occasion in this city." The embellishments and ornaments were distinctive. The bill of fare covered two large closely printed pages.

Poems filled all the newspapers and magazines. The most enjoyable now undoubtedly was by John G. Saxe, contributed to *Harper's Weekly,* September 11, 1858:

How Cyrus Laid the Cable

> Come listen all unto my song,
> It is no silly fable;
> 'Tis all about the mighty cord
> They call the Atlantic cable.

Bold Cyrus Field he said, says he,
"I have a pretty notion
That I can run a telegraph
Across the Atlantic Ocean."

Then all the people laughed and said
They'd like to see him do it;
He might get half-seas-over, but
He never could go through it;

To carry out his foolish plan
He never would be able;
He might as well go hang himself
With his Atlantic cable.

But Cyrus was a Valiant Man,
A fellow of decision;
And heeded not their mocking words,
Their laughter and derision.

Twice did his bravest efforts fail
And yet his mind was stable;
He wa'n't the man to break his heart
Because he broke his cable.

"Once more, my gallant boys!" he cried
"Three times!—you know the fable—"
"I'll make it thirty," muttered he,
"But I will lay the cable."

Once more they tried—hurrah! hurrah!
What means this great commotion?
The Lord be praised! the cable's laid
Across the Atlantic Ocean!

Loud rang the bells—for, flashing through
Six hundred leagues of water,
Old Mother England's benison
Salutes her eldest daughter.

O'er all the land the tidings speed,
    And soon in every nation
They'll hear about the cable with
    Profoundest admiration!

Now long live James, and long live Vic,
    And long live gallant Cyrus,
And may his courage, faith and zeal
    With emulation fire us.

And may we honor evermore
    The manly, brave, and stable,
And tell our sons to make them brave
    How Cyrus laid the cable.

Then had come an anticlimax colossal. On the day of the banquet, a message had been received that the wire, which up to that time had received only state and official messages, was now open to the public. It was the last message to be sent over the cable of 1858. Something had happened to the long wire which at one place lay three miles below the surface of the ocean. The cable was dead, and it was ten years, 1867, before the next, and the successful, cable was laid across the Atlantic from the hold of the steamer *Great Eastern*.

The last word concerning the episode, at least for a decade, was spoken by Artemus Ward: "Cyrus Field's Fort is to lay a sub-machine tellegraf under the boundin billers of the Oshun and then hev it Bust."

V

TOUCH New York City at any time during the 1850's and you will need your superlatives. Take the episode of the first American World's Fair, opened in 1853 as an

"Exposition of the Industry of all Nations." "World's Fair Number Two" Willis termed it. World's Fair Number One had been held in London in 1851, and it had been advertised as the First International Exposition ever attempted. The great Crystal Palace which housed the exposition in all its parts was regarded as the eighth wonder of the world, an edifice according to the many who had never seen India to be compared even with the Taj Mahal. The ceremonies opening the exposition had been resplendent and moving. The young queen of the realm, her royal court, and many of her ministry had honored it with their presence.

To adolescent New York, with its P. T. Barnum, its $200,000-mansioned A. T. Stewart, its Horace Greeley, and James Gordon Bennett, this was a challenge. Why not a World's Fair of the West to be held in the American London, with a Crystal Palace of New World size? Why not indeed? And scarcely two years after the London opening—July 4, 1853, it was—occurred the American opening, an affair that impressed even New York City. As usual, enormous crowds, military pomp, roaring cannons, and clanging bells. Instead of the Queen there was the new President of the United States, the handsome and courtly bachelor Franklin Pierce, resplendent in the uniform he had worn as General in the Mexican War, riding with dashing horsemanship his war steed Black Warrior. Ten thousand of the elect were admitted the first day, all of them notables according to the public prints, and the day was glorious.

But the leading wonder was the great building that housed the exposition, the Crystal Palace replica of the

London structure, a building covering three acres with a dome that glittered like minarets in the *Arabian Nights*. Looking for mere prose, I found this contemporary description:

The building itself is another Crystal Palace, as it is constructed entirely of iron and glass, like the European model, though differing from that in design and arrangement. About 1,250 tons of the former material, and 39,000 square feet of the latter, were demanded in its construction. The edifice, 365 feet in length and breadth, is in the form of a Greek Cross, surmounted by a dome 100 feet in diameter, at the intersection. Its extreme height is 148 feet, and its internal arrangements are such as to admit 111,000 square feet on the ground floor, and 62,000 square feet of galleries, or, substantially, nearly four acres of room.

It is distressing to learn that this grandiose exhibition ended in financial failure. Its location at Forty-second Street and Sixth Avenue, then Reservoir Square, now Bryant Park, was then regarded as out of the city in a spot not easily accessible. Moreover, it was kept closed on Sundays when many people would have been seeking holiday amusement. When the Fair closed its doors, the Crystal Palace became a City problem. Barnum, after much urging, at last accepted the presidency of the corporation, but even Barnum found it a white elephant that was beyond all management. Minor expositions were held in it from time to time, one of them in October, 1858, ending in what might have been a colossal tragedy. With three thousand people in attendance, the building, in spite of its much advertised glass and iron materials, caught on fire and soon was a roaring furnace. By what seems like a miracle, all within escaped. In fifteen minutes the great tower fell, crushing everything into tangled ruins.

Like all World's Fair palaces, it was like the dream of a night—a bubble that glistens for a moment and is gone. For Horace Greeley, however, it was a dream that did not fade. He wrote:

It was a thing to be seen once in a lifetime. As we grow in wealth and strength, we may build a much greater Crystal Palace and accumulate therein more imperial treasures than we could now afford to purchase; but a second Fair cannot bring the exhilaration and glory of the first.

CHAPTER XII

HIAWATHA

In 1854, LONGFELLOW, AGED FORTY-FOUR, ABANDONED HIS lifework of teaching, for which he had so thoroughly prepared himself, to make poetry his sole profession. He would build now that "tower of song with lofty parapet" of which so long he had dreamed. It was "no middle flight" he would take. He would write an American epic with gods and demi-gods on earth among men. And that meant Indians.

Ever since Chateaubriand, the "noble savage" theme had been presented as the one hope for an *American* literature. After the early "Leather-Stocking Tales," the *North American Review* had reopened the subject with Bostonian logic. N. P. Willis had argued that Indian life and Indian legend were our one hope for a native literature. Several poets had tested the materials, notably Eastburn in *Yamoyden* and the young Whittier in *Mogg Megone,* but all such work, Indian fashion, had "bitten the dust."

Undeterred by these failures, Longfellow gathered

materials for an Indian epic. His outline for a poem completely *American* was perfect:

> Legends and traditions
> With the odors of the forest,
> With the dew and damp of meadows,
> With the curling smoke of wigwams,
> With the rushing of great rivers.

But though he professed to have heard the music of these legends

> From the lips of Nawadaha,
> The musician, the sweet singer,

he threw the legends into a meter no Indian ever listened to—and practically no American white man—the meter of the Finnish epic, the *Kalevala*. Parkman, before he wrote of Indians, had lived in an Indian village, and doubtless had heard Indian music, so far as they had music. Not Longfellow. Being a Harvard professor, he went to sources academic: he went to the Harvard library. There he found Schoolcraft's *Algic Researches*. Hiawatha, then, is two white-men steps away from the Indian legends, and both of the men had taken liberties with the historical facts. This, however, can be forgiven. It seems to be the privilege of poets to make history fit their poems rather than poetry fit history. This privilege we concede the poet.

But an Indian poem we demand should have Indians in it, and as the early reviewer in *Harper's Magazine* put it, Longfellow's "Indians are what unicorns are among animals." A modern historian and ethnologist, J. N. B. Hewett, of the Smithsonian Institution, has examined the legends with scientific thoroughness, and building on his findings, Emily C. Davis has written:

If the real Hiawatha that Longfellow never knew could stride back from the happy hunting ground where he has been hunting all these four centuries, and if he found his way to a modern public school, he would be a puzzled redskin. He would hear seven-year-olds piping lustily in his honor:

> "Smiling answered Hiawatha:
> In the land of the Dacotahs
> Lives the Arrow-Maker's daughter,
> Minnehaha, Laughing Water."

For half an hour, the distinguished unseen guest would listen to rippling lines about Hiawatha's bride Minnehaha, Hiawatha's ingenuity in concocting a birchbark canoe, Hiawatha's success in bringing the gift of corn from the gods to the Indian. And after that, we can imagine the shade of Hiawatha stumbling forth, and murmuring sadly to himself (doubtless, by this time, in the meter Longfellow himself used) as follows:

> "And I thought my deeds remembered.
> Such is fame—O Hiawatha."

Legends and traditions of real Indians, a mythology that would thrill the souls of genuine savages, would be of the nature of Sioux victory-chants after the battle that annihilated Custer's troop. According to the Algonquin legends, the real Hiawatha ate his enemies slain in battle. But Longfellow's Hiawatha was a feminized Indian, a Victorian gentleman, and his wooing might have been done on the lawns of an English manse by a fountain with water poured by a water-nymph. He keyed him to the tones of his *Voices of the Night,* had him conceived and born

On the Muskoday, the meadow
In the moonlight and the starlight.

The only thing really Indian about the poem is the Indian summer haze that softens all its outlines, but even this atmosphere is Indian only in name: it was borrowed from German romantic poets.

Completely is the poem in the key of the feminine fifties, even to its utterly bad villain and its supremely beautiful heroine. To sentimentalize the Indian is to translate him into a white man. There was no Minnehaha in the Algonquin or in the Ojibway mythology. She is a forest nymph after the Greek pattern created by the poet from a waterfall with a musical name—"Minnehaha, Laughing Water." And in fullest chord with the emotional fifties, she must die a Little Eva death at the climax of the tale.

Which is all true, and as criticism all useless. Realism finds scant welcome in the domains of poetry. The poet creates his own world, and if he can make readers accept it at his own values he has won the supreme honors possible for poets. And Longfellow's poem was all but unanimously crowned by the American, and even the English, people. In the book-markets it sold like *The Wide, Wide World*. Fifty thousand copies it took to supply the demands of the first few months. I can think of but one other poem published before the Civil War, or perhaps after it, that became the best-seller of a year: Wigglesworth's *Day of Doom*.

The conservative critics of two nations exhausted their superlatives in praising it and in elevating it to the rating

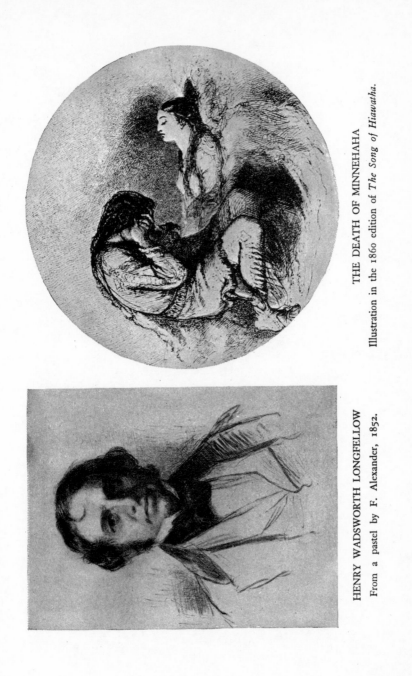

HENRY WADSWORTH LONGFELLOW
From a pastel by F. Alexander, 1852.

THE DEATH OF MINNEHAHA
Illustration in the 1860 edition of *The Song of Hiawatha*.

of an acknowledged classic, a rating that still holds after the passing of two generations. And it is well. Time has spoken.

Even as I, a twentieth-century realist, deplore its unreality, historical and racial, I am compelled to record that when as a young student fitting for college I read the poem for the first time, I was held by it to the end and could not enough praise its romantic beauty and its ability to transport me into a world in which I felt my soul was native. More than once I have heard "The Famine" canto given in an oratorical contest, and always has it won first prize, with the audience deeply moved. *Hiawatha,* whatever its realistic defects, has won the American people, at least that vast majority that have ended their education with the eighth grade. For the *people,* it was the supreme poem produced during the feminine fifties.

And voluminously was it parodied, no poem more extensively. The time-beat of the measure, the "frequent repetitions," and the picturesque namings were easily imitated. Soon the newspapers were spreading such merry doggerel as:

> He had mittens, Minjekahwun,
> Buckskin mittens made of deer-skin;
> Mittens with the fur-side outside,
> Mittens with the skin-side inside.
> When he turned them inside outside,
> When he turned them outside inside,
> Then the warm side, fur-side, in was,
> And the cold side, skin-side, out was;
> When he turned them outside inside,
> When he turned them inside outside.

"John Phœnix" in a merry canto entitled "The Song of Nothing Shorter" translated it into a California epic of gold-rush days:

> At the Mission of Dolores,
> Near the town of San Francisco,
> Dwelt an ancient Digger Indian
> Who supported his existence
> Doing "chores" and running errands.

Like the ancient Arrow-Maker, this worthy also had a daughter,

> And her name was "Tipsydoosen"
> Or ye young grass-hopper eater.

And at the climax, while the Indians on their jews'-harps were celebrating, young Amos Johnson

> Rushed tumultuously from his grocery,
> Crying, "Dern your Indian uproar;
> Stop that noise and 'dry up' quickly,
> Or, by the Eternal Jingo!
> I'll ..." here he saw Miss Tipsydoosen,
> And the heart of Amos caved in,
> As he afterwards told Miss Stebbins
> That she "just completely knocked him."
> Why should I continue longer?
> "Gentiles," well you know the sequel,
> How the bright-eyed Tipsydoosen,
> Now is Mrs. Amos Johnson.

At least five parodies were issued as volumes:

Plu-ri-bus-tah. A Song That's-by-no-Author. "A Deed Without a Name." Perpetrated by Q. K. Philander Doesticks, P. B., 1856.

The Song of Milkanwatha, second edition. 1856.

*The Song of Drop o'Water, by Harry Wandsworth
Shortfellow*, Mrs. Mary Victoria Cowden-Clark.
London 1856.
Wa-wa-wanda. A Legend of Old Orange. 1859.
The Song of Higher-Water, James W. Ward. 1868.

The Doesticks volume is coarse and conventional, and
the others are best read by title and passed. *The Song of
Milkanwatha* is best of the five. The simile in "Hiawatha's Wooing" he befuddles in this homely fashion:

> Just as, to a big umbrella
> Is the handle, when it's raining,
> So a wife is, to her husband;
> Though the handle do support it,
> 'Tis the top keeps all the rain off;
> Though the top gets all the wetting,
> 'Tis the handle bears the burden;
> So the top is good for nothing,
> If there isn't any handle,
> And the case holds, vice versa.
>   In this way, did Milkanwatha
> Reason, when he was a-thinking,
> Thinking of his Pogee-wogee,
> Of the blue-eyed Sweet Potato,
> In the Village of the Noodles.

Parodies were cast up from lands even beyond the ocean,
even from the Wonderland area explored by Alice. At
least Lewis Carroll himself essayed the meter in a "little
poem" entitled "Hiawatha's Photographing." This his
introduction, in seeming prose:

[In an age of imitation, I can claim no special merit for this
slight attempt at doing what is known to be so easy. Any
fairly practised writer, with the slightest ear for rhythm, could

compose, for hours together, in the easy running metre of the
"Song of Hiawatha." Having, then, distinctly stated that I
challenge no attention in the following little poem to its merely
verbal jingle, I must beg the candid reader to confine his criticism to its treatment of the subject.]

> From his shoulder Hiawatha
> Took the camera of rosewood,
> Made of sliding, folding rosewood;
> Neatly put it all together.
> In its case it lay compactly,
> Folded into nearly nothing;
> But he opened out the hinges,
> Pushed and pulled the joints and hinges,
> Till it looked all squares and oblongs,
> Like a complicated figure
> In the Second Book of Euclid.

Thereupon the photographer proceeds to photograph one
by one all the individuals of a family, until utterly maddened by his efforts,

> ...He left that happy party,
> Neither did he leave them slowly.
> Left them in a mighty hurry,
> Stating that he would not stand it,
> Stating in emphatic language
> What he'd be before he'd stand it.

Having one's photograph taken in the 1850's was indeed
almost as painful an ordeal as a dental operation, and the
photographer had much to endure, especially when his
subjects were children or maiden ladies.

The poem ran the gantlet of the critics with no one
taking middle ground. In November, 1855, Longfellow
wrote in his journal:

"Some of the newspapers are fierce and furious about *Hiawatha*." In December he wrote:

"There is the greatest pother about *Hiawatha*. It is violently assailed and warmly defended. Six English papers I have already received on my side and as yet only one against me." And a little later:

"The publishers are just going to press with the ninth and tenth thousand of *Hiawatha*. Critics may assail it as they please—*e pur si muove*." And on January 1, 1856: "*Hiawatha* going at the rate of 300 a day."

All his friends praised the book inordinately. Schoolcraft read it "with high gratification," and the English, who had never lived with Indians, praised it for its accurate picturings of the noble savage. This was *American* literature. Criticism thus palliated, Longfellow could endure, but the parodies angered him. In February, 1856, he noted: "*Hiawatha* parodies come from all quarters— even from California." The swarm increasing, he went down to his publisher and asked that action be taken. This was not criticism: it was insult.

"Have you seen our sales sheets recently?" asked Fields, smiling blandly. The poet had not seen them and he read them with astonishment. "Hadn't we better let them go on advertising the book, Mr. Longfellow?" And the poet with the figures before him was Yankee enough to quit instantly his complaining and even to smile blandly with Fields.

Never had Longfellow written for the masses. Literature, he ruled, should be kept upon the heights. In his journal, June, 1857, he noted: "Had an offer of one thousand dollars for ten poems of any length from the New

York *Ledger*. Declined. I do not wish to write for any newspaper." Three times this figure, however, in later years removed his prejudice. In 1874 he noted: "Sam Ward came to lunch. He has negotiated with Bonner for 'The Hanging of the Crane' (for publication in the New York *Ledger*). I am to have $3000. It is a great sum. It was not my asking, but his offer."

But though he wrote with no thought of the newspaper-reading masses, it was they who bought his books and it was they who gave him what to-day is his most enduring fame. In a critical period of American literary history, Longfellow presented popular literature that was on the high levels of its time. *Hiawatha* may not be true to history or to ethnology, but as poetry of beauty and soul it undoubtedly brought to the uncultured many of America a new vision of real poetry.

CHAPTER XIII

THE GUNMAKER OF MOSCOW

*T*HOUGH ONLY A FEW STILL LIVE WHO ACTUALLY HAVE read *The Gunmaker of Moscow*, its name is still widely known, and almost single-handed this name has kept alive two other names: Sylvanus Cobb and the New York *Ledger*. Its original readers who gave it its fame never saw it as a book. Not till 1888, after its author's death, did it become a separate publication. Three times it was issued as a serial in the *Ledger*, first in 1856, then in 1859, and then in 1880.

Had Horatio Alger, also a product of the 1850's, attempted when at his best to throw into fiction Robert Bonner, founder and editor of the *Ledger*, he would have failed, so completely does bare truth outmarvel mere romance. Bonner started in true Alger fashion. A penniless Irish immigrant, he was fifteen when he first saw American soil. His first real job, printer's devil in the office of the Hartford, Connecticut, *Courant*, launched him on the career that made him famous. At twenty, a skilful typesetter and proof-reader, New England seemed too small for him and he headed for New York City.

The year was 1844. He found employment first in the office of the *Mirror,* and by 1851 he was able to maintain a small printing plant of his own. By mere chance a moribund market sheet, the *Merchant's Ledger,* devoted to the dry-goods trade came to him at a cost ridiculously low, and it devolved upon him to edit it. Of dry goods he knew nothing, and to run the thing as a newspaper to compete with Greeley and Bennett and Raymond was out of the question. But to drop the thing was also out of the question: all his savings were in it. He must edit it and make money from it—but how? Diligently he began to study the literary climate, and by a kind of evolution there grew at length, step by step, a totally new thing. First, he dropped the word "Merchant's" from the title. Then he dropped the news, supplying its place with popular articles highly moral. Then he admitted fiction. The greater reading public, he found, was the middle-class element that had homes and growing families. Not at all were they "high-brows" enamoured of the *Atlantic Monthly* and *Putnam's Magazine* type of literature, but they insisted on clean, moral reading, provided it be interesting and thrilling and sweetened with sentimentalism eight lumps to the cup. Even church-members, he found, would read fiction, even melodrama and *Arabian Nights* sensation, if they were assured that the stuff had been rigorously deloused and pronounced strictly moral. Again, he found that the American people dearly loved lions, royalty if possible, and if imported nobility were not to be had, current great popularities would do—men and women in the newspaper headlines, great authors, preachers, statesmen. They should have them, and to the full.

His first exhibit was a literary lioness, Mrs. Sigourney, "the Mrs. Hemans of America." She was to be, at a breath-taking price widely advertised, a regular contributor. Who would not read everything published in a journal contributed to by Mrs. Sigourney, and let the children read it? Soon was added another literary lioness: Fanny Fern, whose *Fern Leaves from Fanny's Portfolio* was outselling all the new books of the year. It took money to secure a monopoly of Fanny Fern's pen. Soon it was town's talk that her story in the *Ledger* cost the paper $100 a column. And was Bonner not filling column after column of the *Herald,* at unheard of prices, with her mere name?

It was the period when great efforts were being made to buy Mount Vernon by subscription as a national shrine. Edward Everett was to—and did—give a hundred lectures on George Washington, all the proceeds to go to the fund. Suddenly the whole country drew a long breath of astonishment: Bonner had offered Everett $10,000 for a series of articles in the *Ledger* to be entitled "The Mount Vernon Papers," the money to be turned over by him to the fund, and Everett had accepted—Everett, "the ex-ambassador, ex-secretary, ex-president of Harvard University, ex-editor of the Greek Reader, the scholar, the exquisite, the one aristocrat of 'the universal Yankee nation.'" Believe it or not!

Soon Bonner had added to his list of contributors Bancroft, Bryant, Dickens, Alice Cary, Mrs. Stowe, Halleck, and other celebrities whose pens could be purchased. Once he ran a series of papers by twelve college presidents, then another by twelve leading clergymen. He induced Greeley, Raymond, and Bennett, the ruling editors of newspaper New York, to write articles for him, advertised the fact with superlatives, then published all three papers in a single issue of his paper. When Henry Ward Beecher for $20,000 agreed to contribute a novel to the *Ledger,* and his *Norwood* began in its columns as a serial, the religious journals were aghast. Bonner was delighted: the more furious their attacks, the more it advertised the *Ledger.*

From the first he was an advertiser, in many ways the first great advertiser produced by American journalism. Like Barnum, he was a born showman. Upon every one of his newly acquired museum-pieces he threw a limelight that often was an original addition to the devices of advertising. His methods were evolved from the conditions he had to encounter. For instance, Bennett of the *Herald* refused his advertising, telling him that it was against his rules to run display ads and illustrations. Whereupon Bonner asked him if he would consent to run a whole column set in ordinary type. Bennett consented, and the result was a solid column with the single repeated sentence:

Read the New York Ledger.

All New York talked of it. Then he tried the device on a larger scale. He paid $2,000 for a whole page of the *Herald,* filled it solid with the single repeated sentence:

Fanny Fern writes only for the Ledger,

and compelled Bennett to issue his paper that day as a quadruple sheet, "the first of this size ever issued in America." Businessmen prophesied ruin from such fan-

tastic extravagance. Bonner's pastor, learning of the un-
heard-of price he had paid for a single advertisement,
came to expostulate with him. It was sheer waste, he
argued: it meant ruin. A much smaller advertisement
would have been sufficient.

"Had I used a small ad would you have come to expostulate?" asked Bonner.

"No," answered the pastor.

"Right," said Bonner. "You have proved that I have
got the secret of advertising. All New York is as astonished as you are."

For a long period he poured all his profits into advertising. He paid as high as $27,000 in a single week. In
one year he paid $150,000. His expenditures, copiously
advertised, became the talk of the nation. When the first
Atlantic cable was being laid by the government ships
Niagara and *Agamemnon,* he made arrangements to
have a complete story by Dickens cabled over the moment
the line was laid. The cable broke in mid-ocean, but
Dickens was paid $5,000 for his story sent by mail in the
usual way. His success he attributed to his advertising.
"I get all the money I can lay my hands on and throw it
out to the newspapers," he once declared, "and before I
can get back to my office there it all is again and a lot
more with it."

The *Ledger* soon had a circulation of nearly half a
million copies, a remarkable figure for its day. In 1860
the *Ledger* plant burned and the printing of the paper
was done by a dozen plants throughout the country
while in all the newspapers appeared Bonner's advertisement:

Unless we are burned out more than once a week, the New York *Ledger* will be ready Monday mornings on all the news-stands of the United States, the Sandwich Islands, and New Jersey.

Bonner's general plan for his paper was much like George H. Lorimer's for his *Saturday Evening Post* of later years: he had in each issue a variety of material so that all readers could find something to interest them. He induced Jesse Grant, father of the General, to write a life of his famous son, and publish it serially in the *Ledger*. He convinced, at a more-than-Fanny-Fern price, Horace Greeley to write his autobiography for him as a serial. And while these were running, alongside of them would be Mrs. Southworth's *The Hidden Hand* romance, Leon Lewis's thrilling *Kit Carson's Last Trail,* Fanny Fern's mawkish goody-goodyness, and Sylvanus Cobb's amazing mélange, and the novel *Norwood* by the most popular preacher in all America.

And the plan worked, surpassed even the latest triumphs of the *Saturday Evening Post* of to-day. The subscription price for the weekly *Ledger* was $3.00, or not much over five cents a copy, and the paper from the first admitted no advertising. Relying wholly upon his subscription list, Bonner became a millionaire, housed his plant in one of the finest buildings in New York, erected for himself a noteworthy mansion, and at length supported a stable with the leading race-horses of the world. When did mere literature ever yield greater returns than that?

In the meantime all the standard authors derided the *Ledger,* even while they were appearing at sensational prices in its columns. In 1858, Godkin in a letter to a friend wrote of the *Ledger:*

It is filled with tales of the Demon Cabman, the Maiden's Revenge, the Tyrant's Vault, and a great variety of "mysteries" and "revelations," and, in short, barring its general decency of language, belongs to as low and coarse an order of literature as any publication in the world. By the lavish use of puffery à la Barnum, the proprietor, a journeyman printer four or five years ago, has amassed a large fortune.[1]

Sylvanus Cobb, against whom chiefly the criticisms as to sensation were directed, admitted that he used sensation, but his sensationalism, he added, was never immoral or damaging to the morals of readers. His wife, who was his final biographer, defended him as "sensational in the best sense of the word, but never sensual. He never appealed to the passions of men; he never sought to excite the lower, baser nature of his readers. His most glowing pictures, exciting and realistic though they were, were always elevating, never debasing. His pen wielded a marked influence for good always and everywhere."

This side of Cobb was kept always in sight of *Ledger* readers by Bonner. Was not Cobb a prominent churchman, a leading Mason, a man at the head of many reform movements? Was not vice always punished in his romances, and virtue amply rewarded? After such explanations the most religious and prudish of readers could plunge into the most melodramatic of his fictions— "Karmel the Scout," "The Mystic Bride," "The Scourge of Sefton Dale," "The Wild Knight," "The Brigands of

[1] Algernon Tassin, *The Magazine in America* (New York, Dodd, Mead & Company, 1916), p. 304.

Como"—and feel no twinge at all of conscience, for surely tales so pronouncedly moral, so uniform in their punishments of villains and of vice, could do even young people no harm.

Constantly was Bonner's hand on the pulse of his time. Though himself the leading horseman of his day, he allowed no horse-racing in his *Ledger*. One of his rules, never broken by his writers, was that every horse in a *Ledger* story must be named "Dobbin," and no horse must be allowed to trot a mile in less than four minutes.

The circulation of the *Ledger* was unprecedented in its day. Bonner set the figure at 400,000. "One news company—the American—takes all, except what are called the mail subscribers, which go direct from the office of publication. That Company takes weekly nearly 350,000 copies, and pays cash for them. About 50,000 are sent by mail; 40,000 copies go to Boston, 25,000 to Philadelphia, 12,000 to Baltimore, 7,000 to St. Louis, 6,000 to Providence, and so throughout the country."

That the paper exerted a profound and widespread influence cannot be doubted. More than any other man, Bonner put a blight on "the flowering of New England" at the time when its richest fruitage was due to come. Fiction in the atmosphere of the 1850's turned feminine, overripe, and sickly-sweet with its Fanny Fern moralizings; and it turned rapidly into the sensationalism that soon was to reach the extremes of the Beadle and Adams thrillers.

Bonner's career as a horseman deserves an article by itself. His sensational record-breakers like Dexter, Peerless and Maud S., which he never allowed to race for

ROBERT BONNER ENTERTAINS GENERAL GRANT

Lithograph of Dexter, 1869, in possession of the New York Historical Society.

money, kept him as much in the public eye as did his *Ledger*. He invited the President and Senators and other prominent men in the public eye to ride with him after Dexter, a ride sure to be front-page news the next day.

II

WHEN Fanny Fern's *Fern Leaves from Fanny's Portfolio* had reached a sale of 70,000, and her novel was in everybody's mouth, the marvel-loving Bonner, who like Barnum was ever in search of drawing "specimens," had invited her to join the *Ledger* staff with a salary that took her breath away. Hardly realizing what she was accepting, she eagerly removed to New York and began a job which to-day would be termed the running of a weekly newspaper "column." That was in 1854. Two years later she was married to James Parton, the biographer, but she edited her column without a break for fifteen years, or almost until her death in 1872.

Her kindred feminist Grace Greenwood, greatly impressed by this at-that-time-unparalleled feminine exploit, threw it into superlatives after the manner of the times:

Fourteen years ago Fanny Fern made an engagement with Mr. Bonner of the New York *Ledger* to furnish an article every week for his journal, and thereby hangs a tale, the most wonderful fact in this veracious biography. Behold! from that time to this she has never failed one week to produce the stipulated article on time! Think, my reader, what this fact proves! What habits, what system, what thoughtfulness, what business integrity, what super-woman punctuality, and O Minerva—Hygeia—what health!

Aspasia was, Plato says, the preceptress of Socrates; she formed the rhetoric of Pericles, and was said to have composed

some of his finest orations; but she never furnished an article
every week for the *Ledger* for fourteen years.

Elena Lucrezia Comoso Piscopia—eminently a woman of
letters—manfully mastered the Greek, Latin, Arabic, Hebrew,
Spanish, and French; wrote astronomical and mathematical
dissertations and received a doctor's degree from the University
of Padua. Laura Passi, Novelli d'Andrea and Matelda
Tambroni were honored with degrees and filled professors'
chairs in the University of Bologna; but as far as I have been
able to ascertain, by the most careful researches, not one of
these learned ladies ever furnished an article for the *Ledger*
every week for fourteen years. Corinna, for her improvisa-
tions, was crowned at the Capitol in Rome, with the sacred
laurel of Petrarch and Tasso; but she never furnished an article every week for the *Ledger* for fourteen years.

Miss Burney, Miss Porter, Mrs. Radcliffe, Miss Austin, Miss
Baillie, Miss Mitford, Miss Landon, Mrs. Hemans, Mrs. Gaskell and the Brontës did themselves and their sex great honor
by their literary labors; but not one of them ever furnished an
article for the *Ledger* every week for fourteen years. Neither
Mrs. Lewes nor Mrs. Stowe could do it, George Sand wouldn't
do it, and Heaven forbid that Miss Braddon should do it!

III

MARVELOUS for a woman, perhaps, but note this jotting
from the journal of Sylvanus Cobb, Jr., written in 1886:

Wrote to Mr. Bonner. I had written for him thirty years, on
Saturday last—the 6th. I began March 6, '56. I have written
one hundred and twenty-four long stories; eight hundred and
sixty-two short stories; and two thousand one hundred and
forty-three scraps from two to six pages each.

Cobb's first "article of agreement" signed by Mr. Bonner, one renewed every five years to the end of the
author's life, read thus:

I promise to write exclusively for Bonner; and to write to the amount of one novelette once in eight weeks and two short sketches a week, and more if at any time he may need. In return he is to pay me fifty dollars a week, payable weekly. This agreement to continue for five years.

Cobb's first "novelette" for serializing under this contract was *The Gunmaker of Moscow,* the most popular fiction of its decade, never, however, a best-seller volume since Bonner never allowed it to escape from the columns of the *Ledger* until after the death of its author. In its class unquestionably it is a classic. It has movement that never for a moment stops, its dialogue is crackling and brilliant, its dramatic climaxes are telling and satisfying. Of course by no possibility could such a train of events have happened even in the Russia of Peter: the hero is a superman and the arch villain an impossible devil, and the black monk an artificial mystery, yet one who has started the book is powerless to leave it until confronted by the unwelcome *Finis.* To test its quality consider some of the chapter headings:

> The Gunmaker and the Monk
> The Duel
> Before the Emperor
> The Mask Falls From a Villain's Face
> A Strange Discovery
> An Astounding Affair
> The Plotter Is at Work
> The Mystic Tribunal
> What Happened at the Duke's Bath
> Thwarted but not Subdued
> Transactions of a Night
> Strange and Complicated

Since no one to-day reads *The Gunmaker,* allow me to reproduce its bombshell surprise ending. The leading villain, Olga, Duke of Tula, and his villainous tool, the hump-backed priest Savotano, but for the hidden-hand work of the mysterious black monk, would have killed his chief opponent the Gunmaker, married the Countess Rosalind who madly loves the gunmaker hero, and then have caused the overthrow of the Czar. The plot at last ripe, the demon Duke, who now has the Countess in his power, is compelling her to marry him:

The broken-hearted girl wiped the tear from her eye, and in a moment more she was as cold and passionless as before.

"Lead on, Zenobe. I shall walk without help."

Without looking around, the Moslem maiden led the way to the hall. She walked slowly, and she fancied she could hear the beating of her mistress's heart. In the hall stood the duke with some half dozen of his own male attendants. He took the hand of the countess as she approached him, and gazed earnestly into her face; but did not speak. He led her towards one of the drawing rooms, and when they entered there they found the hump-backed priest already in waiting. Rosalind came well-nigh fainting when she saw the miserable villain ready for his work. She knew now that the priest was like the master.

"You see, my dear Countess," spoke the duke, in a low, hypocritical tone, "that we have all prepared. I trust we shall have no trouble before this holy man."

This last sentence was spoken in a threatening tone, but it had no effect upon Rosalind. She hardly heard the words he spoke.

"Come, father," said Olga, turning now to the priest. "We are ready."

Savotano moved forward and mumbled a Latin prayer. Then he looked upon the twain before him, and directed them to kneel.

"No! no! no!" gasped the fair countess, trembling for the first time. "I cannot do that!"

"Kneel!" hissed the duke between his clenched teeth. And as he spoke he grasped the maiden more firmly by the arm and forced her down. She uttered a quick cry of pain as she felt the unmerciful grip, but she could not resist the strong arm of her persecutor.

"Now go on!" the duke cried, as he held the maiden down. "Go on, Savotano, and let the business be done as soon as possible."

"Hold!"

It was a voice of thunder which spoke thus, and it came from the door. The duke started to his feet, and beheld Ruric Nevel, the gunmaker, approaching the spot. But the youth came not alone. Behind him came the huge bulk of Vladimir the monk. And more still—back of the monk came the widow, Claudia Nevel, and the boy Paul. And then there was, besides all this, a heavy tramp of feet in the hall, and the clang of steel.

"Hold! Stop this accursed mockery!" Ruric shouted, as he strode up the apartment.

"Miserable dog!" gasped the duke, mad and frantic with rage, "How dare you come hither?"

"Look you, proud duke," the monk interposed, coming quickly forward, "I am at the bottom of all this. *I* have come to stop this foul work!"

Rosalind had started to her feet when she first heard Ruric's voice; and now, as the monk spoke, a ray of hope darted to her soul, and with a quick bound she reached her lover's side.

"Ruric! Ruric!" It was all she could say; and with a gushing, whelming flood of tears she pillowed her head upon his bosom, and his stout arms were wound fondly about her.

"Fear not," he whispered, "for, oh! Rosalind, thou art safe now."

The mad duke saw the movement, and with a bitter curse he started towards them.

"Now by the living gods!" he shouted, with his fists clenched and his eyes flashing fire, "you have come to your death! What, ho, there!—Without! Slaves, where are you?"

In a moment more the side door was thrown open, and a dozen of the duke's servants rushed in.

"Ha!" Olga cried, "you are in time! Seize these dogs! Kill them on the spot if they offer one act of resistance. At them now! Down with the dogs!"

"HOLD!" It was Vladimir who spoke, and every arm dropped as they heard that voice. It was different from the voice they had heard the fat monk use before.

The duke staggered as though a thunderbolt had burst at his feet.

"Who art thou?" he gasped, staggering further back.

"Olga—Duke of Tula"—spoke the monk, in tones which sounded strange for him, because they were so different from those he had been wont to use, "I am thy master!"

As he spoke he threw open the long black robe which enveloped his person and cast it upon the floor at his feet, and there let it lay, a huge pile of wadding and stuffing. The vast rotundity of his person was gone, and the strange man now stood in his own fair form. His chin—that prominent chin—was no more hidden, and he was but a small man—not much larger than the boy Paul who stood near him. Next he placed his hand to his head and tore away the tight skull-cap, and the ring of gray hair came away with it leaving a cluster of glossy hair floating down over the neck and shoulders!

"*It is the* EMPEROR!" gasped Savotano, staggering back.

"Aye!" cried Peter, turning his darkly-flashing eyes upon the staggering duke. "I am your Emperor. Paul, Paul, go and call the guard."

The boy hastened from the palace, and when he returned he was followed by a party of the Imperial guard.

"Mercy! mercy! sire!" gasped the duke, sinking down on his knees.

But the emperor answered him not. He only turned to his guard and bade them secure the duke and the foul priest.

The romance quickly ends with the Gunmaker dubbed by the Czar "Duke of Tula," with Rosalind his happy bride. In the light of modern history, the story of the Russian monarchy threatened with destruction by the plotting of a scheming priest seems very plausible.

Cobb was now on his life-time job, and in thirty years not once did he break the contract, though it called for six or seven novels a year, to say nothing of short stories and sketches. It was like furnishing dimension lumber on a contract, so much every two months. Bonner was constantly changing his specifications, ordering now a Gipsy story, now a story of the American Revolution, now a tale laid in the Apennines, now a religious tale of Roman days to key with some religious movement of the times. When a story was reaching its final instalment, Bonner might suddenly order at the last moment three more chapters, since he had discovered another serial was ending in the same number. And Cobb at once added the chapters. It was a part of the day's work.

The Cobb type of novel demanded unlimited powers of invention. It must be cut into instalment parts, each approximately three chapters long, and each instalment must end with an intense moment, an uncompleted climax. The hero, for instance, is led out by the enemy to be shot. Blindfolded he stands against the wall. The commander holds up his hand and when he drops it the squad will fire. It is an awful moment.

[*To be continued in our next*]

One can hardly touch the man anywhere without adding a "believe it or not." For instance, though he wrote this incredible mass of fiction, only once did he publish a book—the biography of his father. Not one of his *Ledger* novels did he ever see in book form. After his death Cassell & Co. issued a few of them: *Karmel the Scout, The Gunmaker of Moscow, Orion the Goldbeater, The Smugglers of King's Cave,* and *The Painter of Parma.* Perhaps there are others. In addition to his incredible mass of magazine stuff, he left behind at his death the manuscripts of twelve novels never in print. Dr. Holmes in his description of the landlady's daughter noted that she read Byron, Tupper, and Sylvanus Cobb, Jr. In other words, she was a reader of the *Ledger.* Of course she was.

After having read the climactic ending of the *Gunmaker* romance, one is ready to agree to the full with the characterization made by Sam Walter Foss, author of the lyric "The House Beside the Road." Foss for years was librarian of the Somerville, Massachusetts, public library:

Uncle Seth on the Modern Novel [1]

Them novelists who write to-day, w'y, they hain't got the
    trade.
There ain't a one that knows jest how a story should be made;
Not one who understands the thing, not one who does the job,
An' not a one who slings himself like ol' Sylvanus Cobb.
Ah, ol' Sylvanus Cobb, my boy, w'en he was on the deck,
We had a story-teller then of giant intelleck.

[1] In *Dreams in Homespun* (Boston, Lee and Shephard, 1897), pp. 71-73. Used with their permission.

The hero of a story now he don't git in no row:
No Injuns, an' no piruts, an' no villains, anyhow.
The hero of to-day is tame; hain't got no whiz an' whirl;
Sets still an' lets some other chap go in an' court his girl:
The novelists who write to-day have all mistook their job;
Not one has got the glor'us gift of ol' Sylvanus Cobb.

Sylvanus took *his* hero where a hero ought to go,
In scrapes an' awful dangers where he seemed to have no
    show;
He drowned him, shot him, scalped him, but every reader
    knew
Sylvanus knew his business well and he would pull him
    through.
He bruised him, banged him, buried him, an' did a han'some
    job,
But still we knew the chap was safe with ol' Sylvanus Cobb.

He'd git the chap in dungeons deep, with soldiers all about,
To fill his body full of shot if he should once git out;
Sylvanus was too shrewd for that, an' allus had in stock
A subterranus passageway through which the chap could
    walk.
An' though he slashed an' slaughtered him, he understood his
    job;
We knowed that we could trust the man with ol' Sylvanus
    Cobb.

We'd see the hero's funeral, we'd hear the parson pray,
We'd see his coffin in the tomb, all neatly packed away,
But that didn't worry us a bit. Above the yawnin' grave
We knowed Sylvanus still was there, an' he had power to save.
We'd leave him in the grave content, an' we didn't care a pin.
We knowed Sylvanus knowed the trick to git him out ag'in.

While Sylvanus led his hero we were not a bit afraid,
Though he marched ag'in an army an' he faced a cannonade;

Though a mine should cave in on him, though a whirlpool
   sucked him in,
We all trusted to Sylvanus to produce him sound ag'in.
An' Sylvanus allus done it. Oh, he understood the job;
We knowed that we could trust the man with ol' Sylvanus
   Cobb.

Give me them good ol' days of guns, of snakes, an' gapin'
   jaws,
Of wolves an' ragin' catamounts, with blood upon their paws;
W'en six-foot heroes courted girls that they had snatched away
From out a bloody bandit's clasp, an' tramped him into clay.
I wish we had some writers now who understood the job,
Some writers who could sling themselves like ol' Sylvanus
   Cobb!

Like Fanny Fern, Cobb was a Maine Yankee. He was
born in Waterville, son of a distinguished Unitarian minister. A restless lad, he ran away at eighteen to enlist in
the Navy for a three years' voyage. At twenty-one he was
home again, workman in his father's printing office, married and settled down. Uncolleged, educated in the Navy
and the printing office, he found that he could write
and at once plunged headlong into the making of popular fiction. Gleason, editor of the *Flag of Our Union,*
discovered him, added him to his staff of contributors,
and quickly was flooded with his writings. Soon he was
in wide demand as a maker of wild melodramatics. At
one time he was writing under six pseudonyms.

Then Bonner discovered him and turned the tide of
his fiction into the *Ledger,* at times running his work as
written by Sylvanus Cobb, Jr., and at others as by Colonel
Walter Dunlap, author of *Lorinda the Princess; or the
Sultana's Diadem.* As Sylvanus Cobb, Jr., he won hesi-

tating readers. Surely the son of the nationally-known preacher Sylvanus Cobb could do readers no harm.

The voice of criticism, however, has been almost without exception condemnatory. The readers of the *Atlantic Monthly* class have classed him with the sub-literary writers in the lowest areas of fiction. Seldom is he mentioned by literary historians, the most-read writer of fiction in the America of his day, perhaps. A few have praised him. Nasby the humorist classed him as the leading novelist of his generation, the Walter Scott of America. Shillaber in a criticism in *The Carpet Bag,* written before Cobb had gone to the *Ledger,* spoke highly of his work. Noting that it was a time of literary gloom, he found only a beam or two to light the darkness:

Chief among this class stands the name of Sylvanus Cobb, Jr. With a most fertile fancy, he combines great power of delineation, and the scenes he draws are the embodiments of the genius of a true artist. Though of the *violent* school of writers, he possesses a nice power of discrimination and a correct taste, which leads him to avoid the *disgusting* in literature, so much in vogue with his contemporaries; and his stories—however killing or thrilling in their character—never lose sight of probability. A true artist in the strictest sense of the word, his pictures—even those of the most sanguinary sort—bear the same comparison with nature as his, who, with a glowing brush, exaggerates in coloring, to meet the requirement of defective vision, and yet retains the just proportions and fair consistencies of nature. Mr. Cobb has been a most prolific writer, and no one has been more extensively copied and admired. We take pleasure in awarding to him our estimate of his ability and worth.

There is a story that Emerson, delivering once a lecture in East Boston, spoke contemptuously of "the yellow-colored literature of the Sylvanus Cobb, Jr., type." Cobb's brother who was present approached Emerson after the lecture and asked:

"Mr. Emerson, did you ever read one of Mr. Cobb's novels?"

Emerson never had read one.

"Then do you think it is honest to make the statement you did?"

Thereupon Emerson promised to read one of the novels. Meeting Cobb's brother some months later in the Old Corner Bookstore, Emerson told him he had read a story by the *Ledger* author:

While it is not in my line of reading, I confess that when once I had begun it I could not leave it unfinished. And it will be sufficient for me to say to you that I have never, since that East Boston lecture, nor can I ever again, hold up the stories of Mr. Cobb as an illustration of yellow-covered or merely sensational literature. In sentiment and language that story was not only unobjectionable, but elevating.

Bonner himself never ceased advertising Cobb for the high moral qualities of his fiction. He wrote:

I value his writings and pay highly for them, because they are just what they are—pure in morals, honest and noble in sentiment, simple in diction, plain in construction, and thoroughly adapted to the taste and comprehension of the people. I am glad to have the issue distinctly made on the character of his productions, because certain starveling *litterateurs* whose articles have been rejected by me over and over again, are in the habit of decrying Cobb, and sneering at Cobb, and raving and swearing about Cobb, and drinking "confusion to Cobb" and all because these same men, for the most part, control and give tone to what is called "literary criticism" in certain quarters.

No one criticized the character of Cobb as a citizen and loyal friend. After his death praise of his life was universal. Out of the 323 pages of his wife's biography, only 66 are devoted to his literary life. She gave 50 pages to him as a good master Mason, 50 more to his work as a temperance worker, a church man, and a patriot.

Artemus Ward, according to his own statement, was at one time a reader of the *Ledger*. In his Fourth of July oration which he professed to have delivered in Connecticut in 1859, he was loud in his praise of Yankee institutions with one notable exception:

I like your skool houses, your meetin houses, your enterprise, gumpshun, &c., but your favorit Bevridge I disgust. I allude to New England Rum. I seldom seek consolashun in the flowin Bole, but tother day I worried down some of your Rum. The fust glass indused me to sware like a infooriated trooper. On takin the secund glass I was seized with a desire to break winders, and arter inbibin the third glass I knockt a small boy down, pickt his pocket of a New York Ledger, and wildly commenced readin Sylvanus Kobb's last Tail.

IV

Cobb's melodramatic tales had been subdued for home reading, but unsubdued types were springing up like devil's-paintbrush on fallow fields. And to a degree they were modeled after Cobb's patterns. The dime novel is usually assigned the date 1860 for its birth year, and its godfather has been one Beadle, a New York publisher, who began a series of "yellow-backed" fictions, Number 1 of which was *Malæska: the Indian Wife of the White Hunter,* by Mrs. Ann S. Stephens, followed by such titles as *Alice Wilde, the Raftsman's Daughter,* by Mr. Metta

THE DEATH OF THE WHITE HUNTER

Illustration from Ann S. Stephens, *Maleska*, 1860.

V. Victor, and *Chip, the Cave Child,* by Mrs. Mary A. Denison. Advertised as "dollar books for a dime" they sold rapidly.

But stories of dime-novel texture one may find in quantities long before the Beadle date of 1860. There were Robert Montgomery Bird's *The Hawks of Hawk Hollow* and *Nick of the Woods,* and the wild tales of E. Z. C. Judson, signed "Ned Buntline," tales by a man whose own life had been of dime-novel texture. And there had been "Professor" Joseph Ingraham.

In a decade full of anticlimaxes there is no stranger anomaly than that of this Maine Yankee born in 1809. In histories of American literature he is simply mentioned because of his phenomenal best-seller *The Prince of the House of David,* a narrative centering about the birth of Christ, a sensation even in the wonder year 1855. He had followed this popular hit with *The Pillar of Fire,* a story of Israel in bondage, and *The Throne of David,* all of them best-sellers perfectly in key with the middle-class spirit of the decade. Undoubtedly they did much to remove the prejudice against the novel, a prejudice in America not confined to the puritanical areas. Were these not Biblical narratives written by a minister of the Gospel, arguments that two decades later were to popularize the love-stories of the Reverend E. P. Roe?

But Ingraham had been in reality *a* if not *the* father of the dime novel, or, as termed in England, the "shilling shocker." Leaving his native state in his late boyhood, he had migrated to Mississippi where for a time he had been a teacher and had acquired the title "Professor." Then attracted by the picturesque legends of the Gulf

shores he had written his *Lafitte, the Pirate of the Gulf,*
1836, following it with a headlong series of historicated
blood and horror shockers, fiction utterly wild-cat, not
stopping till he had created at least eighty volumes.
Finally, as if de-hypnotized by some occult power—
Methodists might call it conversion—he suddenly went
into complete reverse, studied theology, became the rector
of a series of Episcopal churches, married the daughter
of a wealthy planter, established a school for young ladies
at Nashville, Tennessee, became rector of the leading
church of Mobile, Alabama, wrote his three religious
romances, and devoted the money received from their
sale to a campaign to suppress his earlier volumes which
had been a serious handicap in his career as a pastor. Evidently he did a thorough job for these novels are now rare.

I can touch only the beginnings of the dime-novel
chapter in the history of American fiction. The story of
this peculiar type belongs to the decade of the sixties and
beyond. But the Beadle and Adams novels, each 32 pages
long, each bringing to its author $50, novels in yellow
paper covers, obeyed to the full the middle-class moral
demands of the fifties. Great bales of them were sent to
the army during the Civil War. Highly were they proper.
Right and justice invariably won in the end. The villain
might triumph up to the last chapter, but never did he
finally win. Unmentionable depravity and all profanity
worse than "darnation" or "dog-gone it" never soiled the
pages of these moral thrillers; blood might flow in
streams, but only the unutterably bad villains, usually
Indians, "bit the dust." Highly moral these early yellow-
backs.

CHAPTER XIV

NATIVE HUMOR BECOMES
RESPECTABLE

THE VERY INCONGRUITY OF THE AMERICAN PEOPLE, MIX-
tures from all nations, and the vast heterogeneousness of
the American background, made from the first for
humor. It was born among the American masses, in
camps and logging gangs, in the rough masses of men
digging the long canals and manning the covered-wagon
trains headed for the unknown West. Deemed, like newspaper stuff, wholly unliterary, it was for long excluded
from the major magazines. The newspapers took it just
as they took all other news whether good or bad, and it
perished daily just as the news perished. After the unprecedented success of Shillaber's Mrs. Partington, publishers became more venturesome. In 1853, D. Appleton
and Company issued *The Flush Times of Alabama* by
Joseph G. Baldwin, papers that had originally appeared in
the *Southern Literary Messenger*. The author considered
the book of pioneer quality:

The scheme of the articles he believes to be original in design and execution—at least, no other book with which he is

acquainted, has been published in the United States designed
to illustrate the periods, the characters, and the phases of
society, some notion of which is attempted to be given in this
volume.

Evidently he was unaware of Longstreet's *Georgia
Scenes,* but nevertheless he was right in denominating
it a pioneer book. It represents the humor of a back-
country legal circuit. The most of his characters are law-
yers whose court cases usually could yield humor of the
variety which in later days Lincoln was to furnish in such
fullness. Redolent is the book of what now are considered
unique American additions to the world's store of humorous devices. Everywhere overstatements and understate-
ments of the varieties soon to be made use of so freely
by Mark Twain and others. For instance: He regretted
"that he did not have a chance of blowing a hole through
his carcass with his Derringer that a bull-bat could fly
through without teching airy wing." "He feels on the
subject as a man of delicacy feels in alluding to a rope
in the presence of a person one of whose brothers 'stood
upon nothing and kicked at the United States.'"

Undoubtedly in his characterization at length of the
old lawyer Ovid Bolus, Esq., he has made alive for us
one who can defend with success the title of leading
member of the American Tall-Story Club:

Bolus' lying came from his greatness of soul and his com-
prehensiveness of mind. The truth was too small for him.
Fact was too dry and commonplace for the fervor of his
genius. Besides, great as was his memory—for he even remembered the outlines of his chief lies—his invention was still
larger. He had a great contempt for history and historians.

He thought them tame and timid cobblers; mere tinkers on other people's wares—simple parrots and magpies of other men's sayings and doings....

There was nothing narrow, sectarian, or sectional in Bolus' lying. It was on the contrary broad and catholic. It had no respect to times or places. It was as wide, illimitable, as elastic and variable as the air he spent in giving it expression. It was a generous, gentlemanly, whole-souled faculty.

Unlike most of the Southwestern humor of the period, these sketches are free from horse-play and farce and often present characterizations made with realistic details.

II

THE YEAR 1855 introduced four new humorists: Frederic S. Cozzens, Charles G. Leland, Mortimer M. Thompson, and George H. Derby.

Cozzens was a belated Knickerbocker whose sketches, first issued in *Putnam's Monthly,* he republished as *The Sparrowgrass Papers,* 1856, illustrated with comic designs by Darley. The humor is of the Irving type, never, even when a balky horse acquired of a Yankee trader becomes a character, lapsing into slapstick exaggeration:

It is a good thing to live in the country. To escape from the prison walls of the metropolis—the great brickery we call "the city"—and live amid blossoms and leaves, in shadow and sunshine, in moonlight and starlight, in rain, mist, dew, hoarfrost, and drouth, out in the open campaign, and under the blue dome that is bounded by the horizon only.

And to find this rural Eden, he and his wife go where "asparagus" they find is pronounced "sparrowgrass," and where farming is not at all according to their dreams.

A pleasant book, parent of a whole later series of city-farmers-in-the-country books.

One final section of the volume I find especially note-worthy—the "Californian ballad" entitled "Ye Battail of Rocky Canyon." Cozzens, though a New York City wine merchant, evidently read the California papers, and, in a December, 1854, number, discovered the account of a fight unequaled even in the *Iliad,* and at once he rendered it into a ballad to be placed chronologically as Exhibit A in all anthologies of early poetry Californian.

Three miners, it appears, Captain Jonathan R. Davis of South Carolina in command, were at work in Rocky Canyon extracting nuggets and such, when they were set upon by twelve Mexican bandits. Two of the miners fell at the first fire:

> James McDonald, of Alabama,
>   Fell at the feet of Doctor Sparks;
> "Doctor," said he, "I'm as dead as a hammer,
>   And you have a couple of bullet marks.
> This," he gasped, "is the end of life."
>   "Yes," said Sparks, " 'tis a mighty solver;
> Excuse me a moment—just hold my knife,
>   And I'll hit that brigand with my Colt's revolver."

But the brigand got *him,* for

> Horrible, terrible, frightful, dire,
> Flashed through the vapor the foot-pad's fire,
> Frequent, as when in a sultry night
> Twinkles a meadow with insect light;
> But deadlier far as the Doctor found,
> When, crack! a ball through his frontal bone
> Laid him flat on his back on the hard-fought ground,
> And left Captain Davis to go it alone.

Thereupon the Captain lets loose his Colts and six of the bandits "bite the dust." Then

> Half of the band that still survives,
> Comes up with long moustaches and knives,
> Determined to mince the Captain to chowder,
> So soon as it's known he is out of powder.
>
> Six feet one, in trousers and shirt,
> Covered with sweat, and blood, and dirt;
> Not very much scared (though his hat was hurt,
> And as full of holes as a garden squirt),
> Awaiting the onslaught, behold him stand
> With a twelve-inch "Bowie" in either hand.
> His cause was right, and his arms were long,
> His blades were bright and his heart was strong.

But the ballad is four hundred verses long and the epic fight is stopped at times for Homeric similes. Suffice it if I record only the results. Captain Davis killed all twelve of the bandits single-handed, though watched by a crowd of men who had been attracted by the firing but who, according to the recording newspaper, "being satisfied that they were all strangers," took no hand. It then added, "Although we counted twenty-eight bullet holes through Captain Davis' hat and clothes (seventeen through his hat and eleven through his coat and shirt), he received but two very slight flesh wounds."

The poet records that "for fear the story might be lost in the perishable pages of the daily press," he had had it published in the more enduring pages of "the immortal *Knickerbocker Magazine.*"

III

CHARLES G. LELAND's first book, *Meister Karl's Sketch Book,* was lost in the remarkable out-pouring of books in the wonder year 1855. It was not until 1868 that his "Hans Breitmann's Party" made him a humorist universally known and quoted.

Mortimer M. Thompson (Q. K. Philander Doesticks) by his own confession added nothing to the devices of humor save "a lingual garb so quaint, eccentric, fantastic, or extravagant, that each lender would be sadly puzzled to know his own. It is undoubtedly this trick of phrase, this affectation of a new-found style, which has caused their wide-spread newspaper notoriety." Few humorists have been so frank. Of his *Doesticks What He Says* volume he could remark, "The book, like Hodge's razors, was made to sell."

A more original humorist of the '55 vintage was George H. Derby, of the United States Army, who early in 1849 had been interned in California to superintend engineering operations. After graduating at West Point he had served in the Mexican War, and then, transferred to the Topographical Bureau, had served on exploring expeditions in Minnesota. In California until 1856, he conducted three exploring expeditions in the gold regions and was in charge of various government projects. His humorous sketches were made with no thought of publication save as they might appear in the California papers. Diversions of a commander strenuously occupied with official business, they were miscellaneous in the extreme and totally unrevised. Usually they were illustrated with his own drawings, more humorous than the accompanying text. Always was he original. For instance, as a scientist and engineer, he criticized the writings of the period as inaccurate and vague. Unconsciously he was an extreme realist before the term "realist" had been invented. The adjective system of the English language, he believed, was inaccurate by all scientific measurements:

We have but three degrees of comparison—a very insufficient number, certainly, when we consider that they are to be applied to a thousand objects, which, though of the same general class or quality, differ from each other by a thousand different shades. Thus . . . we have but half a dozen expressions to convey to one another our ideas of inequality . . . We say of a lady, "She is beautiful"; "She is *very* beautiful"; or "She is *perfectly* beautiful";—descriptions, which, to one who never saw her, are no descriptions at all.

As a scientist enamoured of absolute accuracy, he proposed an adjective system to be arranged according to a grading system with 100 as perfect. By this system a piece of literature might have this appearance:

As a 19 young and 76 beautiful lady was 52 gaily tripping down the sidewalk of our 84 frequented street, she accidentally came in contact—100 (this shows she came in close contact) with a 73 fat, and 87 good-humored looking gentleman, who was 93 (i.e., intently) gazing into the window of a toy shop. Gracefully 56 extricating herself, she received the excuses of the 96 embarrassed Falstaff with a 68 bland smile, and continued on her way. But hardly—7—had she reached the corner of the block, ere she was overtaken by a 24 young man, 32 poorly dressed, but of an 85 expression of countenance; 91 hastily touching her 54 beautifully rounded arm, he said, to her 67 surprise—

"Madam, at the window of the toy-shop yonder, you dropped this bracelet which I had the 71 good fortune to observe, and now have the 94 happiness to hand you."

Blushing with 76 modesty, the lovely (76, as before, of course) lady took the bracelet—which was a 24 magnificent diamond clasp—(24 *magnificent,* playfully sarcastic; it was probably not one of Tucker's) from the young man's hand, and 84 hesitatingly drew from her beautifully 38 embroidered reticule a 67 port-monnie. The young man noticed the action, and 73 proudly drawing back, added—

"Do not thank me; the pleasure of gazing for an instant at those 100 eyes (perhaps too exaggerated a compliment), has already more than compensated me for any trouble that I might have had."

She thanked him, however, and with a 67 deep blush and a 45 pensive air, turned from him, and pursued with a 33 slow step her promenade.

As Derby himself has recorded, the episode that made all California laugh and even made for him a national reputation was his editorship for a short period of the San Diego *Herald* during the absence of its regular editor Judge J. J. Ames. Instantly reversing the politics of the paper, and filling it with wrath-compelling personalities —samples of which he reproduced in his *Phœnixiana* volume—he, according to his own story, was given by the editor on his return a tempestuous welcome:

We rose, and with an unfaltering voice said: "Well, Judge, how do you do?" He made no reply, but commenced taking off his coat.

We removed ours, also our cravat.

*   *   *   *   *   *   *   *   *
*   *   *   *   *   *   *   *   *

The sixth and last round, is described by the pressman and

compositors as having been fearfully scientific. We held "the Judge" down over the Press by our nose (which we had inserted between his teeth for that purpose), and while our hair was employed in holding one of his hands, we held the other in our left, and with the "sheep's foot" brandished above our head, shouted to him, "Say Waldo." "Never," he gasped. ...At this moment we discovered that we had been laboring under a "misunderstanding," and through the amicable intervention of the pressman, who thrust a roller between our faces (which gave the whole affair a very different complexion), the matter was finally settled on the most friendly terms—"and without prejudice to the honor of either party." ... This ends our description of this long anticipated personal collision, of which the public can believe precisely as much as they please. If they disbelieve the whole of it, we shall not be at all offended, but can simply quote as much to the point, what might have been the commencement of our epitaph, had we fallen in the conflict,

Here Lies Phœnix.

D. Appleton and Company, who had dared to bring out *The Flush Times of Alabama,* made a more daring venture when they published two years later the much more boisterous specimen of wild western humor, *Phœnixiana.* Derby himself had had no time to make such a book. Judge Ames for whom he had edited the San Diego *Herald* collected the various papers from California newspapers and in his preliminary word explained that "while the following pages are collected with the permission of the Author, and thus presented in a book-form, he has himself not been consulted in any manner in relation to the order of arrangement of its content."

The distinction given it by its publication by the Appletons, and the fact that it appeared during the period when

California was in everybody's mind as a land where anything could happen, a land of romance like the Bagdad of the *Arabian Nights,* gave to the book a tremendous impetus. The Southwestern native humor had had no such advertisement, and as a result the California type of humor, as used by Derby, became fixed as the matrix from which was molded what later was universally recognized as the new American humor. His influence on Artemus Ward, Mark Twain, Orpheus C. Kerr, Nasby, and the later group of humorists was great. Cacography, Derby did not make use of, but exaggeration was seldom absent from his pages. Solemnly would he proclaim the utter truthfulness of a story infinitely impossible. "If the son of the reader ... should look confidingly into his parent's face, and inquire—'Is that true, Papa?' reply, oh, reader, unhesitatingly—'My son, it is' " and the story might be like this:

He glanced over the first column of Phœnix's Pictorial when he was observed to grow black in the face. A bystander hastened to seize him by the collar, but it was too late. Exploding with mirth, he was scattered into a thousand fragments, one of which striking him probably inflicted some fatal injury, as he immediately expired, having barely time to remove his hat, and say in a feeble voice, "Give this to Phœnix." A large black tooth lies on the table before us, driven through the side of the office with fearful violence at the time of the explosion. We have enclosed it to his widow with a letter of condolence.

Often he uses the device that may be termed specific exaggeration. He records how two men tripped over a rope in the dark "and then followed what, if published, would make two closely-printed royal octavo pages of profanity." So popular, he declared, was the Phœnix *Herald* that "we have now 782 Indians employed night and day mixing adobe for the type molds."

Freely he used irreverence as a humorous device and peculiarly he delighted in euphemistic statement. The father of Joseph Bowers, he explains, was "engaged in business as a malefactor in western New York, but was annoyed greatly by the prejudices of the bigoted settlers. He emigrated suddenly, however, with such precipitation in fact that he took nothing with him of his large property but a single shirt, which he happened to have about him at the time he formed his resolution. Finally he ended his career of usefulness by falling from a cart in which he had been standing, addressing a numerous audience, and in which fall he unfortunately broke his neck."

Allow me to quote two paragraphs from my *History of American Literature since 1870:*[1]

It was Derby who wrote the first Pike County Ballad. "Suddenly we hear approaching a train from Pike County, consisting of seven families, with forty-six wagons, each drawn by thirteen oxen." Elsewhere he has described the typical "Pike": "His hair is light, not a 'sable silvered,' but a *yeller,* gilded; you can see some of it sticking out of the top of his hat; his costume is the national costume of Arkansas, coat, waistcoat, and pantaloons of homespun cloth, dyed a brownish yellow, with a decoction of the bitter barked butternut—a pleasing alliteration; his countenance presents a determined, combined with a sanctimonious expression." Now rises o'er

[1] New York, The Century Co., 1915.

the plains in mellifluous accents, the grand Pike County
Chorus:

> "Oh, we'll soon be thar
> In the land of gold,
> Through the forest old,
> O'er the mounting cold,
> With spirits bold—
> Oh, we come, we come,
> And we'll soon be thar.
> Gee up, Bolly! whoo up, whoo haw!"

Not much was added to Western humor after Derby. Mark
Twain's earliest manner had much in it that smacks of
"Phœnix." The chapters entitled "Phœnix Takes an Affection-
ate Leave of San Francisco," "Phœnix Is On the Sea," and
"Phœnix in San Diego" might have been taken from *Rough-
ing It*. Just as truly the chapters "Inauguration of the New
Collector" and "Return of the Collector," "Thrilling and
Frantic Excitement Among Office Seekers" might have been
written by Orpheus C. Kerr. Yet despite such similarities, the
later school did not necessarily filch from "Phœnix": they
learned their art as he had learned his from contact with the
new West. All drew from the same models.

Derby's illustrations, done with pen and ink, are often
more humorous than the sketches they embellish. For his
volume *The Squibob Papers*, 1859, he made eight full-
page cartoons, one for each stanza of the old Yankee
ballad entitled in *The United States Songster*, 1836, "The
Pizing Sarpent." Derby's text, greatly different from the
Songster version, has additions and rephrasings to such a
degree that it can almost be claimed as an original Phœnix
product. The doubling of the tragedy and the death of

LAMENTATIONS ON SPRINGFIELD MOUNTING

George H. Derby ("John Phœnix"), *The Squibob Papers,* 1865.

the maiden are not in the earlier versions. Derby's form
of the ballad follows:

On Springfield Mounting, thar did dwell
   A likely youth, I knowed him well;
Leftenant Carter's only son,
   A comely youth, nigh twenty-one.

One Monday mornin, he did go,
   Intew the meadow for to mow;
And all ter once, he thar did feel
   A Pizen sarpent bite his heel.

Quick as he felt the sarpent bite
   He raised his scythe, with all his might
He struck ter once a deadly blow,
   That laid the pizen creeter low.

He tuk the riptyle in his hand,
   And straight he went tew Molly Bland;
Oh! Molly, Molly, here you see
   A pizen sarpent, what bit me.

Zerubbabel, why did you go,
   Intu the meadow for to mow?
Oh! Molly Bland, I thought you knowd
   'Twas Daddy's field, and must be mowed.

Then Molly Bland, she squatted down,
   And sucked the pizen from the wound;
But oh! she had a rotten tewth,
   The venom soon affected both.

Oh, then they ware all spotted o'er
   With all the colors that the sarpent wore,
They laid 'em both upon a bed,
   And they swelled up and di-i-ed!

Then when they had gin up the ghost,
  From "Springfield Mounting" they went post;
And they larfed, and sung, as up they went,
  As chipper, as if there wa'nt no pizen Sar-*pent*.

The realism and the dialect are Derby's own, and the
irreverence of tone and the open disregard of old seriousness and sentiment are wholly in the new California
manner.

Of the many different versions of this ballad, the one
my mother used to sing when I was a boy ended with
the stanza, of great use to me in later years:

  Now all you maids a warning take
  From Molly Bland and Tommy Blake;
  And mind when you're in love don't go
  Out in the meadow for to mow.[2]

Derby died of sunstroke in Florida where he was in
charge of a government project in 1861.

IV

THE PUBLISHED books of Charles F. Browne (Artemus
Ward) belong to the sixties, his earliest volume, *Artemus
Ward, His Book*, appearing in 1862. His apprenticeship,
however, belongs wholly to the fifties, and of this period
let Mark Twain who knew him so thoroughly tell the
story:

[2] The original version, written as a song, dates from the eighteenth century.
The author is said to have been Nathan Torrey of Springfield, Mass., and the
year 1761. Springfield Mountain is now Wilbraham, Mass. Derby was a native
of Dedham, not far away. See "Elegy of a Young Man Bitten by a Rattle-
snake" in E. E. Hale's volume *New England History in Ballads*, 1904. See
also *The Journal of American Folk-Lore*, vol. 13, pp. 105-112; vol. 18, pp.
295-302; vol. 22, pp. 366-367; vol. 28, p. 169. The original text is said to
be in existence, but I have never seen it.

He looked like a glove-stretcher; his hair, red, and brushed well forward at the sides, reminded one of a divided flame. His nose rambled on aggressively before him with all the strength and determination of a cow-catcher, while his red mustache, to follow out the simile, seemed not unlike the unfortunate cow.

He never had any regular schooling: he was too poor to afford it for one thing, and too lazy to care for it for another. He had an intense ingrained dislike for work of any kind; he even objected to see other people work and on one occasion went so far as to submit to the authorities of a certain town an invention to run a tread mill by steam. Such a notion could not have originated with a hard-hearted man. He was a dutiful son and his first act, when money began to come in on him from his lectures, was to free from incumbrance the old homestead in his native town and settle it upon his aged mother.

His first literary venture was type-setting in the office of the old Boston Carpet-Bagger, and for that paper he wrote his first squib. He tried every branch of writing, even going so far as to send the Smithsonian Institute—at least so he himself said—an essay entitled "Is Cats To Be Trusted?" He soon tired of settled life and poor pay in Boston, and wandered off into the country to better his fortune, obtaining a position in Cleveland as a reporter at $12 per week. It was while in Cleveland that he wrote his first badly-spelled article, signing it "Artemus Ward." He did not think much of it at the time of writing it, but it gave him a start that speedily sent him to the top of the ladder without touching a single rung.

His letters, published in the Cleveland *Plain Dealer*, 1858-1860, and duplicated in the New York *Vanity Fair*, gave him his start. Leaving Cleveland, he became a member of the staff of *Vanity Fair* and on the resignation of its editor, Charles Godfrey Leland, became himself the

GEORGE H. DERBY

"John Phœnix." From an engraving after the portrait by F. B. Carpenter.

SYLVANUS COBB, JR.

Ballou's Pictorial, 1852.

BENJAMIN P. SHILLABER

Ballou's Pictorial, 1856.

CHARLES F. BROWNE

"Artemus Ward." *Century Magazine*, 1901.

editor. Settled employment, however, did not suit him, and he was again on the move. At New London, 1861, he gave his first lecture, and so successful was he that he determined to make lecturing his profession.

But his literary life belongs to the 1860's. He died in London, England, in March, 1867.

v

In the Boston area, especially among the Harvard elect, American humor in the late fifties, and beyond, centered about a Dr. Holmes-like "Skit" entitled "The Lay of the One Fishball." So fundamentally Harvard was it that as late as 1888, in the college song book of that year, it was the second song in the collection, following "Fair Harvard." Its author was George Martin Lane, Ph.D., Göttingen, 1851; Professor of Latin, Harvard, 1851-1894. That this seeming trifle should outlive all its author's scholarly volumes which for years were of international significance is one of the anomalies of literature.

The poem was first published in 1857, where I do not know. The authentic text, which differs from the songbook version, has been supplied by Charles Eliot Norton, as follows:

THE LAY OF THE ONE FISHBALL

1. There was a man went round the town,
   To hunt a supper up and down;
   There was a man, etc.

2. For he had been right far away,
   And nothing had to eat all day.

3. He feels his cash to count his pence,
   And all he had was just six cents.

4. "Wretch that I am, it happens meet,
   Why did I leave my Kirkland Street!

5. "None but a fool a wife forsakes,
   Who raspberry jam and waffles makes.

6. "If I were now safe out of town,
   I'd give my bran-new dressing-gown.

7. "But yet I'll make a start and try
   To see what my six cents will buy."

8. He finds at last a right cheap place,
   And stealeth in with bashful face.

9. The bill of fare he runneth through,
   To see what his six cents will do.

10. The cheapest of the viands all,
    Was 12½ for two fishball.

11. The waiter he to him doth call,
    And whispers softly, "One fishball."

12. The waiter roars it through the hall,
    The guests they start at *"One fishball!"*

13. The waiter brings one fishball on,
    The guest he looks abashéd down.

14. The scantness of the fare he sees:
    "A piece of bread, now, if you please."

15. The waiter roars it through the hall,
    "We don't give bread with one fishball!"

16. Then whoso orders one fishball
    Must get bread first or not at all.

17. And who would two with fixins eat,
    Should get some friend to stand a treat.

Few facetiæ of equal caliber have had such distinguished treatment as this Harvard *jeu d'esprit*. In the opening days of the Civil War it was thrown into the form of an elaborate opera score in Italian by Professor Francis James Child: *Il Pesceballo. Opera Seria: In Un Atto. Musica del Mæstro Rossibelli-Donimozarti.* Cambridge, 1862. On the verso of each page was the Italian text and on the recto the poetic translation by James Russell Lowell. The version, made for the Sanitary Commission, was performed several times in Cambridge and Boston, and a goodly sum of money was realized for the use of the soldiers. In 1899 the Caxton Club reissued the little volume in an edition limited to 210 copies with an introduction written by Charles Eliot Norton. Concerning the origin of the ballad he wrote this:

The theme of the Pesceballo was suggested to him by a local ballad which had had great vogue, written not many years before by his classmate and lifelong friend Lane, the genial and eminent professor of Latin at Harvard. I send you its genuine text. The account of its origin is given in a recent memoir of Mr. Lane by Professor Morgan. He says: "Many fables about the origin of this song have been told, and one was even printed with the song itself; but I know from Professor Lane's lips that it was based upon an adventure of his own. Arriving in Boston one day after a journey, he found himself hungry and with only twenty-five cents in his pocket. Half that sum he had to reserve to pay his carfare to Cambridge. With the rest he entered a restaurant, 'with modest face,' and ordered a half portion of macaroni. What followed is described, doubtless with humorous exaggeration, in the ballad itself. During the late Civil War it was worked over into a mock Italian operetta, Il Pesceballo, by Professor Child, with an English version by Professor Lowell!"

Child's Italian version is a rare bit of humor. In a footnote, he explains to mythical Italians who may read the opera the mysteries of the Boston fishball:

Il Pesceballo (*corruzione della voce inglese Fish-ball*) *è un prodotto della cucina americana, consistente in una combinazione di stoccofisso con patate, fatta nella forma di pallottole, simili alle nostre polpette, e poi fritta. Msgr. Bedini, nel suo* Viaggio negli Stati Uniti, *c' insegna che la detta pietanza si usa massimamente nella Nuova-Inghilterra, ove, secondo quel venerabile, viene specialmente mangiato a colazione nelle domeniche."*

The opera opens with a student chorus, thus rendered by Lowell:

> Hesper doth peer now,
> Make we good cheer now,
> With the new daylight
>   Back to the oar!
>
> We're your true nightlarks!
> Truce to all learning
> Till, with the morning,
>   Comes the old bore!
>
> Drinking and smoking,
> Laughing and joking,
> These are what students
>   Love to the core!
>
> We have to study
> Flossofies muddy,
> 'Ologies, 'Onomies,
>   'Ics by the score!
>
> All the strange lingoes,
> Law, too, by jingoes!
> Ever new sciences
>   We must explore!

> Drinking and smoking,
> Laughing and joking,
> These are the pleasures
> Night hath in store.

Few have known that Lowell, following Child's Italian with extravagant variations, ever wrote a complete opera like this. It must have been done with the pen, somewhat blunted, that had written the *Fable for Critics*. This, for instance, at the crisis moment of the tragedy:

THE STRANGER *in a rich tenor:*

Now, waiter, bring to me the bill of fare.
(*aside*) Ye pangs within, what will not hunger dare?

THE WAITER *in basso profundo:*

Here is the bill of fare, sir,
Of what there is for supper,
Long as the Proverbs of Tupper,—
Command, then, *s'il vous plait!*

> Soup, with nothing, twenty coppers,
> Roast spring-chicken, three and nime,
> Ditto biled (but then they're whoppers!)
> Fish-balls, luscious, two a dime,
> Two a dime, sir, hot and prime, sir,
> Fried codfish-balls, two a dime!
> There's the bill, and cash procures ye
> Any viand that allures ye....
> Best of all, though, 's the fish-ball, though,
> We have made 'em all the fashion·
> Come to try 'em as we fry 'em,—
> *Presto!* liking turns to passion!
> There we carry off the banner,
> 'Taint so easy, neither, that ain't,—
> But, you see, we've got a patent,—

Do 'em in the Cape Cod manner,—
That's the way to make 'em flavorous!
Fried in butter, tongue can't utter
How they're brown, and crisp, and savorous!

S. Peace, waiter, for I starve meanwhile,—but hold:
Bring me *one* fish-ball, *one,*—(*aside*) curst lack of gold!

Moment of horror! crisis of my doom!
Led by the dreadful Shape, I sought this room
With half a dime! A slender sum, and yet
'Twill buy one fish-ball! Down, weak pride, forget
Thy happier—but what prate I? Thought of dread
If, with one fish-ball, they should *not* give bread!

W. Here's your *one* fish-ball, sir—(*sarcastically*) you ordered
one?

S. Thanks,—and with bread to match, 'twere not ill done.

W. (*with fury*). With one single fish-ball, is't bread ye are
after?
So wild a presumption provokes me to laughter!
So mad a suggestion proves, out of all question,
Howe'er the test shun, you're mad as a hornet!
I trample it, scorn it, so mad a suggestion!
It fills me with fury, it dumbs me with rage!

S. With one dainty fish-ball do *you* bread rufuse me?
It's *you* are the madman yourself, sir, excuse me!
My wish was immodest? Of men you're the oddest!
In straight-waistcoat bodiced, go hide ye in Bedlam!
Your fish-balls, *there,* peddle 'em! learn to be modest,
And tempt not a stranger half-starving to rage!

Chorus. O'er one paltry fish-ball d'ye make such a rumpus?
For gracious sake, neighbors, we'd rather you'd thump us!

The entrance of the landlady calms the tumult. The
opera ends in pure slapstick. A messenger enters inquir-

ing for a stranger of noble mien, half starved, and with coin of small amount. Assured that this man has been actually present, the messenger cries:

> 'Tis he I've sought for years, CARRARA'S COUNT!
> L. Art speaking sooth?
> MESS. Of course; why this amaze?
>   A harsh stepfather turned him out to graze.
>   An exile long—mark now the hand of Fate!
>   The old man's dead, and his'n the estate.

He questions the stranger to make sure of his identity:

MESS. Are you a Paduan?

S. No, of Bergamo!

MESS. Then 'tis the Count. 'Tis *He!*—One further test:
    Wear you a locket with the family crest?

S. Not I!

MESS. 'TIS HE!!!!—Yet, might I be so bold,—
    Shows your left arm a roseate button-mould?

S. Not in the least.

MESS. 'TIS HE!!!! Conviction strong!
    Salute him all!

CHORUS.   I thought so all along.

CHAPTER XV

A WOMAN SEES THE JOKE

WHEN EUROPEAN CIVILIZATION WAS PLANTED IN THE NEW soil of America, certain unique growths sprang up, just as the jimson weed, or Jamestown weed, is supposed to have come from the first English settlement. The unlimited individualism of the western and southwestern borders, from which were evolved such uniquenesses as David Crockett and Mike Fink and the Missouri Pikes, produced also a new "sport" growth from the old trunk of humor, one as indigenous as was the black bear of the Missouri swamps. When first this type of humor broke into print it was classed by the East with the other arts of the trans-Alleghenian border, something crude and native and destined to be outgrown. Totally sub-literary was it considered and rarely was it quoted in the major magazines. As an illustration of its rating, consider the history of the volume *Georgia Scenes*, 1835, which was all but suppressed by its own author after he had become a prominent clergyman and college president.

With the opening of the 1850's, American humor was

running in two channels: this border humor, for the most
part unpublished, and humor of the conventional types
that might have been written overseas as well as in America. The frontier types had, in the East, evolved what
may be called the Yankee-Doodle variety, "Yankee"
meaning Down-Easter, and "Doodle" Old English for
player on the "doodlesack," a rural clown. Judge Halli-
burton had made him as "Sam Slick," a Yankee clock-
maker, Seba Smith had sent him as "Jack Downing" to
the Maine legislature and then to Washington as adviser
to President Jackson; and Lowell had made him, as
"Hosea Biglow," a rural poet with a political message,
rendering him respectable and fit for Boston readers by
adding a Harvard divine, the Reverend Homer Wilber,
as editor.

II

WHEN Benjamin P. Shillaber died in 1890, aged 76, the
Boston press called him "the pioneer of American newspaper wits. When he started the Mrs. Partington papers,
he had the field to himself. Then the broad-ax and sledge-
hammer vagaries which now pass for humor in the
West were quite undreamed of. The 'funny man' and
the paragraphist had not made their début in the daily
press. Shillaber opened a career for those now indispensable adjuncts of journalism, and his first Partington
squib was greeted with laughter throughout the country
and it created a demand for more."

During the decade of the 1840's, Shillaber, a staff
worker on the Boston *Post,* had thrown into the paper
from time to time these so-called "squibs" characterizing
a woman he had found in Sydney Smith's anecdote of a

Mrs. Partington who had tried to sweep back the Atlantic with her broom. Later, with a recollection perhaps of Tony Lumpkin, he had added "that plaguey Ike," the first in a long line of literary bad boys, the most famous of which was to be Tom Sawyer. All through the decade and beyond these sketches were regarded as highly humorous newspaper ephemeræ, copied freely by all the exchanges, laughed at and thrown away with the paper that contained them.

Then in 1851, Shillaber determined to reap from the popularity he had created by publishing his squibs in a weekly illustrated quarto of eight pages to be entitled the *Carpet-Bag.* Humorous papers had never flourished in America save in the matter of numbers. Americans undoubtedly were a laughing people inordinately fond of jokes, so why not an American *Punch?* Over and over attempts had been made to furnish such a journal. During the 1840's there had been *The Jester, Yankee Doodle, Judy, John Donkey,* and others, all of which had speedily perished for want of support. During the 1850's upwards of fourteen such papers sprang up like mushrooms and as speedily perished. And among them had been the *Carpet-Bag,* which after two difficult years joined the procession to the scrap-heap. Certainly it was not lack of quality, not pernicious anæmia, that caused its death. It was a classic among the early American "funny papers." Artemus Ward set type for it, contributed to it, and learned much from its columns. But America was not ready. As one contemporary expressed it, "Our people don't want their wit on a separate dish." The 1840's in the history of American humor was the newspaper period.

Humor was hardly to be classed as literature. As an adjunct to political discussion as in the case of the *Downing Letters* and the *Biglow Papers* it could be sold in book form, but not in the form of a weekly publication wholly humorous.

Literary humor was to be found in the major magazines. The Clark brothers, Lewis Gaylord and Willis, had furnished masses of it for the *Knickerbocker Magazine*. The "Editor's Table" of that periodical was considered by many to be equal to the best English work. Charles Godfrey Leland's humor was rated high. When *Harper's Magazine* was started in 1850, Lewis Gaylord Clark, so long the editor of *Knickerbocker's,* was chosen to conduct the "Editor's Drawer," an omnibus receptacle soon enlarged to six and seven pages. Soon he was publishing letters in which he had been hailed as the prince of American humorists because of "the exhaustless fund of humor he serves up on his monthly board." "From all quarters and corners of this great country! from the farthest Down East to the most distant West (if that point has yet been settled)—from the frozen North and sunny South we have letters like the leaves of autumn for numbers...bearing their grateful testimony to the genial influence of this never-failing reservoir of mirth." So wrote the pathetic editor.

Sorry stuff it seems to-day. In an hour's reading of late I never once smiled. But humor after all is a fashion. Wit dies with its period—at least the most of it. The 1850's handled it often as if it were an explosive. Horace Greeley lectured on it, condemned cacography as a humorous device, and excluded puns. So did Bennett.

"Our wit goes into the newspaper columns," he ruled, and there it ended.

It was not until 1854, a year after the failure of the *Carpet-Bag*, that Shillaber dared to venture the publication of a Mrs. Partington volume. He had issued two volumes of poetry, but were his newspaper "squibs," popular as they undoubtedly had been as ephemeræ, worth risking as a book when they had failed to keep the *Carpet-Bag* alive? An examination of his *Life and Sayings of Mrs. Partington* shows the timidity with which he approached its publication. Like Lowell in his *Biglow Papers* he diluted the mass of plebeianism, which is Mrs. Partington and Ike, with unchallenged literary matter. Even in his second volume, *Mrs. Partington's Knitting-work; and What Was Done By Her Plaguey Boy Ike*, he introduced sentimental short stories, miscellaneous characterizations, and dozens of poems, all of it wholly unconnected with the title characters.

But the popularity of the two books was sensational. The first volume sold 30,000 copies as soon as printed, and the second sold 10,000 copies before publication. The Mrs. Partington volumes have the distinction of being the first non-political pieces of humor thrown into book form to become veritable best-sellers. During the 1840's American humor had been newspaper material; during the 1850's it overflowed into books. From Shillaber's creation of Mrs. Partington sprang the whole school of literary comedians headed by Derby and Browne. During the two years of the *Carpet-Bag*, Samuel L. Clemens was an employee in the printing office of Orion Clemens in Hannibal, and undoubtedly he read the issues of the magazine which came as an "exchange" to his brother's office. That he contributed such sketches to it as his "The Dandy Frightening the Squatter" is very probable. That he had read the Mrs. Partington papers before he wrote *Tom Sawyer* is more than probable. Tom's Aunt Polly, in all save vocabulary, must have been a sister of Mrs. Partington's, and Tom himself is only Ike as he would have been had he lived on the Mississippi at Hannibal. When the first Partington volume appeared, Clemens was in New York or Philadelphia as a tramp printer, and must have known of the book which was being enthusiastically mentioned in all of the papers. As a type-setter on city journals he may have set up notices of it.

III

LATER American humor, then, was started with a humorous "female." The elements of her humor were few. Most of the laughter she caused her early readers came from her copious use of Malaproprieties. A few of them are still laugh-provoking:

"Truth is stranger than friction."

"Sweet are the uses of advertisements."

At Saratoga, observing a man who "had just emptied the eighth tumbler down his spacious gullet" she observes "How folks can make a mill-race of their elementary canal is more than I can see into:"

"People may say as much as they please about the excellence of the schools, but for my part I think they are no better than they ought to be. Why, do you know," continued she, in a big whisper, "that Isaac's teacher has actually been giving him instructions in *vulgar* fractions?" She took off her spectacles and rubbed the glasses, in her excitement putting them on bottom side up.

As a moralist she was completely in step with her times. "Intemperance is a monster with a good many heads, and creeps into the bosoms of families like any conda or an allegator, and destroys its peace and happiness forever. But, thank Heaven! a new Erie has dawned on the world, and soon the hydrant-headed monster will be overturned. Isn't it strange that men will put enemies into their mouths to steal away their heads?"—"Don't you regard taking snuff a vice?" one asked, innocently.—"If it is," she replied, with the same old argument, "it is so small a one that Providence won't take no notice of it; and, besides, my oil-factories would miss it so."

A little of this is all that modern readers can endure. After passages like this, one feels like closing the book. It is as A. Ward would express it, "much too much":

'Tis nothing but change, change. Only yesterday, as it were, I was in the country, smelling the odious flowers;—to-day I am in Boston, my oil-factories breathing the impure execrations of coal-smoke, that are so dilatory to health. Instead of the singing of birds, the blunderbusses almost deprive me of conscientiousness. Dear me! Well, I hope I shall be restrained through it all. They say that the moral turpentine of this place is frightful, but it isn't any use to anticipate trouble beforehand.

Oliver Wendell Holmes and Henry Ward Beecher highly commended the volumes, and not alone for the humor they contained. Shillaber made the kindly old lady with her wisdom, her patience with Ike, her benevolence, her genuine morality, a living character, one that the reader can feel and love as he loves his old grandmother. Ike was enough to try the patience of an angel, but she never lost her temper. "The boy," she would say, "is the least understood of anything in the animal kingdom," and though she herself never understood Ike she never was harsh with him.

Ike undoubtedly added the humor to the Partington books in their own day and in ours as well. He and his dog Lion are in every play. Ike is just home from attending the dedication ceremonies at the Franklin statue:

"But the occasion was very obtrusive," continued she, brightening up like a jolly old warming-pan, "and if I didn't see the statue, somebody else did; so it's just as well." She smiled again, and subsided into a calm, while Ike, with three chairs, and Lion harnessed to a table, filled with a clothesbasket, four chairs, and a water-bucket, was "making believe" a car in a procession on his own account. Lion didn't seem to enjoy it.

Ike was not a bad boy, in the wicked sense of the word bad; but he had a constant proclivity for tormenting every one that he came in contact with; a resistless tendency for having a hand in everything that was going on; a mischievous bent, that led him into continual trouble, that brought on him reproaches from all sides, and secured for him a reputation that made him answerable for everything of a wrong character that was done in the neighborhood. A barber's pole could not be removed from the barber's door and placed beside the broker's, but it must be imputed to "that plaguey Ike"; all clandestine pulls at door-bells in the evenings were done by "that plaguey Ike"; if a ball or an arrow made a mistake, and dashed through a window, the ball or the arrow belonged to "that plaguey Ike"; If on April Fool's day a piece of paper were found pasted on a door-step, putting grave housekeepers to the trouble and mortification of trying to pick up an imagined letter, the blame was laid to "that plaguey Ike"; and if a voice was heard from round the corner crying "April Fool!" or "sold" those who heard it said, at once, it was "that plaguey Ike's."

Not all the humor of the volumes is to be found in the sayings and doings of Mrs. Partington and Ike. Dr. Spooner, for example, contemplating one of Ike's escapades, launches into a sermon:

How strange it is that boys take so naturally to cruelty and violence! In the time of boyhood, the reason has not got control, and hence temptations to tyranny and wrong have at this time potent force. We all remember the tale of a child—not a caudality, but a narrative—who seeing a picture of the holy martyrs torn to pieces by lions, in the days of Nero, wherein one, according to perspective, that was in the background, appeared smaller; and, as it appeared to be taking no part, the child, instead of being horror-stricken at the scene, remarked, with considerable anxiety, that the little lion wouldn't get any martyr, if he wasn't very quick!

Other Partington books like *Partingtonian Patchwork,* 1873; *Ike and His Friends,* 1878; *Mrs. Partington's New Gripsack,* 1890; and *Mrs. Partington's Grab Bag,* 1893, the most of which went into several editions, have kept alive the Shillaber tradition.

IV

THE STORY of the next best-selling book of humor, also feminine, was almost a duplication of Shillaber's experience. The author of *The Widow Bedott Papers* was Frances Miriam Berry of Whitesboro, New York, in 1847 married to the Reverend Benjamin W. Whitcher. At the time of her death in 1852 she had written no book and had contemplated no book. Like Shillaber, she had simply written sketches for a newspaper.

According to Alice B. Neal, widow of Joseph C. Neal,

author of the volume of humor entitled *Charcoal Sketches,* 1838, a work pronounced by Lewis A. Godey as equal to *Pickwick,* and considered by Dickens so original that he secured its republication in London, "the Bedott papers were first widely introduced to public notice through the columns of Neal's *Saturday Gazette,*" Philadelphia. "Its editor," she continued, "Joseph C. Neal, the well-known author of the *Charcoal Sketches,* was struck by the originality and clearness of the first of the series, when submitted among the mass of contributions, which crowd a weekly paper. It was scarcely in print before the author's name began to be asked by subscribers, casual readers, and brother editors, some of whom attributed them to Mr. Neal himself. They could scarcely be made to believe that sketches so full of humor, so remarkable for minute observation of human nature, were the work of an unpracticed pen."

In 1846, after the appearance of a few of the papers, she had lost faith in her Bedott creation, and was about to end her work "in the comic vein," but Neal had urged her to continue. "All the world is full of Bedott," he wrote. "Our readers talk of nothing else, and almost despise 'Neal' if the widow be not there. An excellent critic in these matters said to me the other day that he regarded them as the best Yankee papers yet written, and such is indeed the general sentiment." As a result the papers continued.

A year later (1847) Neal died, and his widow took over the editorship of the newspaper and continued the Bedott series intermittently until 1852 when Mrs. Whitcher died. Seemingly the papers, despite their newspaper popularity, died with her. Doubtless they never would have been heard of again had Mrs. Neal, three years later, not rescued them from the old files of the paper, arranged them in chronological order, and issued them in New York as *The Widow Bedott Papers, With an Introduction by Alice B. Neal,* 1855.

The popularity of the book was instant and unprecedented, greatly exceeding that accorded to the Partington first volume. Over a hundred thousand copies were demanded, and new editions were issued in 1856, 1864, 1880, 1883, and 1893. Again a volume of humor, a "female" central, had become a best-seller. As a result, following it, had come a deluge of humorous volumes.

V

THE VOLUME centers about the amorous ambitions of the Widow Bedott and their final fruitage. When the reader first sees her, she is in the depths of gloom. The late deacon, her sainted consort, now that he is dead, has assumed a perfection that only poetry can express:

> He never jawed in all his life,
>   He never was unkind—
> And (tho' I say it that was his wife)
>   Such men you seldom find.
>
> I never changed my single lot—
>   I thought 'twould be a sin—
> For I thought so much of Deacon Bedott
>   I never got married agin.
>
> If I was sick a single jot
>   He called the doctor in—
> I sot so much store by Deacon Bedott
>   I never got married agin.

> And since it was my lot to be
> The wife of such a man,
> Go tell the men that's after me
> To ketch me if they can.

But as time went on, other deaconly traits began to occur to her mind:

> But now he's dead! the thought is killing,
> My grief I can't control—
> He never left a single shilling
> His widder to console.

Soon she began to take pains with her caps. A letter written by Jefferson Maguire, of Coonville, gives a new turn to the story:

A distinguished stranger arrived at Scrabble Hill some two weeks since. Who do you guess it is? Why, no less a personage than the Widow Bedott, interesting relic of Deacon Hezekiah Bedott. She has actually inflicted herself upon father's folks for the whole winter. What a time they'll have of it, won't they? Mother is so well disposed, that she tries to put up with it cheerfully; but nevertheless, it is pretty evident that she looks upon Aunt Bedott as a prodigious bore...On Sunday morning I said to her, when mother wasn't by, "Well, aunty, where do you go to meeting to-day?" "Where do I go to meetin'!" said she, "What a question! Why, where should I go but to my own meetin'?" "Oh," said I, "I thought perhaps you'd like to hear Elder Sniffles, he's such an interesting preacher." "What!" said she, "me go to the Baptist meetin'! I hope you ain't in arnest, Jeff; why I'd as soon go to the theatre as go there. I have a sufferin' contempt for the Baptists. They think nobody can't git to heaven without bein' dipped, dippin' 's a savin' audience with them. Why, come to think, I remember that Elder Sniffles. When I was here afore, yer mother and me was in to Mr. Hugle's one evenin'—they're

Baptists ain't they? and Elder Sniffles and his wife come in there to call. If my memory serves me, he's ruther a tall, scrawny man, with eyes that looks like a couple o' peeled onions, and kind o' squintin' tew, and seems to me he hadn't no hair hardly." "O!" said I, "you'd scarcely know him now, he's got a wig and wears spectacles, which improves his appearance vastly." "Well, I should think it needed improvin'," said she.

"By the way, aunty," said I, "did you know that Mrs. Sniffles was dead?" "You don't say so!" said she. "Yes," said I: "she died only a few weeks ago. I feel sorry for the elder—he must be so lonesome." "So do I," said she with a sigh. "It's a dredful thing to lose a companion, and I s'pose the Baptists feel it as much as anybody."

Instantly she decides to hear the Reverend Shadrack Sniffles preach, and having heard him, experiences so complete a change of heart that only poetry could express it:

> I heerd him preach—I heerd him pray—
> I heerd him sweetly sing,
> Dear suz! how I did feel that day!
> It was a dretful thing!

> Full forty dollars would I give,
> If we'd continnered apart—
> For though he's made my sperrit live,
> He's surely bust my heart!

Immediately her best cap she set with all her skill, but soon she found that another poetess, Hugelina, copious creator of sonnets, was also luring him with song—poems that to her were abomination unutterable, poems that she tore into shreds as violating all the canons of a sacred art. In chapter after chapter are described the widow's amorous wiles, her Thanksgiving dinner with all the dishes dear to an elder's heart, her lament over her own death, which surely was imminent, poured out where the cold elder could hear it, she of course unconscious of his nearness:

> Here sleeps Prissily P. Bedott,
> Late relic of Hezekiah,
> How mellancolly was her lot!
> How soon she did expire!

> She didn't commit self-suicide,
> 'Twas tribulation killed her.
> O, what a pity she hadn't a' died
> Afore she saw the elder!

Then, all but fainting in his arms, came triumph. The elder proposed before he knew it and instantly she accepted him. Then came the hallelujah chorus:

> The heart that was scornful and cold as a stun,
> Has surrendered at last to the fortinit one;
> Farewell to the miseries and griefs I have had,
> I'll never desert thee, O Shadrack, my Shad!

Which was the beginning of Shadrack's education.

No one, not even Lowell, has more truthfully presented the down-East dialect of the early nineteenth century. Despite the uxorious widow who gives the book its title, the chief characters in the thirty papers of the volume are the small Yankee towns of Scrabble Hill, Slabtown, Coonville, and Wiggletown. To read the book is to move into the small village circle of a century ago with its trivial gossips, its jealousies and feuds, its widows and widowers and love-sick swains, its pumpkin pies and potato puddings and Thanksgiving "chicken-and-turkey eatings," its sewing societies and church doings and its Yankee peddlers. Nobody is omitted. Completely was it in the key of its times, and yet its "local color" and its dialect brought out three different editions of it in the eighties and the nineties when regional picturings were the fashion in fiction, and its biting realism, as in its graphic description of what happened at the donation party at the parsonage, would make it timely even to-day.

CHAPTER XVI

A CABLE LINE ACROSS THE STYX

*T*HE EARLY FIFTIES, ALREADY NEUROTIC AND JITTERY, were suddenly inundated with another wave of emotion, one as unforeseen and unprepared-for as an invasion from Mars. And even now it is open to question as to just what happened. Using contemporary terms, the "knockers" suddenly appeared: the name came from Willis who had had experiences. As usual in the fifties, *cherchez la femme;* as usual in the fifties, two or three country maidens, like the Brontës in England, and like the Warner sisters and the Carys.

The "knockers" were the Fox sisters, two of them prominent: Margaret, born 1836, and Kate, born 1839, and the knockings were first heard in their farm-house at Hydesville, New York, when Margaret was eleven years old. Later the family and the rappings removed to Rochester, and the world began to hear of "the Rochester rappings." That was in 1848.

Convinced that the mysterious noises were signals from the spirit world, the sisters, so report ran, evolved a system whereby three knocks signified "yes" and silence after a question "no." News of the phenomena spread as by radio. Thousands visited the Fox home, and in 1849 the sisters gave exhibitions in a public hall in Rochester and were subjected to tests by various committees, all of which retired perplexed. The term "medium" was applied

THE FOX SISTERS
Ballou's Pictorial Drawing-Room Companions, 1856.

to the girls, a term never before so used. They were looked upon as necessary apparatus for communication between the two worlds, just as the proposed Atlantic cable would be a medium for communication between the two nations.

Then in May, 1850, they went to New York City, Margaret aged fourteen, Kate aged eleven, and with them their mother and an elder married sister, and began a series of "demonstrations" at $100 a night. New York, as usual, overdid the matter, visited the sisters in crowds and came away with spooky stories of revelations from the spirit world which soon were reported on the front pages of newspapers. N. P. Willis recorded in the *Home Journal* under the title "Post-Mortuum Soiree," his own experiences at one of the séances. He had received what he called "the following pokerish note":

Mrs. Fox and her daughters, having received communications from the spiritual world, would be happy to see Mr. Willis at Barnum's Hotel, at any hour most convenient to himself.

"Not being entirely persuaded, as yet," he wrote, "of our own omniscience, we are unwilling to decline knowing anything more; and we, therefore, accepted the invitation to pass an evening with the 'Knockers'!" Arriving at the designated place he was greatly surprised at the company he found:

Our host was Rev. Rufus W. Griswold, and, present, were Fenimore Cooper, Rev. Dr. Hawks, William Cullen Bryant, Mr. Bancroft, General Lyman, Tuckerman the Essayist, Dr. Francis, Dr. Marcy, Mr. Bigelow, of the *Evening Post,* Mr. Ripley, of the *Tribune,* and one or two others. On our way in we saw the "Knocking Party," of four ladies, looking for the house—into which (it is perhaps essential to state) they had never before entered, and the floors and walls of which they had had no opportunity, of course, to cram with accomplices and hammers. A stout lady, of the ordinary small-town type of maternity, led the way, followed by three young ladies considerably prettier than the average. The two Misses Fox, as well as their married sister, have nerves so plumply clad in health and tranquillity, that it is difficult to reconcile their appearance with the fact that they have been worked upon for two years by the phenomena of unexplained visitations; and indeed throughout the evening, we were struck with their combined good-humor and simplicity, and the ease and unpretendingness with which they let their visitors (from both worlds) have their own way. They evidently won the respect and liking of all present, as the evening went on.

What happened during the evening was reported in full in the *Tribune,* doubtless by George Ripley, who had been the organizer of the then recent disastrous Brook Farm community, and who now was literary editor of Greeley's newspaper.

A half-hour of complete silence began the séance, the spirits not at first responsive. The company in a compact circle about a table listened intently and at length heard faint raps coming from an indefinite somewhere. The rapping grew louder and all was ready for communication with the world beyond the world. The spirits, it seemed, were not to be commanded: they at once took the leadership. With certain members of the company they refused to communicate, notably with Bryant and the other journalists. The first to receive a "rap" after his name was called was Dr. Marcy who later testified that he was satisfied: all his questions had been answered rightly. The next was Henry T. Tuckerman, whose name lives to-day because of Tuckerman's Ravine in the White Mountains. I quote from the *Tribune* report:

Having fixed in his mind the name of an individual, he asked, "Did he live in New York?" No answer. "In Baltimore? In Cambridge? In Boston?"—three distinct raps, which is the sign of an affirmative answer. A negative is indicated by silence. Mr. T. continued, "Was he a lawyer? A merchant?

A physician? A clergyman?" Knocks. "Was he an Episcopalian? A Presbyterian? A Unitarian?"—going over the names of the principal sects. No answer. At the suggestion of a gentleman, Mr. T. asked, "Was he a Christian?" Knocks. Mr. T. then asked the age of the person in a series of tens. "Was he twenty years old at the time of his death? Was he thirty? Fifty? Sixty?" Knocks. "Has he left a family?" Knocks. "Children?" Knocks. "Five? Three? Two?" Knocks. "Did he die in Boston? In Philadelphia? In Albany? In Northhampton? In Bennington?" Knocks. "Did he die of consumption? Of fever? Of cholera? Of old age?" Knocks.

The person in Mr. Tuckerman's mind was the late Reverend Dr. Channing of Boston, who died in Bennington, Vermont, while on a journey. The degree of correctness in the answers may be judged by the reader. It may be stated, however, that for the last years of his life Dr. C. disclaimed the use of all sectarian names, preferring to be called only Christian, and that though under seventy, his physical powers had long suffered from premature exhaustion.

"Mr. J. Fenimore Cooper was then requested to enter into the supramundane sphere, and proceeded to interrogate the spirits, with the most imperturbable self-possession and deliberation." To each one of his questions he got what he declared were correct answers, the person he had in mind being his sister "who, just fifty years ago the present month, was killed by being thrown from a horse." "We were very glad," wrote Willis, "to see Mr. Cooper interested in the 'Knockers' the other evening, for he is one of the few men not afraid of the world, and whatever he sees and believes, with his logical and bold mind, he has the courage to tell, and tell well. The numerous places in which these knockings have been heard, within the past year, show that the ghosts at large have got the trick of it, and the 'demonstration' altogether, to our thinking, is of sufficient extent and respectability to warrant grave attention."

Everywhere, now, spiritualism became a subject for eager discussion. It attracted notable men and women. Dr. Kane, the Arctic explorer, became greatly interested in the Fox sisters and upon his departure for the North provided means for Margaret's education. Upon his return in 1853 she announced that he had married her and she bore his name the rest of her life.

II

Horace Greeley became at length much interested in the sisters and in the whole subject of the world of spirits and of mediums, and he investigated the matter with thoroughness, devoting to his findings a whole chapter in his autobiography. At first he had been skeptical. He had attended an early demonstration by the sisters and had come away disgusted:

I had no desire for a second "sitting", and might never have had one; but my wife—then especially and deeply interested in what pertains to the unseen world, because of the recent loss of our darling "Pickie"—visited the Foxes twice or thrice at their hotel, and invited them thence to spend some week or so at our house. There, along with much that seemed trivial, unsatisfactory, and unlike what might be expected from the land of souls, I received some responses to my questions of a very remarkable character, evincing knowledge of occurrences of which no one, not an inmate of our family in former years, could well have been cognizant.

Greeley and Willis were discussing the matter before Jenny Lind, then in the midst of her New York concerts, and immediately she insisted on being taken to one of the "Manifestations." "I answered," wrote Greeley, "that she could do so by coming to my house in the heart of the city, as Katy Fox was staying with us. She assented and a time was fixed for her call; at which time she appeared with a considerable retinue of total strangers. All were soon seated around a table, and the 'rappings' were soon audible and abundant. 'Take your hands from under the table!' Mademoiselle Lind called across to me in the tone and manner of an indifferently bold arch-duchess." She was certain Greeley was doing the rapping even though he at once put his hands up as if a bandit had appeared.

Greeley, sorely puzzled by the phenomena that seemed so amazing, rejected completely the hypothesis of "jug-glery, knee-joint rattling, toe-cracking, etc.," since the mediums "were often children of tender years, who had no such training, have no special dexterity, and some of whom are known to be awkward and clumsy in their movements. The jugglery hypothesis utterly fails to account for the occurrence which I have personally wit-nessed, to say nothing of others."

Greeley's conclusions as to "spirit-rapping" are worth noting. Allow me to reproduce a few of them:

1. Those who discharge promptly and faithfully all their duties to those who still live in the flesh can have little time for poking and peering into the life beyond the grave. Better attend to each world in its proper order.

2. Those who claim, through the "mediums," to be Shake-speare, Milton, Byron, etc., and try to prove it by writing poetry, invariably come to grief...Even Tupper, appalling as

is the prospect, will be dribbling worse rhymes upon us after death than even *he* perpetrated while on earth.

3. As a general rule, the so-called "spiritual communications" are vague, unreal, shadowy, and trivial. They are not what we should expect our departed friends to say to us...

4. Nearly all attempts of the so-called "mediums" to guide speculators to events yet future have proved melancholy failures. They did not help fish up the broken Atlantic cable, nor find Sir John Franklin, nor dispel the mystery which still shrouds the fate of the crew and passengers of the doomed steamship President.

The spread of what soon developed into the sect called the Spiritualists was rapid. Many who had lost dear friends, like Mrs. Stowe whose son Henry, a freshman at Dartmouth, was drowned in the Connecticut River, found evidences of life beyond death. Mrs. Browning and scores of equally prominent women were sympathetic. After the Civil War, as always after a great and devastating war, there were many who found comfort in the revelations which their mourning hearts so eagerly looked for.

III

As ALWAYS when popular newnesses sweep over a city, as this did over New York, and then over the country and over Europe, the humorists of the time seized upon it as a fertile theme. Q. K. Philander Doesticks (Mortimer M. Thompson) professed to have himself consulted the spirits during the reign of the Fox sisters:

I inquired all sorts of things from all kinds of spirits, "black spirits and white, red spirits and grey." Result as follows.

By means of thumps, knocks, raps and spiritual kicks, I

learned that Samson and Hercules have gone into partnership in the millinery business. Julius Cæsar is peddling apples and molasses candy. Tom Paine and Jack Sheppard keep a billiard table. Noah is running a canal boat. Xerxes and Othello are driving opposition stages. George III has set up a caravan, and he is waiting impatiently for Kossuth and Barnum to come and go halves. Dow, Junior, is boss of a Methodist camp meeting. Napoleon spends most of his time playing penny "ante" with the three Graces. Benedict Arnold has opened a Lager-beer saloon, and left a vacancy for S. A. Douglas (white man)... Joe Smith has bought out the devil, and is going to convert Tophet into a Mormon Paradise.

After the "demonstration," which he reports at length, he went home:

Satisfied that there are more things in heaven and earth than are dreamed of, except by lying "mediums," so called; who, too lazy to work, and too cowardly to get an honorable living by stealing, adopt this method to sponge their bread and butter out of those, whom God in his mysterious wisdom has seen fit to send on earth weak enough to believe their idiotic ravings.

Artemus Ward, who during the whole decade missed nothing that was new and picturesque, always describing it accurately with seeming nonsense, and always ending the account of his visit with a moral burst of eloquent advice, also visited the projectors of deincarnated souls. Asked to select a spirit, he said he desired to converse a few moments with his old show partner Bill Tompkins, long deceased:

"Is the Sperret of William Tompkins present?" sed I of the long hared chaps, and there was three knox on the table.
Sez I, "William, how goze it, Old Sweetness?"

"Pretty ruff, old hoss," replide he.

That was a pleasant way we had of addressin' each other when he was in the flesh.

"Air you in the show bizness, William?" sed I.

He sed he was. He sed he and John Bunyan was travelin with a side show in connection with Shakspere, Jonson & Co.'s Circus...

Sez I, "William, my luvly friend, can you pay me that 13 dollars you owe me?" He sed NO with one of the most tremenjis knox I ever experiunsed.

The Sircle sed he had gone. "Air you gone, William?" I axed. "Rayther!" he replide, and I knowed it was no use to pursoo the subjeck furder.

I then called fur my farther.

"How's things, daddy?"

"Middlin, my son, middlin."

"Ain't you proud of your orfurn boy?"

"Scacely."

"Why not, my parient?"

"Becawz you hav gone to writing for the noospapers, my son. Bimeby you'll lose all your character for trooth and verasserty. When I helpt you into the show bizniss I told you to dignerfy that there profeshun. Litteratoor is low."

He also statid that he was doin middlin well in the peanut bizniss and liked it putty well, tho' the climit was rather warm.

When the Sircle stopt thay axed me what I thawt of it.

Sez I, "My frends I've bin into the show bizness now goin on 23 years. There's a artikil in the Constitooshun of the United States which sez in effeck that everybody may think just as he darn pleazes, and them is my sentiments to a hare. You dowtlis beleeve this Sperret doctrin while I think it is a little mixt. Just so soon as a man becums a reglar out and out Sperret rapper he leeves orf workin, lets his hare grow all over his fase and commensis spungin his livin out of other peple. He eats all the dickshunaries he can find and goze round chock full of big words, scarein the wimmin folks and little children and destroyin the piece of mind of evry famerlee he enters. He don't do nobody no good and is a cuss to society and a pirut on honest people's corn beef barrils. Admittin all you say abowt the doctrin to be troo, I must say the reglar perfessional Sperret rappers—them as makes a bizness on it—air abowt the most ornery set of cusses I ever enkountered in my life. So sayin I put on my surtoot and went home,—Respectably Yures,

ARTEMUS WARD.

IV

In May, 1857, *Harper's Magazine,* in an article entitled "Table-Turning in France," could speak of "the knockers" in the past tense. No craze endures long in New York City:

Thank Heaven, the spirits are at last at rest, and even Judge Edmonds vaticinates, if at all, in private. The radius of the spiritual circle has shrunk into proportions so small as almost to defy measurement. The Foxes have retired to their holes, and the Hares are in cover. Our mahoganies no longer offend the public taste by indulging in acrobatic feats; nor are young ladies given, at the present time, to converse with immaterial essences in their chamber at night. Our grandmothers, poor old souls! rest in peace, and do not rise from the dead to warn us against Gift Enterprises; General Washington has ceased to be dull, by the mouth of a medium, on the Hon. Mr. Giddings and Lawrence Keitt. A flash of common sense has succeeded the heated term of credulity. But they are very busy about spiritualism in France.

Beyond its New York beginnings we shall not pursue the "knockers," certainly not into France.

CHAPTER XVII

"JAPONICA-DOM"

NEW YORK HAS ALWAYS DEMANDED LITERARY LIGHTNESS, fashionable literature, smart-set naughtiness brilliantly presented. In 1850, N. P. Willis, then in his early forties, was writing no more poetry and no more fiction: he had reached the table-land of his last manner (not at all elevated) and he was doing what Nature had prepared him to do: writing "Ephemeræ," "Slipshodities," a column it would be called to-day, but in his own terms a weekly letter which he might entitle "Town Gossip," or "Uppermost Town Topics." The *Smart Set* of the fifties we may call his *Home Journal,* and it was Willis who furnished the "smartness." Never did he cater to the masses for popularity, to "the vulgarians," as he termed them, and seldom to the "upper ten thousand" especially that brainless section of it which he described as "Fifth-Ave.-Noodles—promenading Nobodies bent on ogling the Fifth-Ave.-Nudities." Rather was his audience "the five-dollar-billers"—those who took five-dollar seats at the opera—and "japonica-dom," "the class uptown who usually wear in their hair the expensive exotic commonly

called a japonica." The people who could enjoy his lightness, his quiddities, his gossip, were the well-to-do middle
class, denominated by him "The Few," the home-loving
people on the "central plane":

The vulgar outnumber the possessors of common sense. So
do the aspiring and pretentious. The "central plane" may, in
fact, better be defined as "The Few," whom we have, once
before, tried to fence in, as the parish of the *Home Journal's*
intended ministration.

Willis, like all of the New York writers save Irving,
was not a native of the city. He was born in Portland,
Maine, educated at Yale, and then was added to the edi-
torial board of S. C. Goodrich of Boston, publisher of
The Token and *The Legendary,* both of which annuals
helped the young graduate to cut his literary teeth. Even
as a college undergraduate he had become a contemporary classic with his "inspiration and water" ballads, but
poetry, he soon found, could not express his peculiar
genius. He had started therefore a magazine, made in his
own image, a Boston *Smart Set,* light, witty, gossipy,
worldly—and Boston would have none of it. Boston
smelled brimstone and banked his fires. As a result, the
young editor, mindful of Scriptural advice for such cases,
shook the Boston dust from off his dainty shoes and with
it some hundreds of dollars in due bills never to be paid,
and lit out for New York where brimstone is native and
where the devil is laughed at as the soul of wit. Morris
and his *Mirror* circle took him in at sight and his Boston
magazine with him.

But New York he had soon found was no Bagdad. Spick
and span Fifth Avenue was no nesting place for a young

Byron, his wing feathers now fully fledged. Romance lay in the Old World, and with arguments winged with nothing short of genius he persuaded the moneyless *Mirror* editors to send him to Europe and to support him there, his repayment to be a weekly column-letter made spicy for New York palates. And he fulfilled his part of the contract to the letter. On the pitiful ten dollars a week, doled out irregularly by the *Mirror,* he crashed the most exclusive baronial homes of Great Britain, was entertained again and again like an ambassador, turned the heads of duchesses with *Lara*-like tales of his Mediterranean tour, leaving them convinced that brides of Abydos and of Istambul had on his account been bowstringed by Blue-beard husbands and thrown into the Bosporus. One English duke, indeed, after Willis had spent a week-end at his home, declared that in his opinion the young Don Juan was destined to be President of the United States and that soon. Ah, a rare bird this young Willis. We shall never have another.

But all this in the 1850's was ancient history. Willis and Morris for years had given a weekly banquet of what New York readers thrived on, first in their weekly *Mirror.* Then in 1846 they had started on a new round with a magazine they named the *Home Journal,* later to have as assistant editors James Parton, the biographer, and later Thomas Bailey Aldrich, who used it as a literary teething ring. In 1850, Willis was pouring himself without stint into this new journal.

A rare blend this Willis. No trace of Boston in the blend, despite his father, founder and editor of the *Youth's Companion,* and no Puritanism despite the fact that his close friend at Yale had been Horace Bushnell. Much in the blend there was of Byronism and cosmopolitanism, much of sentimentalism, much of wit and bubbling effervescence; and much there was of worldliness, sheer devil, which makes the mixture still tolerable.

As he comes upon the boards in the 1850's he has ceased to write poems and stories. "Hurrygraphs" now, "Ephemeræ"; New York laid bare in a column to compare even with O. O. McIntyre's glimpsings of the New York moon in our own time. Let me introduce this columnist of yesterday in the terms of his own day. Let me quote from one, Duganne, author of *Parnassus in Pillory*, 1851:

I almost passed by Willis—*"ah miboy!*
Foine morning! da-da!" Faith I wish him joy—
He's forty-three years old—in good condition—
And, positively, he has gained "position."
Gad! what a polish "upper-ten-dom" gives
This executioner of adjectives;
This man who strangles English worse than Thuggists,
And turns "the trade" to trunk-makers or druggists;
Labors on tragic plays that draw no tiers—
Writes under bridges, and tells tales of peers;
His subjects whey—his language sugared curds;
Gods! What a dose!—had he to "eat his words!"
His "Sacred Poems," like a rogue's confessions,
Gain him indulgence for his worst transgressions:
His "Fugitive Attempts" will doubtless live—
Oh! that more works of his were fugitive!
Fate to his fame a ticklish place has given,
Like Mahomet's coffin, 'twixt the earth and heaven;
But be it as it will—let come what may—
Nat is a star, his works—the Milky Way!

At one point, at least, the critic of the fifties is in accord with latter-day estimates: it is his "fugitive attempts" that are the most valuable parts of his writings. He was fundamentally a journalist, a pourer-out, without time for revision, of what the day had brought under his eye. He was one of the earliest of the foreign correspondents for the newspapers, and as such his work is first-hand material for the historian. He actually sat in the presence of most of the notable men of his time, American and European, and always he jotted down his impressions— valuable indeed at this late day. And after the advent of the *Home Journal* he mirrored New York City as not even George William Curtis was mirroring it for the "Easy Chair."

The ending of one of his columns, or "letters" as he called them, will illustrate his weekly variety:

Is my letter long enough? I think it is. Yet I have half a dozen passing topics I meant to touch, while in the vein:— Alboni's arrival—the death of Count D'Orsay—Wallack's welcome return—a book by my old Constantinople friend Honan—one or two new poets whose flights it is time to speak of, etc., etc.

From 1846 to 1855 he interpreted the New Yorkness of New York. He was recorder, philosopher, literary critic, journalist, wit, photographer with words, and always was he sparkling and original. Egotistic?—undoubtedly. One may hurl back at him his own pun: in all his writings,

> Dark as winter was the flow
> Of *I*, sir, rolling rapidly,

yet it is the Willisness of Willis' reporting that is its greatest charm. He was original, even to the coining of a whole new vocabulary. Who has not heard of "the upper ten," meaning the upper ten thousand, New York's aristocracy? "One half, at least, are religious, and the remainder seek refined pleasures, and attend theaters and operas, and are rich enough if they choose to keep a carriage." Writing of the younger generation, in all periods regarded by middle age as a menace, he heads his column: "Juvenocracy in the Ascendant." He mentions "the all-a-gogery of the city on the reopening of the Park Theatre." Newspaper critics made merry with this witty "verbicide" as Dr. Holmes would term it. The Boston *Transcript* manufactured an alleged clipping in the Willis manner on "the all-engrossing topic, the spring style of hats," deftly weaving in many of his typical expressions:

After admitting that "knowingness could no further go" than Beebe & Coster went, Willis winds up thus: "For ourself and ten thousand other workies *whom we could name,* the sadder model of Orlando Fish—timid, proper and thoughtful —is perhaps more appropriate." This passage has produced a great sensation in dandy-dom. The Fish party are in raptures, and could hug Willis to their very bosoms; "the opposition" is in a fury. Nobody can tell what the result may be. Willis dare not venture out, it is thought without a body-guard of Fishites. There are, moreover, many surmises with regard to the character of the "ten thousand other workies" whom Mr. Willis "could name."

The constituent elements of "japonica-dom" and "dandy-dom" may be seen daily in Broadway, between the hours of twelve and three. All the beauty above Bleecker Street wanders at that time down as far as the Park, hazarding even the contamination of the vulgar crowd, in the hope of securing an appetite for dinner. The liveried lacqueys, who oscillate upon a black board behind the carriages of our republican nabobs, sport their gayest trappings: I had the pleasure of seeing one yesterday in a drab "cut-away" with gold lace and yellow facings, and white silk stockings with purple velvet smalls! What is this great country coming to? We Gotham-ites do sometimes make ourselves ridiculous, by aping what as a people we profess to despise. It is rumored that a deputa-tion of English "small-potato" baronets may be expected in this city next summer; and that the object of their transatlan-tic mission is, to establish an aristocratic nucleus among our *"upper ten thousand."*

Willis' literary criticism has been neglected. Few have written more sanely than he of contemporary writers and of literary trends. Constantly he pleaded for an *American* literature, for writers at home who would handle home themes so powerfully that they would be able to shake the English books from the hands of Ameri-can readers. He believed it could be done. For originality he pleaded and for realism in a day when that word had not entered the vocabulary of criticism. Before Mark Twain had left Hannibal, Willis was calling for a Mark Twain:

We have been for years looking at the western horizon of American literature, for a star to arise that should smack of the big rivers, steamboats, alligators, and western manners. We have the Down East embodied in Jack Downing and his imitators. There was wanting a literary embodiment of the Out West—not a mind shining *at* it, by ridiculing it from a distance, but a mind shining *from* it, by showing its peculiar qualities unconsciously. The rough-hewn physiognomy of the

West, though showing as yet but a rude and unattractive outline, is the profile of a fine giant, and will chisel down to noble
features hereafter; but meantime, there will be a literary fore-
shadowing of its maturity—abrupt, confiding, dashing writers,
regardless of all trammels and fearless of ridicule.

He wrote letters of advice to young magazine aspirants
that could be circulated to-day with profit to aspiring
youngsters. He sketched with sure pen the most of the
writers major and minor of his day. Himself a sentimen-
talist, he nevertheless realized to the full the tendencies
of the time, the subtle dangers of the tide of femininity
that was sweeping over the literature of America, North
and South:

Throughout all the middle and lower classes of American
life everything except toil and daily bread is looked at through
the most sentimental and romantic medium. In their notions,
affections, and views of life, the Americans are really the most
romantic people on earth. We do not get this from our English
forefathers—the English are as much the contrary as is possible. We do not get it from our pursuits—what can be more
unromantic than the daily cares of an American? We do not
get it from our climate—it is a wonder how romance, fled
from the soft skies of Spain and Italy, can stay among us. We
get it from books—from the hoisting of the floodgates of copyright—from the inundation of works of fiction. There are
few, we venture to say—few below the more intellectual
classes, whose views of life are not shaped and modelled, and
whose ambitions are not aimed by characters and impulses
found in the attractive pages of "cheap literature."

A book of selections from the critical writings of N. P.
Willis would be, even at this late day, a most thought-
provoking and illuminating volume.

He heard Emerson lecture and took notes like the reporter he was. What was the secret of Emerson's power as a lecturer? He would find out. "The first twenty sentences which we heard betrayed one of the smaller levers of Emerson's power of style, which we had not detected in reading him. He works with surprises.... In delivery his cadences tell you that the meaning is given, and the interest of the sentence all over, when—flash!—comes a single word or phrase, like lightning after listened-out thunder, and illuminates, with astonishing vividness, the cloud you have striven to see into." He then illustrates the device with examples. Next he was impressed with the quality of Emerson's voice:

Emerson's voice is up to his reputation. It has a curious contradiction, which we tried in vain to analyze satisfactorily—an outwardly repellent and inwardly reverential mingling of qualities, which a musical composer would despair of blending into one. It bespeaks a life that is half contempt, half adoring recognition, and very little between. But it is noble, altogether. And what seems strange is to hear such a voice proceeding from such a body. It is a voice with shoulders in it, which he has not—with lungs in it far larger than his—with a walk in it which the public never see—with a fist in it which his own hand never gave him the model for—and with a gentleman in it which his parochial and "bare-necessaries-of-life" sort of exterior, gives no other betrayal of. We can imagine nothing in nature—(which seems, too, to have a type for everything)—like the want of correspondence between the Emerson that goes in at the eye, and the Emerson that goes in at the ear.

In like manner he gives his impressions of Webster whose oration he heard at a Forefathers' Day dinner, of

Edward Everett, of Calhoun and Benton, of Fanny Kemble's readings from Shakespeare, of the visitors from Europe, Samuel Lover and Fredrika Bremer, of Fenimore Cooper whom he visited at Cooperstown, of Fanny Forester and Grace Greenwood, of Poe, and Irving, of Jenny Lind, the biography of whom he published as a volume, and of dozens besides.

But with the advance of the decade of the fifties, Willis' troubles began to multiply. His health failed. After 1854 he was a sick man—an invalid the rest of his life. His robustness of expression in some of his letters brought violent antagonisms. For instance, in his treatment of Emerson as lecturer, he said that even though they had at one time been fellow-Bostonians, he had not gone to hear him preach since he then had the "idea that he was but a new addition to the prevailing Boston beverage of Channing-and-water." Constantly he was called upon to answer such flings; according to his biographer, Beers, "next to Cooper he was the best abused man of letters in America."

Moreover, he was in the New York headlines during the whole decade for another and a very different reason. Trouble seemed to pursue him from every quarter. The actor Forrest, the New York trouble-maker for two decades, was suing his wife for divorce, and Willis considered his charges against her unfounded and unjust. Thereupon Forrest charged him with alienating his wife's affections, a charge most ridiculous in view of the evidence presented, assaulted Willis on the street, knocked him down with his cane, and would have beaten him to a pulp had bystanders not interfered. Then had come

court action. Willis got the verdict and Forrest was compelled to pay $64,000. But for five times the case was
appealed, the judgment against him was in each case
confirmed, but it was not till 1868 that the case was
finally settled.

Broken in health, Willis took a "health trip to the
tropics" and removed from New York City to a country
residence, "Glenmary." His letters to the *Home Journal,*
which he still continued, now became sketches of country life. He died in 1867. His work of value had ceased
a decade before.

II

DURING the 1850's, New York Knickerbockerism was in
its Indian summer. *Knickerbocker,* long the leading
magazine of the city, had been a gentleman's magazine
with—to use a Willisism—the ideals of *Spectator*-dom.
The unique benefit given its editor Lewis Gaylord Clark
was in 1854, when as a personal tribute fifty-four of the
old contributors, comprising all the New York school
old and young and half a dozen New Englanders, furnished gratuitously each an article and a steel engraving
of himself (no women included) for a volume elaborately bound to be called *The Knickerbocker Gallery,*
the ingratiating Clark to have all the profits. It was really
the funeral service of the magazine though the thing
dragged on a pitiful wreck for a decade longer.

The Indian-summer glow came from the younger generation of New Yorkers who would keep literature on
the Irving levels. The cry all through the decade was
that literature was being vulgarized, that as *Harper's*

"Editor's Table" expressed it, "it had gone in pursuit of the million" and to reach them had descended to their level. Realizing that the aristocratic *Knickerbocker's* work was done, a group of the younger literary generation headed by C. F. Briggs and George William Curtis, in order to keep the Washington Irving alpenglow still glorious on the American page, in 1853 established *Putnam's Magazine*. Of this romantic venture Briggs in later days wrote this:

We derive considerable satisfaction in remembering the cosy little dinner in a certain cosy house in Sixteenth Street, at which the plan of the work was discussed and the adventure determined upon. The little party consisted of Mrs. Caroline M. Kirkland, Mr. George Sumner, Mr. Parke Godwin, Mr. George W. Curtis, Mr. and Mrs. Putnam, and the present writer. The chief doubt in the minds of many was whether the country could furnish the requisite number of writers to sustain an original magazine of the better class, but the experiment proved there was plenty of latent talent which only required an opportunity for its development.

In its original form it lasted four years, and, as Briggs expressed it, from its numbers "seventeen books were printed, including *Potiphar Papers* and *Prue and I.*" In 1857 it was merged with *Emerson's*.

The noteworthy little gathering with a publisher reminds one of a similar gathering with a publisher four years later in Boston from which resulted the *Atlantic Monthly*. But *Putnam's* was an Indian-summer creation, marvelous in its beauty, something to be remembered forever, but it was the beauty of a dying tradition. The *Atlantic Monthly* was a midsummer matter, the gathering place for the fruitage of a noteworthy spring planting.

No decade in our history has been put on paper so brilliantly and so exhaustively as the decade of the fifties. The first to mirror it was Willis; then came the Dr. Holmes of the new *Putnam's Magazine,* George William Curtis, with his *Potiphar Papers* and "Easy Chair" papers; and finally came the Autocrat, two series of whose papers ran through the *Atlantic* before 1860.

Potiphar Papers have been classified as satire—wrongly so. Rather are they genial revealings of fashionable life in New York in the early fifties by one forced to live in it and be reckoned with Willis' "upper ten." It is a series of lengthened "Easy Chair" papers revealing the New Yorkness of New York society, graceful picturings from a Gotham angle of "the little farce called life." Its opening paper "Our Best Society" is a classic. It is strewn, to be sure, with passages that date it with almanac-like exactness, as this:

We were quietly ruminating over our evening fire, with Disraeli's Wellington speech, "all tears," in our hands, with the account of a great man's burial, and a little man's triumph across the channel. So many great men gone, we mused, and such great crises impending! This democratic movement in Europe; Kossuth and Mazzini waiting for the moment to give the word; the Russian bear watchfully sucking his paws; the Napoleonic empire redivided; Cuba and annexation, and slavery; California and Australia, and the consequent considerations of political economy; dear me! exclaimed we, putting on a fresh hodful of coal, we must look a little into the state of parties. As we put down the coal-scuttle there came a knock at the door. We said, "Come in," and in came a neat Alhambra-watered envelope, containing the announcement that the queen of fashion was "at home" that evening week.

To his wife he said, "You'll go, of course, for you will meet all the best society of the city, the picked flower of its genius, character, and beauty." But as he had not recently arrived from the moon, he knew precisely what was in store. "We had received other cards, and had perfected our toilette many times, to meet this same society, so magnificently described." If he was to go to this ball he would meet:

We shall meet three classes of persons: first, those who are rich, and have all that money can buy; second, those who belong to what are technically called "the good old families," because some ancestor was a man of mark in the state or country, or was very rich, and has kept the fortune in the family; and, thirdly, a swarm of youths who can dance dexterously, and who are invited for that purpose.

We went to the brilliant ball. There was too much of everything. Too much light, and eating, and drinking, and dancing, and flirting, and dressing, and feigning, and smirking, and much too many people. Good taste insists first upon fitness. But why had Mrs. Potiphar given this ball? We inquired industriously, and learned that it was because she did not give one last year. Is it then essential to do this thing biennially? inquired we with some trepidation. "Certainly," was the bland reply, "or society will forget you." Everybody was unhappy at Mrs. Potiphar's, save a few girls and boys, who danced violently all the evening. Those who did not dance walked up and down the rooms as well as they could, squeezing by nondancing ladies, causing them to swear in their hearts as the brusque broadcloth carried away the light outworks of gauze and gossamer. The dowagers, ranged in solid phalanx, occupied all the chairs and sofas against the wall, and fanned

themselves until supper time, looking at each other's diamonds, and criticizing the toilettes of the younger ladies,
each narrowly watching her peculiar Polly Jane, that she did
not betray too much interest in any man who was not of a
certain fortune. It is the cold, vulgar truth, madam, nor are
we in the slightest degree exaggerating. Elderly gentlemen,
twisting single gloves in a very wretched manner, came up
and bowed to the dowagers, and smirked, and said it was a
pleasant party, and a handsome house, and then clutched their
hands behind them, and walked miserably away, looking as
affable as possible. And the dowagers made a little fun of the
elderly gentlemen, among themselves, as they walked away.

And so through twenty-six pages. No need for more
samples. We have all had experience. It is as modern as
yesterday and it will be modern after we are dead.

The paper "A Meditation by Paul Potiphar, Esq." deals
with a situation that has always been an affliction of
New York—the steady trampling down of fashionable
streets by the great foot of business on its steady march
uptown. Potiphar, whose fashionable mansion had become from long residence a home, every part of which
he knew and loved, must be abandoned, so his wife de-
creed, for were not all the fashionable ones moving to
areas more aristocratic? There must be a new mansion
with modern furniture and decorations if they wished to
keep their place in society. The wife ruled and the new
house was built and furnished at a maximum of cost
after her own designs. Potiphar, dislodged from what
had been for him the solid comfort of his old home,
viewed his new quarters with a critical eye:

The furnishing was certainly performed with great splendor
and expense. My drawing-rooms strongly resemble the ware-

house of an ideal cabinet-maker. Every whim of table—every caprice of chair and sofa, is satisfied in those rooms. There are curtains like rainbows, and carpets, as if the curtains had dripped all over the floor. There are heavy cabinets of carved walnut, such as belong in the heavy wainscotted rooms of old palaces, set against my last French pattern of wall paper. There are lofty chairs, like the thrones of archbishops in Gothic cathedrals, standing by the side of the elaborately gilded frames of mirrors. Marble statues of Venus and the Apollo support my mantels, upon which *or molu* Louis Quatorze clocks ring the hours. In all possible places are statues, statuettes, vases, plates, teacups, and liquor-cases. The woodwork, when white, is elaborated in Moresco carving— when oak and walnut, it is heavily moulded. The contrasts are pretty, but rather sudden. In truth, my house is a huge curiosity-shop of valuable articles—clustered without taste, or feeling, or reason. They are there, because my house was large and I was able to buy them; and because, as Mrs. P. says, one must have buhl and *or molu,* and new forms of furniture, and do as well as one's neighbors, and show that one is rich, if he is so. They are there, in fact, because I couldn't help it. I didn't want them, but then I don't know what I did want. Somehow I don't feel as if I had a home, merely because orders were given to the best upholsterers and fancy-men in town to send a sample of all their wares to my house. To pay a morning call at Mrs. Potiphar's is, in some ways, better than going shopping. You see more new and costly things in a shorter time. People say, "What a love of a chair!" "What a darling table!" "What a heavenly sofa!" and they all go and tease their husbands to get things precisely like them. When Kurz Pacha, the Sennaar minister, came to a dinner in my house, he said:

"Bless my soul! Mr. Potiphar, your house is just like your neighbor's."

I know it. I am perfectly aware there is no more difference between my house and Crœsus' than there is in two ten-dollar bills of the same bank. He might live in my house and I in his without any confusion.

Then we have Minerva Tattle's summer diary at Newport, "The Potiphar's in Paris," and the observations of Kurz Pacha upon the people of New York made to his "Most Sable and Serene Master" at home, a letter purporting to have been translated by the author of the *Potiphar Papers*. This letter unquestionably must be classified as satire.

III

THE MOST popular satire of the decade, however, was the long poem *Nothing to Wear,* first published anonymously in the newly established *Harper's Weekly* in 1857, and then republished in book form, still anonymously. The first edition sold one hundred and forty thousand. Other editions followed, one of them "profusely and elegantly embellished by Hoppin, the first humorous artist in America." William Allen Butler, a lawyer and magazinist of New York City, acknowledged in due time the authorship, and later added other clever satires, none of which need to be disinterred. *Nothing to Wear* is still quotable:

Miss Flora M'Flimsey of Madison Square,
Has made three separate journeys to Paris,
And her father assures me, each time she was there,
That she and her friend Mrs. Harris. . . .
Spent six consecutive weeks without stopping,
In one continuous round of shopping;
Shopping alone, and shopping together,
At all hours of the day, and in all sorts of weather;
For all manner of things that a woman can put
On the crown of her head or the sole of her foot,

NATHANIEL PARKER WILLIS
From a portrait by C. Harding.

JOHN GODFREY SAXE
Ballou's Pictorial, 1855.

A NEW YORK PARLOR OF THE FIFTIES
Ballou's Pictorial Drawing-Room Companion, 1854.

Or wrap round her shoulders, or fit round her waist,
Or that can be sewed on, or pinned on, or laced,
Or tied on with a string, or stitched on with a bow,
In front or behind, above or below:
For bonnets, mantillas, capes, collars, and shawls;
Dresses for breakfasts, and dinners, and balls;
Dresses to sit in, and stand in, and walk in;
Dresses to dance in, and flirt in, and talk in;
Dresses in which to do nothing at all;
Dresses for winter, spring, summer, and fall;
All of them different in color and pattern,
Silk, muslin, and lace, crape, velvet, and satin,
Brocade, and broadcloth, and other material,
Quite as expensive and much more ethereal;
In short, for all things that could ever be thought of,
Or milliner, modiste, or tradesman be bought of,
From ten-thousand-francs robes to twenty-sous frills;
In all quarters of Paris, and to every store,
While M'Flimsey in vain stormed, scolded, and swore,
They footed the streets, and he footed the bills.

* * * * * * * *

The last trip, their goods shipped by the steamer Arago
Formed, M'Flimsey declares, the bulk of her cargo,
Not to mention a quantity kept from the rest,
Sufficient to fill the largest sized chest,
Which did not appear on the ship's manifest,
But for which the ladies themselves manifested
Such particular interest, that they invested
Their own proper persons in layers and rows
Of muslins, embroideries, worked underclothes,
Gloves, handkerchiefs, scarfs, and such trifles as those;
Then wrapped in great shawls, like Circassian beauties,
Gave good-by to the ship, and go-by to the duties.
Her relations at home all marvelled no doubt,
Miss Flora had grown so enormously stout

For an actual belle and a possible bride;
But the miracle ceased when she turned inside out,
And the truth came to light, and the dry goods beside,
Which, in spite of Collector and Custom-house sentry,
Had entered the port without any entry.

* * * * * * * *

And yet, though scarce three months have passed since the day
This merchandise went, on twelve carts, up Broadway,
This same Miss M'Flimsey, of Madison Square,
The last time we met, was in utter despair,
Because she had nothing whatever to wear!

* * * * * * * *

Nothing to wear! Now, as this is a true ditty,
I do not assert—this, you know, is between us—
That she's in a state of absolute nudity,
Like Powers' Greek Slave, or the Medici Venus;
But I do mean to say, I have heard her declare,
When, at the same moment, she had on a dress
Which cost five hundred dollars, and not a cent less,
And jewelry worth ten times more, I should guess,
That she had not a thing in the wide world to wear!

Invited to the great party to be given by the Stuckups, her lover had suggested acceptances be sent, but

The fair Flora looked up with a pitiful air,
And answered quite promptly, "Why, Harry, mon cher,
I should like above all things to go with you there;
But really and truly—I've nothing to wear."

Whereupon, man-like, he called over the great catalogue of her dresses, each of which she rejected with rising scorn.

Here I ripped out something, perhaps rather rash,
Quite innocent, though; but, to use an expression

More striking than classic, it "settled my hash,"
And proved very soon the last act of our session.
"Fiddlesticks, is it, Sir? I wonder the ceiling
Doesn't fall down and crush you—oh you men have no feeling,
You selfish, unnatural, illiberal creatures,
Who set yourself up as patterns and preachers.
Your silly pretence—why what a mere guess it is!
Pray, what do you know of a woman's necessities?
I have told you and shown you I've nothing to wear,
And it's perfectly plain you not only don't care,
But you do not believe me" (here the nose went still higher).
"I suppose if you dared you would call me a liar.
Our engagement is ended, Sir—yes, on the spot;
You're a brute, and a monster, and—I don't know what."
I mildly suggested the words—Hottentot,
Pickpocket and cannibal, Tartar, and thief,
As gentle expletives which might give relief;
But this only proved as spark to the powder,
And the storm I had raised came faster and louder,
It blew and it rained, thundered, lightened, and hailed
Interjections, verbs, pronouns, till language quite failed
To express the abusive, and then its arrears
Were brought up all at once by a torrent of tears,
And my last faint, despairing attempt at an obs-
Ervation was lost in a tempest of sobs.

* * * * * * * *

Well, I felt for the lady, and felt for my hat, too,
Improvised on the crown of the latter a tattoo,
In lieu of expressing the feelings which lay
Quite too deep for words, as Wordsworth would say;
Then, without going through the form of a bow,
Found myself in the entry—I hardly knew how—
On door-step and sidewalk, past lamp-post and square,
At home and upstairs, in my own easy chair,
Poked my feet into slippers, my fire into blaze,

And said to myself, as I lit my cigar,
Supposing a man had the wealth of a Czar
Of the Russias to boot, for the rest of his days,
On the whole, do you think he would have much to spare
If he married a woman with nothing to wear?

IV

AN EARLIER poetic satire of New York society, "The Proud Miss Mac Bride," 1849, by John G. Saxe, a Vermonter, settled for a time in the city, was popular in the fifties. Writing to Griswold who was revising his anthology, Saxe chose this poem to represent him in the volume, begging that it be presented entire. Fragments of the poem, however, must represent it in our survey:

THE PROUD MISS MAC BRIDE. A LEGEND OF GOTHAM

I

O, terribly proud was Miss Mac Bride,
The very personification of Pride,
As she minced along in Fashion's tide,
Adown Broadway—on the proper side—
   When the golden sun was setting;
There was pride in the head she carried so high,
Pride in her lip, and pride in her eye,
And a world of pride in the very sigh
   That her stately bosom was fretting;

II

A sigh that a pair of elegant feet,
Sandaled in satin, should kiss the street—
The very same that the vulgar greet
In common leather not over "neat,"—
   For such is the common booting;

(And Christian tears may well be shed,
That even among our gentlemen bred,
The glorious day of Morocco is dead,
And Day and Martin are raining instead,
  On a much inferior footing!)

III

O, terribly proud was Miss Mac Bride,
Proud of her beauty, and proud of her pride,
And proud of fifty matters beside
  That wouldn't have borne dissection;
Proud of her wit, and proud of her walk,
Proud of her teeth, and proud of her talk,
Proud of "knowing cheese from chalk,"
  On a very slight inspection.

Her father, an honest mechanic, kept a shop where he sold candles and soap:

XIX

Little by little he grew to be rich,
By saving of candle-ends and "sich,"
Till he reached, at last, an opulent niche—
  No very uncommon affair;
For history quite confirms the law
Expressed in the ancient Scottish saw,
  A Mickle may come to be May'r!

Wooers came in swarms, until:

XXXI

Old John Mac Bride, one fatal day,
Became the unresisting prey
  Of Fortune's undertakers;
And staking his all on a single die,
His foundered bark went high and dry
Among the brokers and breakers!

XXXIII

But alas! for the haughty Miss Mac Bride,
'Twas such a shock to her precious pride!
She couldn't recover, although she tried
   Her jaded spirits to rally;
'Twas a dreadful change in human affairs,
  From a Place "Up Town," to a nook "Up Stairs,"
  From the Avenue down to the Alley!

XXXVIII

And to make her cup of woe run over,
Her elegant, ardent, plighted lover,
   Was the very first to forsake her;
"He quite regretted the step, 'twas true—
The lady had pride enough 'for two,'
But that alone would never do
   To quiet the butcher and baker!"

XXXIX

And now the unhappy Miss Mac Bride,
The merest ghost of her early pride,
   Bewails her lonely position;
Cramped in the very narrowest niche,
Above the poor, and below the rich,
   Was ever a worse condition?

V

THE INFLUENCE of Thackeray during the decade popularized home-made satire. *The Book of Snobs* and *Vanity Fair* had dealt with London society. An American Thackeray would naturally deal with New York City, already the largest and richest American metropolis and already possessed of a social set that took itself with seriousness. Undoubtedly aping London usages, it was importing manners and furnishings, and at Saratoga and Newport had supplied itself with summer luxury corresponding in a way with the English Bath and the Continental spas.

Only one other satirist is worthy of note, Donald G. Mitchell, "Ik Marvel," who in 1850 issued anonymously a *Salmagundi*-like periodical, *The Lorgnette, or Studies of the Town by an Opera-goer,* essays and satires dealing with fashions of the day, and had followed it in the *Knickerbocker* with a rambling series in similar vein entitled *Fudge Doings.* Useful volumes the two may be for a study of the New York social set, but of no value as literature.

Mitchell's *Reveries of a Bachelor,* however, issued in the initial volume of *Harper's Magazine,* 1850, non-satirical papers, oversentimental at times and completely in key with the feminine fifties, has long been rated as a minor classic. Remarkably has it held its popularity with readers of every class. Never has it been out of print, a noteworthy statement in view of the fate of most of the other best-sellers of its decade.

CHAPTER XVIII

THE FURBELOWED FIFTIES

No ONE HAS BETTER EXPRESSED CERTAIN CHARACTERISTICS of American literature during the Victorianized 1850's than Bayard Taylor in his *Diversions of the Echo Club*. The group had just misquoted in high glee a stanza from the amazing lyric "Rosalie Lee" by Chivers:

> Many mellow Cydonian suckets,
> Sweet apples, anthosmial, divine,
> From the ruby-rimmed beryline buckets,
> Star-gemmed, lily-shaped, hyaline;
> Like the sweet golden goblet found growing
> On the wild emerald cucumber tree,
> Rich, brilliant, like chrysophrase glowing,
> Was my beautiful Rosalie Lee.

This had started the "Ancient" lecturing on fashions in literature:

Just now the fashion runs to jewelry; we have ruby lips, and topaz light, and sapphire seas, and diamond air.... Then we have such a wealth of gorgeous color as never was seen before —no quiet half tints, but pure pigments, laid on with a pallet-

knife. Really, I sometimes feel a distinct sense of fatigue at the
base of the optic nerve, after reading a magazine story. The
besetting sin of the popular—not the best—authors is the
intense.

Zöilus. Why do you call intensity of expression a sin?

The Ancient. I mean intensity of *epithet:* the strongest expression is generally the briefest and barest. Take the old
ballads of any people, and you will find few adjectives. The
singer says: "He laughed; she wept." Perhaps the poet of a
more civilized age might say: "He laughed in scorn; she
turned away and shed tears of disappointment." But nowadays,
the ambitious young writer must produce something like this:
"A hard, fiendish laugh, scornful and pitiless, forced its passage from his throat through the lips that curled in mockery
of her appeal; she covered her despairing face, and a gust and
whirlwind of sorrowing agony burst forth in her irresistible
tears."

The literary furbelowing extended itself to the outer inventory of books. It seemingly was taken for granted by
all the publishing houses of the mid-century that the feminine buyers of books, and the masculine buyers of books
for the ladies, were more concerned with the surface appearance of the books than with their contents. The book
to be bought must please the eye.

As all students of American literature well know, for
three decades all the bookstores at Christmas and New
Year's had been full of elegant little volumes, bound in
purple and gold, and packed with sentimental verses and
romantic steel engravings and Irvingesque sketches and
tales. During the first decade—from 1826 to 1836—these
were called annuals, in reality little magazines to be issued once a year. In the second decade of their run they
degenerated into "gift-books"—gawdy miscellanies whose

chief value was their external appearance. Gawdy indeed many of them, with sentimental titles: *The Amaranth, The Casket, The Magnolia, The Amethyst, The Dew-Drop, The Forget-Me-Not, The Hare-Bell, The Hyacinth, The Iris, The Jewel, The Lily, The Mayflower, The Moss-Rose, The Ruby, The Snow-Drop, The Violet, The Wintergreen,* and hundreds of others. The majority of the later issues were edited by women, and in their thousands of pages one may find contributions by every writer of the early nineteenth century, including Emerson, Hawthorne, Longfellow, and Holmes.

Of the third phase of this literary rubeola, or, to change my figure, of the terminal-moraine rubbish swept into our decade by an ebbing tide, I shall speak later. After 1850 the concocting of gift-books from the ruins of earlier gift-books became a publisher's "racket." The whole gift-book phenomenon is enormously important. No treatment of mid-nineteenth century literature is complete without a careful survey of it. Recent students have listed some 2,000 different annuals and gift-books published during their amazing run through three decades, and so widely was distribution made that they touched almost every home in America, often again and again.

Out of the annuals grew the conception of *Godey's Lady's Book.* In its early period it was, indeed, to make an Irish bull, an annual published twelve times a year.

II

THE HIGHLY ornamented gift-books with their illuminated title-pages and elaborate rubrications tended to turn the written work of one whole younger generation rococo in style and diction. Young women eager for publication gave themselves gaudily floralized pseudonyms—Fanny Forester, Grace Greenwood, Fanny Fern—and, as did the young Marlowe of Elizabethan days, believed that literature to be effective must be written in "high astounding terms."

By the inexperienced writer generally, literary beauty is defined in terms of "fine writing"—adjectives in the superlative, nouns in gorgeous raiment, everything in Sunday finery.

One may take as typical Grace Greenwood, whose volume *Greenwood Leaves* appeared in 1849, second edition 1851, and sold like a breakfast food in sensational figures. Born Sara Jane Clarke, one of the eleven children of a New York small-town physician, she had at the age of nineteen removed with her father to a small town near Pittsburgh, Pennsylvania, and thus marooned on the outskirts of civilization had evolved her pen-name and had showered languishing tales upon the eastern magazines. Highly moral they were, for was not her great grandfather Jonathan Edwards? And some of them found lodgment, especially a series she sent to the New York *Home Journal*.

Willis, who had not been able to endure another floral "authoress" (his sister Fanny Fern), gave her an abundant entrance to his journal, and in time even immortalized her with an editorial so rococo that it gloriously abandoned all truth. She was, he said,

Born with the Ohio, at Pittsburgh, and destined, like this her foster-river, to have had a sufficiently distinct and important existence of her own, before merging her name in her destined Mississippi. In personal appearance, she is more like an Andalusian than a child of the Alleghanies—her large Spanish eyes, oval outline of face and clear brunette complexion, looking to be of a nativity warmer and nearer the equator than the cold Blue Ridge—and, with her tall person, and fondness for horses and open air exercise, there seems a persistence of Nature in making her as much a personal, as she is a mental, exception to the latitude she lives in.

The most of *Greenwood Leaves* appeared in the *Home Journal,* and after its publication as a volume, Willis slopped over again. On this occasion he wrote to his partner Morris:

Save her from meriting the approbation of dignified critics. Leave this fairest blossom on the rosetree of women for my worship, and the approbation of the few who, like me, can appreciate the value of an elegant uselessness and perceive the fascination of splendid gayety and brilliant trifling.

This early Grace Greenwood that fascinated Willis was manifestly, define the word as you will, sentimental. The part of *Greenwood Leaves* that appeared in the *Home Journal* was a series of heart-throb sketches, with such titles as "Heart Histories," "Sly Peeps into the Heart Feminine," "Destiny in a Rose-Bud," "A Spring Flower Faded."

Enough! But the style that charmed Willis—let me quote from a contemporary critic, one of Willis' feared "dignified critics" perhaps: "If ever there should be a concordance made of her book, the repetition of the word 'gorgeous' would be startling. It occurs on almost every page and only yields now and then to such mild adjectives as 'grand,' 'superb,' and 'delicious.' . . . Sunsets, moun-

tains, trees, churches, paintings, music, and pyrotechnics
are all 'gorgeous.' "

But unlike Fanny Fern who gave to literature all she
had, Grace Greenwood had powers that were never called
forth by the times in which she lived. Her "Copyright"
parodies, which appeared in the Philadelphia *Saturday
Evening Post*, 1849, "a piece of audacious mirth and mis-
chief," she called them, are far more vivacious and witty
than those in Bayard Taylor's volume *Diversions of the
Echo Club*, done with Fitz-James O'Brien and Stoddard
a decade later. No American author of consequence
escaped. Had Poe, for instance, been asked to write a tale
graphically setting forth the need of an international-
copyright law, this is her version of what he would have
written:

A TALE OF HORROR

by E.A.P.

> ... *Tenet insanabile multos
> Scribendi cacoethes.*
> —JUVENAL

I did not see the lad. To that I will take an oath—any oath
you please, on the Bible, the Koran, or Tooke's Pantheon.
I did not see the lad; yet I knew that he was behind me; that
he had followed me for several squares up Broadway. I knew
that he wore but one shoe; I knew also that he was *black,*
though I will again swear that I did not see his *shadow.*
"*How* did I know all this?" impatiently demands my reader.
Simply by my analytical faculty—by resolving thought into its
constituent elements. This was the *magnum arcanum* of my
certain, and at first view, mysterious knowledge of these facts.
Thus I knew that it was *myself,* he was following, because,
amid all the hurrying crowd, he had maintained so close a

proximity, that I could distinctly hear his labored respiration. I knew that he wore but one shoe, by the different sounds made by the two feet in descending. "But how knew you that he was *black?*" I answer, *Ex pede Herculem*—by the peculiar *slapping* sound made by the *bare* foot upon the pavement. That the foot of the Africo-American is *flat,* is a fact sufficiently authenticated by common observation. The somewhat hyperbolical expression, in the popular ballad goes also to confirm it:

"The *hollow* of her foot makes a *hole* in the ground."

Suddenly I turned upon the lad, and said sternly, "Snowball, what want you with me?" The boy absolutely shrieked with surprise and terror, his ebony complexion changed to a ghastly blue, and his enormous eyes rolled up till not a particle of the iris was visible.

When sufficiently recovered, he placed in my hand a soiled and crumpled note, on reading which, I ordered him to conduct me immediately to a place therein designated. On, on, deeper and deeper, into the most squalid and heaven-forgotten portions of the city, I was led by my urchin guide. At length we paused before a tumble-down-castle of a building—the *ne plus ultra* of all wretchedness, where, after pointing up a crumbling flight of stairs, my ragged cicerone held out his hand for a sixpence. An old woman was standing in the doorway—a fleshless, toothless, half-sightless hag, with grizzly elf-locks straggling over her shrivelled face, munching a crust of mouldy bread, forcibly taken from a starving dog. She took no notice of me, as I passed her to ascend to the third story of the house. The first two or three stairs gave way beneath my feet, probably not having felt the weight of a well-fed person for some years. Shaking from me the dislodged spiders and scorpions which were running in all directions, I shudderingly but safely reached the top of the stairway. Here a door obstructed my passage. To this I found no handle, but perceiving a long, black cord hanging through an aperture, I concluded it was what is called a "latch-string," and gave it a vigorous pull. What was my horror to feel it gliding from my grasp! *It was the tail of an enormous rat!* Raising my foot, I levelled the door at once, and ascending a second flight of stairs, found myself in a small and most miserable apartment. On a table before me lay a huge pile of manuscripts, beside a bottle, labelled "Ink," but which had been last used as a candlestick. On a wretched bed in one corner was extended the wasted figure of a man. His emaciation was so extreme that in some places the bones were protruding through the skin! His hair and beard, of great length, were grizzly and matted. His nose was transparent in its thinness, and his eyes were sunken almost into invisibility. On the straw at his feet was perched, what at first I took for a raven, but presently discovered to be a wild-visaged black cat, also fearfully attenuated.

The man was insensible—*in articulo mortis,* in fact—but by a few mesmeric passes, and an intense concentration of will, I was able to revive him for a few moments. He opened his eyes —he knew me—I knew *him!* Ay, this forlorn being was the once distinguished Adolphus Twiggs, the poet and novelist; the most successful delineator of the fashionable and senti-mental which our country has ever known! "Yes, my friend," he said, "you see before you the victim of the miserable com-pensation awarded to native genius, and *of the want of a law of International Copyright!*" Then he added with touching impressiveness, *"Sum quod eris, fui quod sis."*

"How long have you been in this condition?" I asked.

"It is now two years," he replied, "since the Harpers refused to bring out my greatest work, 'Fashionable Flirtations, and Delicate Distresses,' at which time, disgusted with the *punica fides* of both publishers and public, I exiled myself from my kind, and retired to the dignified repose of this garret."

"But, Twiggs, you had a wife?"

"Yes, but I divorced her, *a mensa et thoro.* She was a good creature enough, but no sentiment, no congeniality, and I would not be bored by her. Yes, 'twas a trial, for *inter nos,* Lucy more than half supported us with her needle; but then, what great genius has ever been able long to endure a wife? Since then, that faithful creature (pointing to the cat) has shared my bed and board, and though she can't bring in money, she keeps the rats at a distance, never interrupts me in my inspired moods, and..."

Here a fearful change came o'er the sufferer! The cat, who was rubbing against his face, cried out piteously. Twiggs opened his eyes and murmured, "Oh my poor mews!"—then came the death-rattle—the jaw fell, and the ill-rewarded author was no more!

The bereaved cat gave one unearthly howl, turned and sprang frantically into the street below! This was the more easily done, as there was no pane to obstruct her frenzied passage. I drew to the window, and, sick with horror, gazed downward. *She had dashed her brains out against the pavement!*

Her take-off of Melville in the same series, and her "A Fable from the Burmese" by Fanny Forester, a prose rhapsody woven largely of gorgeous adjectives, are still readable. So, too, are the twenty-six letters which she published, letters sparkling with humor, simple in diction, and realistic in their backgrounds.

In 1852-1853, she spent fifteen months in Europe recording her impressions in *Haps and Mishaps of a Tour in Europe,* 1854, a book unmercifully criticized by the London *Athenæum.* In 1853 she was married to Leander K. Lippincott, of Philadelphia. She edited the *Little Pilgrim,* juvenile magazine, and during the later fifties traveled widely as an anti-slavery lecturer.

III

OF FANNY FORESTER, born Emily Chubbuck, one needs to know that she was exceedingly religious, that she wrote tracts on "How to Observe the Golden Rule," and "How to be Happy," and then Fanny-Fern-like articles, first published in the New York *Mirror* and later gathered for the volume *Alderbrook*. As a result of this book, she attracted the notice of the missionary Adoniram Judson, on leave from his field in Burma, and was employed by him to write the biography of his second wife who had died in India. Over this sainted wife the two wept together, for weeks, he furnishing the facts and she the tearful adjectives, and when the book was done they were married and she went with him to Burma. The biography appeared in 1849, the year before he died. Her death followed four years later at the age of thirty-six.

IV

BUT LITERATURE, after all, is a following of the fashions of a day. Following the World War, sentimentalism and Puritanism were excommunicated as devils which had haunted and enfeebled literature. College classes quoted Mencken and imitated him in smashing condemnations. I remember how a class of graduate students not ten years ago reading *Reveries of a Bachelor,* a volume praised in superlatives by one whole generation, wet with many tears, and still in print, burst into laughter when the dream-child died and the dream wife's coffin was brought in. Where the 1850's cried, the 1930's laughed. It is "sickly sweet sentimentality," they say.

But is it?

"Sentimentalism" changes its definition with every new younger generation.

V

But that the decade was a veritable swamp of fur-belowed sentimentalism is easily shown by exhibiting the almost endless run of gift-books and annuals. The glamo-rous Griswold compiled eight in four years:

> *Poetry of the Flowers,* 1851
> *The Gift of Affection,* 1853
> *The Republican Court,* 1853
> *Gift of Flowers, or Love's Wreath,* 1853
> *Gift of Love,* 1853
> *Gift of Sentiment,* 1853
> *Gift of Love,* 1854
> *Gift of Sentiment,* 1854

Mrs. Sigourney compiled seven; Emily Percival five; T. S. Arthur endless specimens; Mrs. Sawyer and Miss Edgar-ton eighteen volumes of *The Rose of Sharon;* and even Seba Smith could perpetrate two volumes of *Dew-Drops of the Nineteenth Century.*

But the 1850's ended this amazing episode of annuals and gift-books, and ended it in a fiasco of literary racketeer-ing. Surely these gift-books were not bought to be read. According to Faxon, the first to explore the vast Ever-glades of these publications:

The case of *The Wreath of Wild Flowers,* a book of mis-cellanies by John Milton Sterns, published in New York in 1846, and copyrighted in that year, will serve as a final example of how some publishers met the demand for a new annual each year. With the addition of a preliminary poem, and some extra plates, Mr. Sterns' work was used as *Amaranth* in 1851, Boston; *Garland* in 1852, Boston, edited by Emily Percival; *Keepsake of Friendship,* in 1853, Boston, edited by G. S. Monroe; *Tokens of Friendship,* 1854, Boston, and also New York, and finally as *Magnolia,* with a preface date of 1853.

In my history *The First Century of American Litera-ture*[1] I have written this:

Some of the annuals went through as many as twelve repub-lications with different names. A doting husband during this racketeering decade might buy for his wife as a wedding anniversary present in 1849 *The Amaranth;* in 1850, *The Garland;* in 1851, *The Keepsake of Friendship;* in 1852, *The Magnolia;* in 1853, *The Token of Friendship;* in 1854, *The Casket;* in 1869, *Memory's Gift,* and then discover that all the volumes were but reprintings from the old plates of the 1849 *Amaranth,* with changed titles and changed engravings. It is a commentary upon the literary condition of the times that dozens of these flamboyant counterfeits were sold in profitable editions every year, and that no one seems to have complained.

The literary morals of the fifties were loose indeed. To cite but a single example, when N. P. Willis' books had ceased to sell, he republished them with new titles, as new books. His *Pencilings by the Way* he republished in parts with new titles. During the fifties, indeed, he added fif-teen volumes to his list, only two or three of which were new material.

VI

AND, in advertising their books many of the publishers in New York and Boston went to extremes that were little short of book racketeering. Emerson Bennett's novel *The Forged Will* was advertised as "one of the most powerful works in the language." "It will sell a hundred thousand

---

[1] D. Appleton-Century Co., New York, 1935.

copies and have a run equal to *Uncle Tom's Cabin.*" *The Wife's Victory* was presented as "the most splendid picture of American life ever written." "She is now conceded by all critics to be the best female writer now living and her works to be the greatest novels in the English language." And again, "There is no doubt that the *Lost Heiress* is to be the great book of this age." Charles J. Peterson's *Kate Aylesford* was presented to the reading public in 1855 as "the best historical novel ever written in America ... one of the most powerful, thrilling, and absorbing stories ever penned." *Yankee Yarns and Yankee Letters,* by Sam Slick, was "full of the drollest humor that has ever emanated from the pen of any author." One might go on multiplying examples indefinitely, but book "puffery" did not begin with the fifties, nor did it end there.

VII

DURING the late forties the amusement world was widened by the addition of a new popular show—moving pictures two generations before the "movies." Even the overly-pious could attend a panorama exhibition, for it had all the educative elements of a lecture and at the same time it was a show. Panoramas were in high vogue during the fifties. At one time in Boston one might attend "The Ingenious Diorama of the Battle of Bunker Hill," or go to Lui's "Great Moving Panorama of the Mexican campaign," or else see Banvard's "Panorama of the Mississippi River." The last was the one that drew the crowds. The Boston *Journal,* in a contemporary notice, gave this description of "the largest painting in the world":

The immense painting by Mr. Banvard of the panorama of
the Mississippi River is now open for exhibition at Armory
Hall. The picture is represented on canvas three miles in
length, and exhibits a view of the great Mississippi, with its
bends and bayous, its turbid water and its snags, and the
towns and villages, and forests and swamps and plantations,
indeed all the scenery on its banks for the distance of twelve
hundred miles, extending from the mouth of the Missouri
to the city of New Orleans. The drawings were made by Mr.
Banvard from actual observation in the years 1840-'41, and the
work has been in progress to the present time, a period of six
years. The panorama is exhibited by means of upright revolving cylinders, which unfold the painting gradually, in-
tending to represent the scenes which unfold, while travelling
on a steamboat along the channel of this noble river.

Then as now, moving-picture shows prospered finan-
cially. In Boston alone during a six months' run Banvard's
panorama is said to have brought to its owner some fifty
thousand dollars. Special trains brought crowds of people
from all parts of New England and its success in other
cities was similar. Longfellow was thrilled by the picture
and from it derived suggestions for backgrounds in *Evan-
geline*. The title of one of Whittier's books issued in the
fifties was "The Panorama."

A painting measured in miles seemed to Europe a
peculiarly American phenomenon. The French critic
Philarète Chasles, writing for the *Revue des Deux Mondes,*
quoted in high glee an advertisement he had once seen in
London of another panorama American size:

GIGANTIC, ORIGINAL AMERICAN PANORAMA.

In the great American saloon can be seen the prodigious moving Panorama of the Gulf of Mexico, the Falls of St. Anthony

and the Mississippi, painted by J. R. Smith, the great American artist, covering four miles of canvas, and representing nearly four thousand miles of American landscape.

Artemus Ward, home from his tour of the extreme West, found in the highly popular panorama a device

BRIGHAM YOUNG AT HOME
A scene from *Artemus Ward's Panorama*, 1869.

for giving something like unity to the incoherent miscellany that he was to call a lecture. It was a stroke of genius. He would make the panorama a running joke and in doing so, all unwittingly, he was to be one of the elements contributing to the decline of the device. At once he ordered thirty-one crudely-drawn pictures of Western scenes, his artist being William Hilliard, chief scene-painter for Niblo's Garden, New York, and around them he wove the lecture materials that were to prove so amusing to his audiences in London. Certainly this was American uniqueness. The volume *Artemus Ward's Panorama as Exhibited at Egyptian Hall London*, 1869, reproduces verbatim with illustrations and illuminating foot-notes this notable lecture.

At every point Ward made his panorama the center of his ridiculousness. He had intended, he told his London audiences, to have the finest scenes that could be painted, but failing to secure them on account of the expense, he had determined to get the worst. Looking rapturously at one of his grotesque daubs he would say:

This picture is a great work of art; it is an oil-painting done in petroleum. It is by the Old Masters. It was the last thing they did before dying. They did this, and then they expired. I wish you were nearer to it so you could see it better. I wish I could take it to your residences and let you see it by daylight. Some of the greatest artists in London come here every morning before daylight with lanterns to look at it. They say they never saw anything like it before, and they hope they never shall again!

Then pointing at several brown splotches:

These are intended for horses; I know they are, because the artist told me so. After two years, he came to me one morning and said, "Mr. Ward, I cannot conceal it from you any longer; they *are* horses."

Ward's last recorded joke involved his panorama. Sick unto death in London, his contemplated lecture tour now impossible, he whispered: "It seems a fashion nowadays for everybody to present the Prince of Wales with something. I think I shall leave him—my panorama."

In one of his pictures Ward introduced real "movie" effects. The prairie fire was made realistic by a revolving cloth behind a transparent part of the painting.

CHAPTER XIX

THE MAN WHO HATED BOSTON

OUT OF THE FERMENT OF THE DECADE CAME LITTLE THAT was permanent. The yeasty foam of congressional oratory disappeared early. Fiction degenerated into a "dope" for worried souls seeking escape. Whittier's fiery lyrics and much of Lowell's *Biglow Papers* can be understood now only by means of copious foot-notes. Only *Uncle Tom's Cabin* remains a permanent classic wrought from the materials of its time. As young Bayard Taylor expressed it, "the literature of our day is in a sad state of bewilderment and confusion.... A few effervescing powders would perhaps soothe a public stomach which has been over-dosed with startling effects."

The dosage came, but no one could have foreseen its origin, and its effects certainly were not soothing and were not permanent. In an era of paradox there could have been no greater paradox than the Irish Bohemian Fitz-James O'Brien, come to live by his wits in headlong old New York which was just freeing itself from the last traces of its Knickerbockerism.

O'Brien was perhaps twenty-four in 1852, when, full of letters to New York publishers and littérateurs, he first saw the East River. Into the American literary confusion he was bringing what classic Boston might have termed dangerous baggage: a Villon-like experience gained in old-world literary Bohemias; a Celtic imagination prone to run without leash; a wild tendency toward the horrific, learned, it may have been, from Baudelaire and D'Aurevilly—perhaps in France; a total lack of reverence for old régimes; and a masculine gift of lyricism desultory and lawless but always original and never enfeebled by sentimentalism.

The life of the young adventurer before his arrival in America must at present, and perhaps finally, be rated as legendary. He was born in Limerick, and he must have had an extensive education, though not as William Winter reported (with a saving "perhaps") at Dublin University. His name is not on the University records. That he squandered in London a paternal bequest of 8,000 pounds seems believable. He was in London undoubtedly for some two years, possibly he was in Paris for a time, and from sheer restlessness he had emigrated to America.

And he came at the one moment when such a personality could have become a serious influence. Willis in his day had also brought old-world atmospheres and Bohemian up-to-dateness, but Willis was slipping: he was lapsing into invalidism. That the young Irishman could so swiftly have won the leadership of the young intellectuals of the city is surprising. But was he not a Celt, and was leadership not innate in his race? Moreover, congenial young souls hunt always in packs with the most headlong of them all at the head. Young T. B. Aldrich, his literary pin-feathers sprouting mightily in the New York of Willis, clove at sight to the new leader and for a time actually lived with him, though O'Brien's régime, as he himself expressed it, was: "Sleep all day and live all night." Other excited young souls quickly gathered about him: Taylor; Stoddard; Fitz-Hugh Ludlow, author of the *Hasheesh Eater,* 1857; Henry Clapp; Launt Thompson, sculptor; William Winter, dramatic critic; George Arnold, poet; Stedman; Walt Whitman, his lyre still unstrung but already sounding strange notes; and there were others, less known.

Surprisingly did the magazines open their columns to the young stranger. *Harper's* published thirty of his short stories and many of his lyrics, and all the other magazines seldom refused his offerings. Dramas he produced, several of which had surprisingly successful runs. In less than eight years he had created an enormous miscellany and the most of it he had sold at current rates. Composition troubled him not at all. The prince of entertainers, he could pay for the banquet he was giving by writing lyrics or tales on the table on which they had dined, sometimes ere his guests had departed. The electric quality of his genius one may learn from Taylor's unique volume, *Diversions of the Echo Club.*

The headquarters of the little junto was Pfaff's dingy rathskeller, 647 Broadway, where night after night over steins of beer were discussed all possible things in earth and heaven and some others. Let Bayard Taylor, who alone has recorded anything of these ambrosial nights, describe with a fictitious local name the Bohemian headquarters:

In the rear of Karl Schafer's lager-beer cellar and restaurant —which every one knows is but a block from the central part of Broadway—there is a small room with a vaulted ceiling, which Karl calls his *Löwengrube,* or Lion's Den. Here, in their Bohemian days, Zöilus and the Gannet had been accustomed to meet to discuss literary projects, and read fragments of manuscript to each other. The Chorus, the Ancient, and young Galahad gradually fell into the same habit, and thus a little circle of six, seven, or eight members came to be formed. The room could comfortably hold no more: it was quiet, with a dim, smoky, confidential atmosphere, and suggested Auerbach's Cellar to the Ancient, who had been in Leipzig.

Here, authors, books, magazines, and newspapers were talked about; sometimes a manuscript poem was read by its author; while mild potations of beer and the dreamy breath of cigars delayed the nervous, fidgety, clattering-footed American hours.

According to the *Diversions* volume, once for a period of eight nights they gave themselves over to "echoes," that is each was to be given at random a poet and then in a specified time was to produce a poem as that poet, if present, would write it. Few English and American bards escaped. "The Gannet" seemed devoid of all reverence. Against the protest of all the others, he insisted on echoing the reverenced Whittier, though "Galahad" threatened to "withdraw from the Club." This was the "echo":

THE BALLAD OF HIRAM HOVER

Where the Moosatockmaguntic
Pours its waters in the Skuntic,
    Met, along the forest-side,
    Hiram Hover, Huldah Hyde.

She, a maiden fair and dapper,
He, a red-haired, stalwart trapper,
    Hunting beaver, mink, and skunk,
    In the woodlands of Squeedunk.

She, Pentucket's pensive daughter,
Walked beside the Skuntic water,
    Gathering in her apron wet,
    Snakeroot, mint, and bouncing-bet.

"Why," he murmured, loath to leave her,
"Gather yarbs for chills and fever,
    When a lover, bold and true,
    Only waits to gather you."

"Go," she answered, "I'm not hasty;
I prefer a man more tasty;
    Leastways, one to please me well
    Should not have a beasty smell."

"Haughty Huldah!" Hiram answered;
"Mind and heart alike are cancered:
    Jest look here! these peltries give
    Cash, wherefrom a pair may live."

"I, you think, am but a vagrant,
Trapping beasts by no means fragrant;
    Yet—I'm sure it's worth a thank—
    I've a handsome sum in bank."

Turned and vanished Hiram Hover;
And before the year was over,
    Huldah, with the yarbs she sold,
    Bought a cape against the cold.

Black and thick the furry cape was;
Of a stylish cut the shape was;
    And the girls, in all the town,
    Envied Huldah up and down.

Then, at last, one winter morning,
Hiram came, without a warning:
    "Either," said he, "you are blind,
    Huldah, or you've changed your mind.

"Me you snub for trapping varmints,
Yet you take the skins for garments:
    Since you wear the skunk and mink,
    There's no harm in me, I think."

"Well," said she, "we will not quarrel,
Hiram: I accept the moral.
    Now the fashion's so, I guess
    I can't hardly do no less."

Thus the trouble all was over
Of the love of Hiram Hover;
    Thus he made sweet Huldah Hyde
    Huldah Hover, as his bride.

Love employs, with equal favor,
Things of good and evil savor;
    That, which first appeared to part,
    Warmed, at last, the maiden's heart.

Under one impartial banner,
Life, the hunter, Love, the tanner,
    Draw, from every beast they snare,
    Comfort for a wedded pair!

It was "The Ancient" who remarked, "I have noticed the lack of a younger generation of poets." Such a lack unquestionably there was. Rhymed sentimentality flourished, mostly feminine, but nothing virile and compelling. "Put some tender, thoroughly obvious sentiment into rhyme which sounds like the melody of a popular song, and it will go through hides which are impervious to the keenest arrows of the imagination." And such was the poetry of the fifties.

American poetry unquestionably was out of joint, and for a moment it might have seemed that O'Brien had been born to set it right. Unquestionably he had poetry in his soul, but never did it come out save in flashes of intuition. He was great only in moments. His failing was ephemeralness: he lacked stability. As expressed in the *Diversions* volume: "A great deal of all modern literature is ephemeral, created from day to day to supply a certain definite demand, and sinking out of sight, sooner or later." O'Brien, from spendthrift habits, acquired perhaps while scattering his patrimony in London, demanded luxury, and to secure it meant headlong work without aim or finish for the mere money he earned.

In inspired moments, however, he did some of the best poetical work of the decade—poetry great in passages. His monody on Dr. Kane who died, aged 37, after his memorable voyage to the Arctic, is noteworthy. I quote but the opening stanza:

> Aloft, upon an old basaltic crag,
>> Which, scalped by keen winds that defend the pole,
>> Gazes with dead face on seas that roll
>> Around the secrets of the mystic zone,
> A mighty nation's star-bespangled flag
>> Flutters alone:
> And underneath, upon the lifeless front
>> Of that drear cliff, a simple name is traced!
> Fit type of him, who, famishing and gaunt,
>> But with a rocky purpose in his soul,
>> Breasted the gathering snows,
>> Clung to the drifting floes,

By want beleaguered, and by winter chased,
Seeking the brother lost amid that frozen waste.

His poem "The Prize-Fight," a bestial exhibit, graphic as a daguerreotype, and as revealingly realistic, leaves little to the imagination. So with his "Song of the Locomotive," "The Demon of the Gibbet," "The Zouaves." His long poem, *The Sewing Bird,* perhaps his best work, is a song for men. Let me begin with Canto x:

Up in a wild California hill,
Where the torrents swept with a mighty will,
And the grandeur of nature filled the air,
And the cliffs were lofty, rugged, and bare,
Some thousands of lusty fellows she saw
Obeying the first great natural law.
From the mountain's side they had scooped the earth
Down to the veins where the gold had birth,
And the mighty pits they had girdled about
With ramparts massive, and wide, and stout;
And they curbed the torrents, and swept them round
Wheresoever they willed, through virgin ground.
They rocked huge cradles the livelong day,
And shovelled the heavy, tenacious clay,
And grasped the nugget of gleaming ore,
The sinew of commerce on every shore.
Their beards were rough and their eyes were bright,
For their labor was healthy, their hearts were light;
And the kings and princes of distant lands
Blessed the work of their stalwart hands.

Then high o'er the shovel's and pickaxe's clang
Loudly the song of the Sewing Bird rang:—
"See, see, see, see!
This is the place where MEN should be!"

XI

She saw a region of mighty woods
Stretching away for millions of roods;
The odorous cedar and pine-tree tall
And the live-oak, the grandest among them all,
And the solemn hemlock, massive and grim,
Claiming broad space for each mighty limb.
When she heard the clang of the woodman's axe
Booming along through the lumber-tracks,
And she heard the crack of the yielding trunk,
As deeper and deeper the keen axe sunk,
And the swishing fall—the sonorous thrill—
And the following stillness, more than still.
Then, moving among the avenues dim,
She saw the lumbermen, giant of limb;
The frankness of heaven was in each face,
And their forms were grand with untutored grace;
Their laugh was hearty, their blow was strong,
And sweet as the wood-notes their working song,
As they hewed the limbs from the giant tree,
And stripped off his leafy mystery;
They breathed the air with elastic lungs,
They trolled their ditties with mirthful tongues,
To see it would do a citizen good,
With what unction they relished their homely food;
For their hunger was keen as their trenchant axe,
And their jokes as broad as their brawny backs.

Then the Sewing Bird sang again and again,
As he soared o'er the sonorous woods of Maine,
"See, see, see, see!
This is the place where MEN should be!"

Not at all was the little group that drank beer at Pfaff's
a measurable body. It varied from night to night. Some-

times Walt Whitman came, defending, perhaps, his new *Leaves of Grass,* but on such ambrosial *Noctes* there was present no Christopher North. Howells, who dropped in on a memorable night, found himself wholly out of key. He had been a contributor to the literary outlet of the Bohemians, the *Saturday Press,* started in October, 1858, with Henry Clapp, Jr., arch-hater of "brownstone morality," as editor, and with O'Brien and Thomas Bailey Aldrich as assistants, and he had recorded what he saw:

It would not be easy to say just why the Bohemian group represented New York literature to my imagination, for I certainly associated other names with its best work, but perhaps it was because I had written for the *Saturday Press* myself, and had my pride in it, and perhaps it was because that paper really embodied the new literary life of the city. It was clever, and full of the wit that tries its teeth upon everything. It attacked all literary shams but its own, and made itself felt and feared. The young writers throughout the country were ambitious to be seen in it, and they gave their best to it; they gave literally, for the *Saturday Press* never paid in anything but hopes of paying, vaguer even than promises. It is not too much to say that it was very nearly as well for one to be accepted by the *Press* as to be accepted by the *Atlantic,* and for the time there was no other literary comparison. To be in it was to be in the company of Fitz-James O'Brien, Fitz-Hugh Ludlow, Mr. Aldrich, Mr. Stedman, and whoever else was liveliest in prose or loveliest in verse at that day in New York. It was a power, and although it is true that, as Henry Giles said of it, "Man cannot live by snapping-turtle alone," the *Press* was very good snapping-turtle. Or, it seemed so then; I should be almost afraid to test it now, for I do not like snapping-turtle so much as I once did, and I have grown nicer in my taste, and want my snapping-turtle of the very best. What is certain is that I went to the office of the *Saturday Press* in

FITZ-JAMES O'BRIEN

From a drawing by Sol Eytinge, Jr., in William Winter, *Poems and Stories of Fitz-James O'Brien*, 1881.

THOMAS BAILEY
ALDRICH

Photographed at nineteen. From Mrs. Thomas Bailey Aldrich, *Crowding Memories*, courtesy of Houghton Mifflin Company.

New York with much the same sort of feeling I had in going
to the office of the *Atlantic Monthly* in Boston, but I came
away with a very different feeling. I had found there a bitterness against Boston as great as the bitterness against respectability, and as Boston was then rapidly becoming my second
country, I could not join in the scorn thought of her and said
of her by the Bohemians. I fancied a conspiracy among them
to shock the literary pilgrim, and to minify the precious emotions he had experienced in visiting other shrines; but I found
no harm in that, for I knew just how much to be shocked,
and I thought I knew better how to value certain things of the
soul than they. Yet when their chief asked me how I got on
with Hawthorne, and I began to say that he was very shy and
I was rather shy, and the King of Bohemia took his pipe out
to break in upon me with "Oh, a couple of shysters!" and the
rest laughed, I was abashed all they could have wished, and
was not restored to myself till one of them said that the
thought of Boston made him as ugly as sin; then I began to
hope again that men who took themselves so seriously as that
need not be taken very seriously by me.

O'Brien who had defined Bohemians as writers "who
cultivate literature and debts, and heedless of the necessities of life, fondly pursue the luxuries," like the rest of his
group hated Boston with the whole range of his vocabulary, yet he boasted when his stories "The Diamond Lens"
and "The Wondersmith" made the *Atlantic*.

And the literary New Englanders in the same measure
damned New York. Senator George F. Hoar, recalling
the Concord days of the Curtis brothers, could say in his
old age: "I think if George W. Curtis had dwelt almost
anywhere but in New York City, he would have been a
very powerful influence in the public life of his generation. But he did not find any congenial associates in the

men of New York who had any capacity to effect much good."

Much criticism has been expended upon O'Brien's short stories—far too much. He had invention unquestionably, and he had moments of brilliancy, but he wrote with headlong haste, he lacked discipline, he lacked sincerity. His "What Was It?" so praised by his contemporaries, was thrown off in the odds and ends of two or three evenings. A dash of genius is in it. The motif of it as handled later by Maupassant in his *Le Horla*, by Ambrose Bierce in his "The Damned Thing," and by F. Marion Crawford in his "The Upper Berth," shakes the soul of a reader. But its inventor, after his first stroke of horror, ends his tale in a sprawl. The invisible "what was it?" was made visible by having a plaster cast made of the body of it, and that cast, according to the writer, now reposes in a museum. None of his tales command their reader to the end. They lack the perfect body this distinctive genre demands, and they lack that something indispensable to great art which we may denominate Soul. Almost wholly to-day is he unread.

Much has been made of this "Bohemian" episode—too much. It was simply a picturesque "Midway Pleasance" in a picturesque decade. George W. Curtis, who from the vantage point of *Harper's* "Easy Chair" observed the ten years and missed nothing worth recording, wrote in October, 1859, what is undoubtedly the last word concerning the phenomenon:

Bohemia is the realm of vagabondage. It is the modern sphere of the spirit that formerly coursed the world for adventure—but now prefers to explore the universe in a microcosm, and finds a metropolis the best of all. Men of an indomitable irregularity and indolence, who live by their wits and for self-indulgence are Bohemians. They are a genial, generous fraternity, in whom you may securely look for the kindly, but not surely for the stern and heroic virtues. They are the great company of "good fellows," who have a secret contempt for the processes by which money is acquired, but a profound enjoyment of the pleasures it purchases... Bohemia is a fairy land upon the hard earth. It is the Arcadia in New York or London, in Paris or Rome... Respectability is the converse of the Bohemian idea. There are plenty of men among them worthy of respect—but none who are technically respectable. If they are the lees of society, as has been injuriously urged, they are the richness which settles at the bottom of the cup. Respectability is the pale, thin, emasculated liquor that floats upon the surface and is easily seen through. Bohemia is the nimble essence, the fat substantiality, which "ascends to the brain" and begets their glorious phantasies.

O'Brien's literary career in New York lasted only eight years. Then had come the Civil War, and, Irishman that he was, he enlisted among the very first, he was rushed to the front, and in a minor skirmish in 1862 he received wounds from which he died. What he might have written had he lived, and had age cooled the tumult within him, it is useless to conjecture.

II

I HAVE said that the literary sons of the Brahmins were all daughters. Note in the period after the war the recorders in fiction of the New England decline: Rose Terry Cooke, Sarah Orne Jewett, Mary E. Wilkins, Elizabeth Stuart Phelps, Annie Trumbull Slosson. And outside of New England note the rise of Constance Fenimore

Woolson, Mary Hartwell Catherwood, Frances Hodgson Burnett, Mary Hallock Foote, Mary N. Murfree, Margaretta Wade Deland, Grace King, and Alice French. During this feminine efflorescence period an editor for the *Atlantic* had to be imported from the virile West, and following him came another importation, the ex-editor of the New York *Saturday Press* and ex-editor of the New York *Home Journal,* a man who had learned the fundamentals of magazine editorship from N. P. Willis and George P. Morris and Henry Clapp, Jr., "King of Bohemia" and arch-hater of Boston and of "brownstone morality."

Thomas Bailey Aldrich was a New Englander by birth—Portsmouth, N. H., 1836—but his early environment had been largely outside of his native region. After three years in New Orleans, in 1852 he had entered his uncle's counting room in New York to be trained for a business career. But poetry had intoxicated the lad, and poetry to his practical old uncle was a disease of adolescence that must be eradicated even if it required heroic treatment. Once when the youth showed him a check which the editor of *Harper's Magazine* had given him for a poem, his uncle had burst out: "Why don't you send the damned old fool one every day?" After three years in the office the young poet had gotten his fill of business, had broken loose, secured a minor position on Willis' journal, and until 1865, when he was 29, had worked as a hack writer and minor editor in literary New York. The ten years had been his college course in literature.

During this decade he published eight books, mostly

poetry. Could he at the end of this apprenticeship have faced his literary self and bade it stand and answer, it would have said: I feel three natures struggling within me. First, the Dickens-fed sentiment and sentimentalism of the times, that had expressed itself in 1855 in his "Ballad of Babie Bell" (the spelling characterizes it). Logic abdicates when writers publish. The lyric had appeared in a commercial newspaper, then it had leapt from its non-literary columns and had swept over the country even as Harte's "The Heathen Chinee" was to sweep a decade later. It was the talk of the poetic year, but Whitman's *Leaves of Grass,* which had been published the same moment, made not a ripple. Then had followed the over-ripe lushness of a copious adolescent fruitage, poems like "The Course of True Love Never Did Run Smooth," an Arabian love story dedicated to his fellow poet, also a lotus-eater, Stoddard, "under whose fingers this story would have blossomed into true Arabian roses." Holmes with this exotic nosegay in his hand remarked upon "the sandal-wood sweetness" that breathed from it, "the semi-voluptuous excess of color and odor" and advised the youngster not to allow his "tendency to vanilla-flavored adjectives and patchouli-scented participles" to stifle his "strength in cloying euphemisms." Lowell was to say the same thing to the young Howells: "You must sweat the Heine out of you as men sweat out mercury."

The second nature within him, a talent long suppressed, had been aroused and rendered keen by his contacts with the Bohemian group of whose whole eight years he had been a part. Later, when disciplined by Boston contacts and his daily work on European journals for the eclectic

Every Saturday, his wit and brilliancy grew to equal even that of Dr. Holmes.

The third element in his nature, a growing sense of the seriousness of life and the realism that forces itself upon increasing years, tended to erase little by little the New Yorkness of his literary apprentice years. Contact with the Brahmins, especially with Dr. Holmes, gave a patrician touch to his prose, perhaps his greatest addition to the short-story art of his period. But life in Boston never rendered him a complete Bostonian. Dr. Holmes never could convince him that the *Atlantic* office was the universe, or even the hub of the solar system. "There is a finer atmosphere," he would admit, "than in our city"— note the pronoun which stood for New York. "I'm not genuine Boston: I'm Boston plated." Yet from his earlier, New-York-written volumes, he dropped nearly everything when he selected the materials for his definitive collection. One of his early volumes *A Year's Life,* he found so out of key with his later self that he destroyed every copy he could find.

As a poet he never reached the heights: his Bohemian training had forbidden that. Greater was he as a prose-writer. His contacts with French fiction, then enamoured of artistry, made his short-story work highly influential. But I am wandering from the 1850's.

Aldrich as a poet, like so many others whose blossoming was in the feminine decade before the war—Taylor, Stoddard, George Arnold, Stedman, William Winter—was a thwarted soul, really a paradox. With a mighty epic enacting before their very eyes, they read Theocritus and wove bouquets of Arabian roses.

CHAPTER XX

IN MINOR KEY

ONE CANNOT BE TRUSTED TO FEEL UNTIL ONE HAS LEARNED to think," ruled Ambrose Bierce. But the great mass of the American readers, for the most part women, did not think at all. A pioneer people, especially the feminine half, on lonely borders or isolated farms, with telephone and radio and automobile and rural postal delivery undreamed of, are more susceptible to melancholy and heart-aches than those nearer civilization. Women in an urban population, with their infinitude of social contacts, even in the barren fifties felt it less keenly; yet even with them there were maladjustments and discontent. America, even at the present day, is a land adolescent, and adolescence is always susceptible, over-dreamful, overfilled with sentiment until it slops over into sentimentalism. The *alma-mater* songs of American colleges are for the most part in minor key.

It is not difficult at all, as one explores the vast swamp of the feminine fiction of the pre-Civil War period, to answer the startled question of Artemus Ward, himself a product of the fifties, "Why these weeps?" Women cried over *The Wide, Wide World* and the novels that followed it, because the stories renewed their own experiences of maladjustment and vanished dreams and personal loss. It was not the novel that made them cry but their stirred memories. Or it may be because the novel stirred their imagination and they cried in sympathy with the persecuted hero or heroine. Tears gave relief to their lonely souls. Women seemed to want to cry. They unfolded their clean handkerchief when they opened their book. I have seen the advertisement of a feminine novel of the decade which gave as a climactic inducement to buyers the information that "as a tear-compeller the author surpasses even Mrs. Stowe."

Tear-compelling was a device even of the clergy. Often at lacrimose moments handkerchiefs would flutter all over the congregation. In 1854 the Atlantic steamship *Arctic* collided in mid-ocean with another steamer and many of the passengers perished. When Henry Ward Beecher told the story on a Sunday following to his great Brooklyn congregation "there was not a dry eye in the house."

It was autumn. Hundreds had wended their way from pilgrimages;—from Rome and its treasures of dead art, and its glory of living nature; from the sides of the Switzer's mountains; from the capitals of various nations; all of them saying in their hearts, "We will wait for the September gales to have done with their equinoctial fury, and then we will embark; we will slide across the appeased ocean, and in the gorgeous month of October we will greet our longed-for native land and our heart-loved friends."

And so the throng streamed along from Berlin, from Paris, from the Orient, converging upon London, still hastening towards the welcome ship, and narrowing every day, the circle of engagements and preparations. They crowded aboard. Never had the Arctic such a host of passengers, nor passengers so nearly related to so many of us.

The hour has come. The signal ball fell at Greenwich. It was noon also at Liverpool. The anchors were weighed; the great hull swayed to the current; the national colors streamed abroad, as if themselves instinct with life and national sympathy. The bell strikes; the wheels revolve; the signal gun beats its echoes in upon every structure along the shore, and the Arctic glides joyfully forth from the Mersey, and turns her prow to the winding channel, and begins her homeward run. The pilot stood at the wheel, and men saw him. Death sat upon the prow, and no eye beheld him. Whoever stood at the wheel in all the voyage, Death was the pilot that steered the craft, and none knew it. He neither revealed his presence nor whispered his errand.

And so hope was effulgent, and lithe gayety disported itself, and joy was every guest. Amid all the inconveniences of the voyage, there was still that which hushed every murmur—"Home is not far away." And every morning it was still one night nearer home! Eight days had passed. They beheld that distant bank of mist that forever haunts the vast shallows of Newfoundland. Boldly they made it; and plunging in, its pliant wreaths wrapped them about. They shall never emerge. The last sunlight has flashed from that deck. The last voyage is done to ship and passengers. At noon there came noiselessly stealing from the north, that fated instrument of destruction. In that mysterious shroud, that vast atmosphere of mist, both steamers were holding their way with rushing prow and roaring wheels, but invisible.

At a league's distance unconscious, and at nearer approach unwarned—within hail, and bearing right towards each other, unseen, unfelt—till in a moment more, emerging from the gray mists, the ill-omened Vesta dealt her deadly stroke to the Arctic. The death-blow was scarcely felt along the mighty hull. She neither reeled nor shivered. Neither commander nor officers deemed that they had suffered harm. Prompt upon humanity, the brave Luce (let his name be ever spoken with admiration and respect) ordered away his boat with the first officer to inquire if the stranger had suffered harm. As Gourley went over the ship's side, O that some good angel had called to the brave commander in the words of Paul on a like occasion, "Except these abide in the ship, ye cannot be saved!"

They departed, and with them the hope of the ship; for now the waters, gaining upon the hold, and, rising up above the fires, revealed the mortal blow. O, had now that stern, brave mate, Gourley, been on deck, whom the sailors were wont to mind—had he stood to execute efficiently the commander's will—we may believe that we should not have had to blush for the cowardice and recreancy of the crew, nor weep for the untimely dead. But apparently each subordinate officer lost all presence of mind, then courage, and so honor. In a wild scramble, that ignoble mob of firemen, engineers, waiters, and crew rushed from the boats, and abandoned the helpless women, children and men to the mercy of the deep! Four hours there were from the catastrophe of the collision to the catastrophe of sinking.

O, what a burial was here. Not as when one is borne from his home among weeping throngs, and gently carried to the green fields, and laid peacefully beneath the turf and the flowers. No priest stood to pronounce a burial service. It was an ocean grave. The mists alone shrouded the burial-place. No spade prepared the grave, nor sexton filled up the hollowed earth. Down, down they sank, and the quick returning waters smoothed out every ripple, and left the sea as placid as before.

II

FROM THE CHURCH to the theater is but a step. In 1853, Dion Boucicault arrived in New York and soon he was dominating the American stage. Dickens dramatizations he freely produced, then *The Poor of New York,* and many Irish plays. Always the *motif* of his dramas was human suffering, and always was there a pathetic climax calling for tears. The most popular of his pre-Civil War plays was undoubtedly his adaptation entitled *The Octoroon, or Life in Louisiana.* Completely was it in the key of the times, sensational as a dime novel, picturesque with surface coatings of Southern local color thickly spread, and tear-compelling to saturation, but unlike *Uncle Tom's Cabin,* it could be played with approval even in the state mentioned in its title. An inflammable subject, yet one with no trace in it of anti-slavery propaganda. Simply and completely was it melodrama, and it was accepted as such.

The great plantation ruined by the villain Yankee manager is to be sold at auction, and with it the beautiful octoroon heroine whose freedom papers he has destroyed. The money that would have redeemed the place is to come by mail, and the houseboy sent for it is delayed by his finding a camera apparatus forgotten by its owner. For a time he plays with it. Then the villain murders the boy to secure the letter in the mail-bag the boy is carrying, and in doing so smashes the camera. Abstracting the money from the letter he then spreads the report that the Indian murdered the boy, and at the auction, despite the opposition of the patrician son of the former owner of the estate, who is madly in love with the girl despite her racial taint, bids her off and prepares to take her away. Then the Indian, a part in the first production of the play taken by Boucicault himself, is caught and is about to be lynched, when

PETE (*Who has been looking about the camera*) 'Top, sar. 'Top a bit! O, laws-a-mussey, see dis! here's a pictur' I found stickin' in that yar telescope machine, sar! look, sar!

SCUD A photographic plate. (*Pete holds his lantern up.*) What's this, eh? two forms! The child—'tis he! dead—and above him—Ah! ah! Jacob M'Closky, 'tis you murdered that boy!

M'CLOSKY Me?

SCUD You! You slew him with that tomahawk; and as you stood over his body with the letter in your hand, you thought that no witness saw the deed, that no eye was on you—the blessed sun in heaven, that, looking down, struck upon this plate the image of the deed. Here you are, in the very attitude of your crime!

M'CLOSKY 'Tis false!

SCUD 'Tis true! the apparatus can't lie. Look there, jurymen. (*Showing plate to jury which had been chosen to try the Indian lest he be lynched*) Look there. O, you wanted evidence—you called for proof—Heaven has answered and convicted you.

M'CLOSKY What court of law would receive such evidence? (*Going*)

RATTS Stop! *this* would! You called it yourself; you wanted to make us murder that Injiun; and since we've got our hands in for justice, we'll try it on *you*. What say ye? shall we have one law for the red-skin and another for the white?

OMNES Try him! Try him!

The end of M'Closky was melodramatic. He escaped, hid in the hold of a river steamboat; about to be taken, he set the boat on fire and leaped overboard. But the Indian trailing him through the swamps finally found him and gave him in full measure a villain's deserts.

But the Octoroon!

Sold to a human devil, and about to be surrendered to

him, takes poison and with music *doloroso* slowly dies, but not until her eager lover brings her the news that is transporting him that the man who bought her cannot hold her. And with the house in a tumult of sobs she gasps her last words.

O! George, you may, without a blush, confess your love for the Octoroon.

Melodrama in every movement, but the fifties were themselves a melodrama.

III

BUT THE religious backgrounds of the era must not for a moment be lost sight of as one tries to interpret it, especially in its sentimental areas. And I know of no better first book for such an interpreter than Lucy Larcom's *A New England Childhood*.

Born on a rocky angle of Cape Ann, Massachusetts, in 1846, she had from her babyhood known of toil and privation, and her training had made her feel that the world of religion was as real as the world revealed by her senses:

Almost the first decided taste in my life was the love of hymns. Committing them to memory was as natural to me as breathing. I followed my mother about with the hymn-book ("Watts' and Select"), reading or repeating them to her while she was busy with her baking or ironing.

Before she was five she could repeat one hundred hymns.

Once a stranger minister visiting her Sunday school had told her class that Jesus was not dead. "He is alive. He loves you and wants you to love him."

My heart beat fast. I could hardly keep back the tears...
He is alive! He loves me! He will tell me how to be good!
I said it over to myself, but not to anybody else. I was sure
that I loved him. It was like a beautiful secret between us two.
I felt him so alive and so near.

Sentimentalism? Not at all. Intensely human it was, and
with thousands of others of her generation it lasted un-
dimmed to the end of life.

Early, like so many of her generation, she found employment in the Lowell mills and she became a contributor to the literary magazines which had been started by
the mill-girls.

The *Operatives' Magazine,* [she wrote], had a decidedly
religious tone. We who wrote for it were loyal to our Puritanic
antecedents, and considered it all-important that our lightest
actions should be moved by some earnest impulse from behind. We might write playfully, but there must be conscience
and reverence within in all. We had been taught, and we believed, that idle words were a sin, whether spoken or written.

In her early *Lowell Offering* poetry and prose, she was,
she says, inclined to "dismalize myself." "The title of one
string of morbid verses is 'The Complaint of a Nobody,'
in which I compared myself to a weed growing up in
a garden. I think I must have had a frequent fancy that
I was not long for this world. Perhaps I thought an early
death rather picturesque; many young people do."

Describing herself, she was describing the New England
generation that had come up in all the corners of the land,
eager, vigorous, self-cultured and hungry for they knew
not what, the feminine generation that was to make its
impress upon the decade before the Civil War.

It is noteworthy that Lucy Larcom's poetry was un-
recognized until, in 1852, she published her tear-compelling lyric "Hannah Binding Shoes," the story of the
maiden whose lover had been lost at sea, but during
a long life had daily expected his return, asking all she
met the same question:

"Have you from the fishers any news?"
Poor lone Hannah, Hannah at the window binding shoes.

IV

BEFORE judging a period, let me hear the songs of that
period. What were the people singing? More than any
other music the fifties were singing hymns. America
then was prevailingly rural, and a large percentage
of the population went to church on Sunday and often
to the mid-week prayer meeting where always there was
singing. Songs in minor measures chorded with their
hard-working lives. A favorite with the old grandfathers
and grandmothers in their feeble years was the old
hymn, so often sung:

> There is rest for the weary,
> On the other side of Jordan,
> In the sweet fields of Eden,
> Where the Tree of Life is blooming,
> There is rest for me.

The factory-girls in the mill-towns along the Merrimac,
all of them from the farms, were very religious. Elizabeth
Stewart Phelps in her story recording the fall in the
early sixties of the Pemberton Mill in Massachusetts when
in full operation, the most of the operatives perishing,

tells of girls pinned under the fallen timbers and slowly burning, but singing as they died,

> We're going home to die no more,

a pathetic tale completely in key with its time. Much sung was the hymn "Shall we gather at the River?" Death constantly faced all Christians. Life was but a brief school-time, then Heaven and "home."

Among the Negroes of the South the new Christianity, which could be added by a strange affinity to the religion of their old Congo gods, worshiped with weird rites and savage music, expressed itself in original exaggerations and wild half-and-half strains called spirituals now, the one totally original creation in the field of American popular song.

But American singing was by no means all religious. The "Tippecanoe and Tyler too" presidential campaign, log cabin and hard cider, had sung General Harrison into the White House.

v

EMOTIONAL music and balladry during the middle years of the century and the part they played in the formation of the spirit of the epoch have never been adequately treated. The sentimental songs of Morris, of "Ben-Bolt" English, Woodworth, and others had helped swell the tide of emotionalism that culminated in the great ninth wave that swept over the 1850's. In this decade came Foster's songs in minor key, and in the decade that followed came the greatest of emotional outbursts, the war between the North and the South.

For a generation, sentimental songs were everywhere. Even Thoreau sang them and in public. Whole families took to the road as song-singers, the most famous of them the Hutchinson family, the sixteen sons and daughters of a New England farmer. Their plaintive songs in close harmony brought lumps into the throats of common people gathered in school-houses and town halls and church vestries. Inflexibly they stood for fundamentalist religion, abolitionism, temperance reform, and during the war loyalty to the flag. The concerts of the Hutchinsons began with a ballad of introduction, the fourth stanza a roll-call of the singers:

> David, Noah, Andrew, Zephy,
> Caleb, Joshua, Jess, and Benny,
> Judson, Rhoda, John, and Asa,
> And Abby are our names.

Their published song book, many of the pieces original with the singers, is a welter of emotionalism, "Mother, home, heaven" in every variety, abolitionism in tearful numbers, temperance, patriotism, and religion in allopathic doses. During the war they sang many recruits into the Union armies. Always their audiences went home humming their tunes and later repeating them on the parlor melodeon.

The effect of this cumulative emotionalism when the war broke out was marked. For the enlisting of volunteers for the armies nothing could have been more effective than the lacrimose chords of the time toned to sentimental verse. In the elements of propagandic song and literary appeal, the North exceeded the South a thousand-fold.

The North had the poets and the musicians, forces as important, perhaps, as cannons and warships. Foster's plaintive minstrelsy presented to the North, which knew little of Negroes, a moving series of pathetic pictures. A Northern minstrel, Walter Kittredge, with a baby organ for accompaniment tramped from town to town, singing his timely song "Tenting To-night on the Old Camp Ground." Soon every one was humming it and with it the pathetic chords of "Tramp, tramp, tramp, the boys are marching." And there was in the air everywhere "Just Before the Battle, Mother," "The Vacant Chair," "Rally Round the Flag, Boys," "Three Cheers for the Red, White, and Blue." Songs enlist armies, keep up the morale of troops and people, and hold the supporting country firm during the days of crisis.

The ebbing wave of this emotional minstrelsy expended itself after the war in the Moody and Sankey Gospel Hymns. But I am traveling beyond my decade.

VI

THE ARTLESS folk-songs of Stephen Collins Foster, tinged, all of them, with tender melancholy, give promise of outlasting all the American classics musical or literary written during the decade and perhaps during the century which followed. Foster was a genius, and his biography, now known to all, has all the ear-marks ascribed to genius. His school education was scanty and his musical training was self-administered. His songs were spontaneous creations. Says his biographer, Mulligan, "He had not had to learn his art by struggle and self-denial, nor to adapt his wares to his market by patience and labor."

STEPHEN
COLLINS
FOSTER

From a daguer-
reotype of 1859
in the Foster
Hall Collection.

"JEANIE WITH
THE LIGHT
BROWN HAIR"

Courtesy of the Foster
Hall Collection, Uni-
versity of Pittsburgh.

And his songs slipped away from him as easily as they had come. Others reaped fortunes from his work, but Foster, the creator of their fortunes, died in the hospital at the age of thirty-seven, with thirty-eight cents in his pocketbook. For "Old Folks at Home" he had received $15. Not a penny did he receive for "Oh! Susanna" or for "Old Uncle Ned," but their publisher netted from them $10,000.

In the "Prefatory Note" to the Library of Congress volume *Catalogue of First Editions of Stephen C. Foster*, 1915, is this paragraph:

Few are the composers whose music survives their generation. Stephen Collins Foster died in New York on January 13, 1864—by a remarkable coincidence this American master of song was born in 1826 on the Fourth of July—and his best music is still a living force in our national life. Many of Foster's songs, of course, belong to the mid-nineteenth century type of sentimental American parlour "ballad," not exactly distinguished by either beauty or skill, but some of his songs possess the beauty and power of imperishable folksongs. Misconception or partisanship may succeed in banishing these songs from our public schools, but Stephen C. Foster's place in the history of music in America is too high to be permanently affected by such efforts.

During his lifetime Foster was relegated to the "Tin Pan Alley" streets of literary and musical art. His songs were "end-man stuff." The literary aristocracy never heard of him. But soon the people everywhere were singing "Oh! Susanna," 1848; "The Camptown Races," 1850; "My Old Kentucky Home, Good Night," 1853; "Massa's in de Cold, Cold Ground," 1853; "Old Dog Tray," 1853; "Nellie Was a Lady," "Open Thy Lattice, Love," "Old

Folks at Home," 1851; and "Old Black Joe." Once heard they are never forgotten. Soon the whole country and beyond were whistling them, or humming them, or singing them. They seemed to express to the full the emotionalism of their time. Though Negro melodies, many of them, there is nothing fundamentally African either in the melodies or the words. Always was there a minor strain. Says his biographer, "When he sang his own songs, there was a plaintive sweetness in his tone and accent that sometimes drew tears from listeners' eyes."

Gospel hymns came from his creative soul: "He leadeth me, Oh, blessed thought!" "What Shall the Harvest Be?" "There is a Land of Bliss Where the Weary are at Rest"; and love songs: "Beautiful Dreamer," "Open Thy Lattice, Love," "Come Where My Love Lies Dreaming"—everywhere in the 174 songs he wrote are mother, home, heaven, love; everywhere are full chords expressing tender melancholy. They are period songs. I know of no better way to realize how it felt to live in the emotional fifties than to hum through the harmonies of Foster. One will remember more of them than one realizes. But they are more than period songs; the whole world is singing them even now.

In the last Florida legislature a bill was introduced appropriating a large sum for building a monument to Foster on a selected site on the Suwanee River, a river Foster never saw, and a river on whose banks are really no plantations. (It did not pass.) Foster, it seems, had chosen the name "Pedee," but disliking the name, had opened his geography and had found the river which he spelled Swanee. Again, Henry Ford bought the Foster house in

Pittsburgh and removed it to Detroit, but, according to Pittsburgh authorities, he got the wrong house.

Garbled have been the accounts of Foster. His songs have been claimed by others. Tales have been spread concerning his unhappy later years. But recent biographers have worked with exactitude, have presented the man as he was. The city of his birth is preparing a million dollar monument to his memory; plans are even now in progress for building a magnificent memorial on the Suwanee River; in the City of Indianapolis has been erected a music hall dedicated to the life and work of Foster, and from the same city is issued from time to time the "Foster Hall Bulletin," an elaborate magazine running over with Fosteriana. There seems to be no danger that the folk-minstrel of America will be forgotten.

CHAPTER XXI

BOSTON BUILDS A MAGAZINE

*T*HAT THE 1850's WAS A PERIOD OF LITERARY TRANSITION during which were sown the seeds that after the storm of the Civil War germinated for a new era in American letters is evident to all who examine the history of the literary magazines of the decade. The magazines of a period are a literary barometer. During the decade came the passing of the magazines of the Philadelphia type. *Sartain's* lost its identity in 1852; *Graham's* in 1859; *Peterson's* merely dragged on; *Godey's Lady's Book,* under the inspiring leadership of Sarah Josepha Hale, who had trained a generation of feminine writers until they were able to take charge of the new fiction of the period, still held its own. But Mrs. Hale was a New Englander with New England ideals and vigor. In New York, *Knickerbocker—A Magazine of Polite Literature,* was now in a saintly senility; *Putnam's,* born in 1853 of aged parents, had died of old age, four years old. And *Harper's Magazine,* which I have seen classed as "a re-print magazine," was dealing out Dickens and Thackeray in allopathic doses, with palliatives of fashion-plates *à la*

Godey's, cartoons in the manner of *Punch,* and a voluminous department of Joe Miller jokes edited by the man
who had nursed *Knickerbocker* into senility. And it had
prospered. At the opening of 1853 it claimed a circulation
of 118,000, and the figure was steadily increased during
the decade. The reading middle-class that had been
swelled to best-seller proportions by Dickens and the
Lady's Book, were eager for literary caviar and were
willing to pay for it.

And Boston had only the venerable *North American
Review,* scholarly and dignified, marching with the pon-
derous step of the old reviewers. Never had Boston had
a popular literary magazine worth mentioning. The
Brahmins had marketed their literary wares, so far as
they had condescended to use magazine vehicles, in
Philadelphia and New York.

As the decade neared the sixties, the financial crash of
1857 mowed wide swaths through the magazine field.
Only the strongest magazines survived, and a study of
these survivors could have told the critics of the time
what the new period in American literature ending with
the century was to be. Few, however, realized what was
happening. The whole nation was trembling on the verge
of civil war, and what is literature in the hurricane of a
war?

Eighteen hundred and fifty-seven was the climacteric
year in the literary history of the decade. Late in this
year, despite the financial crash, Mr. Phillips, head of the
publishing house of Phillips, Sampson & Co., Boston, sat
at a Boston table about which were gathered Emerson,
Longfellow, Holmes, Lowell, Motley, Cabot, and

Underwood, and told them his house would back the magazine they proposed publishing. And for taking the responsibility he gave this reason: A magazine to prosper must have distinctive contributors: we have them here in an abundance no other American magazine has ever had, and the magazine we propose will prosper. You distinguished authors know how to make literature, "but none of you knows the American people as I do." His house went down a year later as a result of the financial crash, but the *Atlantic Monthly* was strong enough to survive. Its birth marks the beginning of a literary epoch.

II

THE "flowering of New England" was running heavily to seed, and to handle this abundant fruitage a base granary or literary elevator had been long needed. Why send Boston products to Philadelphia and New York? New England literature for New England was becoming the new literary Monroe Doctrine. And for the weigher and gager of the new elevator, James Russell Lowell was selected. Thus the *Atlantic Monthly*.

Lowell among the mid-century Brahmins held a curiously anomalous position. He was too young to be classed with Emerson, for Emerson in point of age was old enough to have been his father; and he was too old to march comfortably in step with the youngsters who were beginning to appear even in the closing years of the fifties: Aldrich, Howells, and the rest. He was a Janus personality: one face looking fondly backward into the old régime of his youth, and the other looking eagerly forward into the new world that was to be.

The 1850's had cut his literary life sharply in two. After the death of his wife in 1853 he wrote,

My moon is set; my vision set with her,

and he wrote no more poetry until the tragedy of the war restrung his abandoned lyre and called forth the series of odes which has been widely proclaimed as his best bid for fame. The year 1854, too, was for him a transition one. His election to the chair in Harvard, so long occupied with distinction by Longfellow, reversed the current of his life, sent him into a new profession for which he had to prepare himself. And his preparatory period in Europe brought him vitally in contact with the new tendencies that were reshaping European literature. So when the editorship of the *Atlantic* came to him he brought to it the conservatism of the old régime and the new liberalism that was to rule the period that was to be.

At the very start the new magazine broke into new ground. "The editorship had been given to Lowell at a salary of two thousand five hundred dollars with six dollars a page for his own contributions. This and the regular rate for other contributions was on a scale more liberal than had ever been heard of before." Soon he was bringing newnesses into the magazine unknown in more conventional days. He could ask Whittier to cast the refrain of "Skipper Ireson's Ride" into the Marblehead dialect. He could suggest changes in Emerson's work, and revise without consulting its author the text of an article by Thoreau. All took their revisions in good part except the Walden hermit who in anger withdrew the remainder of his manuscript.[1] Thoreau walked alone. To read him is to feel oneself alone. Constantly is one startled by his conditions and his discoveries. I remember the thrill I once felt while reading this in one of his letters bearing the date August 9, 1850: "I have in my pocket a button which I ripped off the coat of the Marquis of Ossoli, on the seashore the other day."

Thoreau, I said, walked alone.

A pen portrait of him in 1856 by Bronson Alcott has come to us through Odell Shepard's valuable edition of Alcott's journals. With the philosopher as guide, Thoreau visited Whitman in Brooklyn, but neither of the two men overflowed easily and they sat in silence, each "planted fast in reserves, surveying each other curiously, like two beasts, each wondering what the other would do, whether to snap or run. . . . Whether Thoreau was meditating the possibility of Walt's stealing away his 'out-of-doors' for some sinister ends, or pecuniary . . . or whether Walt suspected or not that he had here for once, and for the first time, found his match and more in smelling out 'all Nature,' I cannot say."

Volume 1, Number 1, contained work by fourteen writers, the *Atlantic* charter members. The best known were Longfellow, Emerson, Motley, Charles Eliot Norton, Whittier, Mrs. Stowe, Holmes, Parke Godwin, Lowell, and J. T. Trowbridge. Until Volume 26, articles in the magazine were not signed, and until Volume 9 the names were not given in the indexes of the semi-annual volumes.

[1] In his paper entitled "Chesuncook," Thoreau had written of a towering pine in the Maine woods: "It is as immortal as I am, and perchance will go to as high a heaven, there to tower above me still," and Lowell had struck the sentence out.

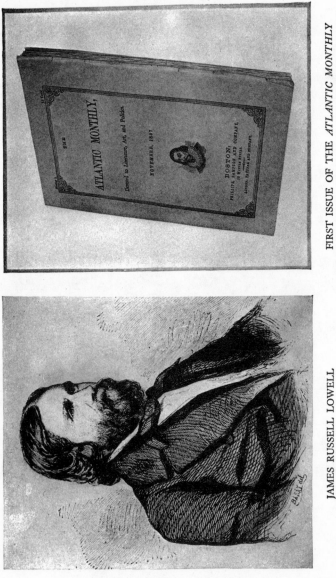

JAMES RUSSELL LOWELL
Ballou's Pictorial Drawing-Room Companion, 1855.

FIRST ISSUE OF THE *ATLANTIC MONTHLY*
November, 1857. Courtesy of the *Atlantic Monthly.*

Guessing who wrote this and that was a favorite topic of conversation. After the first issue of the *Atlantic*, Bostonians greeting each other would say, "Have you seen that poem in the new magazine? What can it mean? Who could have written it?":

> If the red slayer think he slays,
>   Or if the slain think he is slain,
> They know not well the subtle ways
>   I keep, and pass, and turn again.
>
> Far or forgot to me is near;
>   Shadow and sunlight are the same;
> The vanished gods to me appear;
>   And one to me are shame and fame.
>
> They reckon ill who leave me out;
>   When me they fly, I am the wings;
> I am the doubter and the doubt,
>   And I the hymn the Brahmin sings.
>
> The strong gods pine for my abode,
>   And pine in vain the sacred Seven;
> But thou, meek lover of the good!
>   Find me, and turn thy back on heaven.

The title "Brahma" told the whole story: Bostonians should have known that, and they should have known that only Emerson could have written it. But it made a Boston holiday, even attaining the celebrity of being parodied in the newspapers. The season, it seems, had been backward. The winter was on, but no snow for the favorite sport of many. Therefore the parody:

> If the red sleigher thinks he sleighs,
>   Or if this sleighing thinks it's sleighing,
> They know not well the subtle ways,
>   Of snow that comes and goes aga-in.

The new realism was admitted freely into the magazine, and the short story, which had been brushed up anew in France and was coming again to be a ruling literary form, Lowell admitted in unprecedented quantity. During the four years of his editorship there appeared in the magazine some eighty-seven short stories, nearly half of them by women. Volume 5 alone contained thirteen, among them the notable "The Amber Gods" and "Circumstance" by Harriet Prescott (Spofford), "Love and Self Love" by Louisa May Alcott, and "My Own Story" by Mrs. Richard Henry Stoddard. In the first five volumes appeared eleven short stories by Rose Terry (Cooke), pioneer work in local color a decade before Bret Harte and George W. Cable. She had begun as a writer of the Sylvanus Cobb type with idolized heroines and supernaturally black villains, but the influence of Lowell seemed to awake in her new powers. The New England Yankee she portrayed in all his vulgarity and meanness and in all his strength of character. In some of her tales, realism, never tainted with nastiness, goes to the depths of character and situation as in "The Ring Fetter," in "Cal Culver and the Devil," and in "Freedom Wheeler's Controversy with Providence." In Volume 7 appeared "Life in the Iron Mills" by Rebecca Harding (Davis), as grim a piece of realism as one can find in all American literature.

Women writers were taking charge of American fiction, young women who as girls had read *The Lady's Book* and *The Wide, Wide World* and *The Lamplighter.* During Lowell's four years of editorship appeared the early work of Elizabeth Chase (Ackers), Mary Abigail Dodge, Lucretia P. Hale, Julia Ward (Howe), Lucy

Larcom, Nora Perry, Elizabeth Stuart Phelps (Ward), Celia Thaxter, Mrs. A. D. T. Whitney.

The decade of the feminine fifties, so far as literature is concerned, ended with Lowell's editorship of the *Atlantic Monthly*.

But despite his new liberalism and his early perception of the dawning of a new period, Lowell was unable to influence to any marked degree the literary generation with which he found himself regimented. Literary style is not an individual matter; it is the expression of a period and a people. Oliver Wendell Holmes may be taken as a typical example. All his powers until middle age had been centered upon his profession, which was medicine and, as we realize to-day, he had succeeded in it so fully that he is named now with Pasteur and Lister as a pioneer on the frontiers of his subject. What Lowell did to him when, as editor of the *Atlantic,* he turned him perforce to literary creation has never been fully treated. It was like lopping the bearing branches from a richly fruited tree and throwing all the life forces into selected branches capable of producing only a marvelous flowering like Japanese cherry blossoms with inferior fruitage. Always had those sap shoots been present. Once Holmes, years before, had started the *Autocrat* papers, but had abandoned them because his powers were centered upon his profession. For amusement he had thrown off many popular verses. Once he had classed himself:

> I'm a florist in verse, and what *would* people say
> If I came to a banquet without my bouquet?

The feminine fifties had molded the man, and he wrote

in the key of the times, became a best-seller, and soon was hailed as the creator of classics to be rated with Emerson's and Hawthorne's. The Holmes breakfast of 1879, given by his publishers, lauded only his literary creations until President Eliot arose and quizzically questioned them as to who the Holmes was, that they were so wreathing with garlands. "I know him as the professor of anatomy and physiology in the Harvard Medical School of Harvard University for the last thirty-two years, and I know him to-day as one of the most active and hardworking of our lecturers." Eliot, we realize to-day, was not facetious in these remarks, but was two generations ahead of his times. Holmes, the literary man so redolent of the feminine fifties, is now a fading figure, despite his wit and his brilliant breakfast-table monologues. He is now the man of one book, the 1858 *Autocrat* papers, and even this book we realize to-day is merely a babbling mountain brook, delightful, but everywhere shallow and meandering to nowhere. Completely does it belong to the decade that produced it. The life of Holmes should be rewritten, making central what was really his major contribution to his times—his distinctive medical work, his scientific explorations, his religious courage, and his unfailing good citizenship.

CHAPTER XXII

THE IMPENDING CRISIS

*T*HE 1850's TOPPLED OVER INTO THE 1860's WITH CHAR-acteristic melodrama. A chapter as sensational as a Sylvanus Cobb thriller might be written on a dozen events in the closing years of the decade.

The Panama Railroad, a story of jungle-cutting and yellow fever that lasted for five years, was dedicated in 1855 and was in full operation when the decade ended.

The colossal steamship the *Great Eastern,* just before the opening sixties, was a nine-day wonder along the New York water-front.

And who in all America, or in England for that matter, did not know the details of the most famous of early prize-ring fights, the Heenan-Sayers contest?

And in Boston there was a pirate-hanging on an island down the harbor, the execution of the notorious Hicks, with all Boston present to see a dime-novel event with their own eyes.

And with the new decade came the Prince of Wales, son of Queen Victoria and later crowned King Edward VII. American society went wild over the youngster. The

Republic has always boasted of its democracy but always has been thrilled to the soul by royalty in any of its degrees.

In 1856 the Republican Party had been organized and two years later had occurred the famous Lincoln-Douglas debates. Then had come the election of Abraham Lincoln and the secession of the Southern states.

II

ALL THAT the decade stood for was obscured by the smoke of the great war. What would have been, could the conflict have been settled without warfare, can only be conjectured. There had been hopes in the South that a Southern literature could be evolved; that the "flowering of New England" could be matched by a "flowering of the South." *Russell's Magazine* had been started in Charleston, South Carolina, in 1857, to be the *Atlantic Monthly* of the South, and it had run with distinction until the war smothered it. Helper in his book *The Impending Crisis,* the 60th edition of which, issued in 1860, lies before me, declared that "at the late Southern Convention at Savannah a speaker had said, 'It is important that the South should have a literature of her own, to defend her principles and her rights.'"

Helper had agreed with the statement, but had pointed out the obstacles that made such a literature impossible: "Southern men expect to get talent without paying for it." The North has all the machinery for making and spreading literature, he argued. Pointing out that Greeley's *Tribune* in 1857 sold 176,000 copies weekly, and that *Harper's Magazine* issued 175,000 copies monthly, or two millions a year, or 3,000 volumes a day throughout the year, he said:

How is it that the people of the North build up their literature? Two words reveal the secret: *intelligence, compensation.* They are a reading people—the poorest artizan or day-laborer has his shelf of books, or his daily or weekly paper, whose contents he seldom fails to master before retiring at night; and they are accustomed to pay for all the books and papers which they peruse. Readers and payers—these are the men who ensure the prosperity of publishers. Moreover, they pay their writers. Northern publishers can employ the talent of the South and of the whole country to write for them and pour out thousands annually for it, simply because a reading population, accustomed to pay for the service which it receives, enables them to do so.

Though a born Southerner, resident all his life in North Carolina, Helper condemned "the current gabble of the oligarchs about a Southern literature." Duyckinck's *Cyclopædia of American Literature,* 1856, he argued, had biographies and samplings of 569 authors of which 87 were natives of the South; Griswold's *Poets and Poetry of America* presented 141 verse-writers, 17 of them Southerners; and Read in his *Female Poets of America* found 73 Northern poets and 11 Southern.

What has produced this literary pauperism of the South? [he demanded] One single word, most pregnant in its terrible meanings, answers the question. That word is SLAVERY!

The South lacks readers. In the South newspapers and books seem generally ignored, and noisy discussions of village and state politics, the tobacco and cotton crops, filibustering in Cuba, Nicaragua, or Sonora, the price of negroes generally, and especially of "fine-looking wenches," the beauties of lynch-law, the delights of horse-racing, the excitement of street fights, with bowie-knives and revolvers, the "manifest destiny" theory that justifies the stealing of territory contiguous to our own, and kindred topics, constitute the warp and woof of conversation.

Thus Southern literature during the decade as presented by a native Southerner.

But my book has run into the Civil War and must stop.

INDEX

335